Romans

ROMANS

© 2012, 2015, 2018 BEE World

Revision 2018-01. Typo corrections throughout and theological clarifications in Lessons 2 and 6.

For information regarding permissions or special orders, please contact:

BEE World
International Headquarters
990 Pinon Ranch View, Ste. 100
Colorado Springs, CO 80907

ISBN: 978-1-937324-14-8

First Edition

Printed in the United States of America

1 2 3 4 5 6 7 8 9 10

01292018

Contents

Romans

Description of the Course

This course is the second part of your study of Paul's epistles to the Galatians and Romans. In this course you will study Paul's letter to the Romans. You will look at the historical background and examine the vital theological issues in the early church in Rome. You will become better acquainted with the life, character, and ministry of the apostle Paul. You will also gain new insights into Christian life and service as you apply the teaching of this epistle to contemporary situations.

Course Introduction

You are about to embark on a study of one of the most significant books of the New Testament: Paul's *magnum opus*, the epistle to the Romans. This letter has had an enormous impact on the history of the church. The book was a pivotal document of the Protestant Reformation. Both Martin Luther and John Wesley were profoundly impacted by this work and found Christ through its pages.

Romans was Paul's summary of the Christian teaching. There is no more magnificent statement of the doctrines of grace than those found in this letter.

But how will this book affect you? How will the study of this ancient letter make a difference in your walk with God?

Grace. This is the major theme of the New Testament and of this book in particular. This book will give you a magnificent picture of God's grace; His unconditional acceptance of you based upon the finished work of Christ. There is perhaps no more important truth to authentic Christian living. Let us begin.

Objectives of the Course

All of the courses on the Internet Biblical Seminary are based on the conviction that every Christian has a ministry. God has a purpose for your life and ministry. This course has been written to help you incorporate the great truths revealed in Romans into your own life and service for Christ. When you finish this course, you should be able to:

- Appreciate the up-to-date solutions that God supplies in this letter for problems that the Christian must face today and apply them as needed in your life and ministry
- Appreciate more deeply the life, character, and ministry of the apostle Paul and apply the principles that will improve your own life and work
- Discuss the following aspects of the background of the Roman epistle: the date of writing, the occasion for writing, and the recipients of the letter
- Compare what you have studied of Galatians with Romans in terms of content, purpose, theme, occasion for writing, time of writing, style, and the key theological passages
- Explain and trace the development of Paul's teaching on faith throughout Romans
- Use the diagrams, sketches, maps, and a chronological chart when teaching from Romans
- Apply the fundamental principles of inductive Bible study to your study of other Bible passages
- Develop and improve your skills of interpreting other Bible passages as you use the methods that you have learned

Units of Study

The lessons are grouped into two units:

Unit 1: Paul Explains His Gospel

> Lesson 1: Introduction and Preview

> Lesson 2: Man's Need of Salvation

> Lesson 3: God's Provision for Salvation

> Lesson 4: A New Life of Freedom

> Lesson 5: Life in the Spirit

Unit 2: Paul Applies His Gospel

> Lesson 6: Gospel for Jews & Gentiles

> Lesson 7: The Gospel and the Christian

> Lesson 8: The Gospel and the Church

As you plan your study schedule, decide the dates you want to finish each unit. You can then divide this time into study periods for each lesson.

We suggest that you try to do a lesson a week or three lessons per month. You can do this if you study about one hour each day.

Lesson Organization

Please give careful attention to every part of the lesson:

> 1. Title

> 2. Lesson Outline

> 3. Lesson Objectives

> 4. Lesson Assignments

> 5. Word Study

> 6. Lesson Development

> 7. Illustrations

The title, outline, and objectives provide a preview of the lesson. Your mind will be more alert and receptive, and you will learn better because of this preview. The lesson assignments describe how and in what order to complete the lesson. The word study prepares you for special terms in the lesson. The lesson development follows the lesson outline. Its comments, suggestions, and questions all help you reach the lesson objectives. Be sure to check your answers with the ones given for the study questions. These will fix your attention once more on the main points of the lesson. This procedure is designed to make your learning more effective and long-lasting. Take special note of the maps, charts, and other illustrations because they will help you to identify with a part of the early church, sharing its problems and letting the tremendous truths of these letters grip your heart. Also, you will find these illustrations useful in your preaching and teaching.

Author

This course was originally part of a larger course encompassing the study of both Galatians and Romans, in that order. That course was written by Paul A. Pomerville, who at the time was a missionary and director of the Theological Education by Extension pilot project in Indonesia. The original course was edited and revised by BEE World personnel in 1997 and further edited by Doug Filkins in 1999. In 2011, BEE World personnel divided the Galatians and Romans course into two separate courses. Further revisions have been done by BEE World personnel on both courses since that time, resulting in this edition of the course.

Recommended for Further Reading

The only reading required for this course is in your Bible and course book. You can, however, enrich your spiritual life, find help on each Bible passage, and discover a wealth of material for teaching and preaching by referring to any of these commentaries: *Matthew Henry's Commentary; Barnes' Notes on the New Testament; Adam Clarke's Commentary; Pulpit Commentary One Volume New Testament Commentary* by Wesley, Clarke and others; and *A Commentary on the Whole Bible* by Jamieson, Fausset and Brown.

For English speaking students, we recommend any of the following books:

Ball, Charles Ferguson. *The Life and Journeys of St. Paul.* Chicago: Moody Press, 1971 edition. A thrilling, popular biography.

Bruce, F.F *Epistle of Paul to the Romans.* Grand Rapids: Eerdmans, 1969.

Eerdman, Charles R. *The Epistle of St. Paul to the Romans.* Philadelphia: Westminster Press, 1929. A rather condensed expositional study.

Newell, William R. *Romans Verse by Verse.* Chicago: Moody Press, 1972 printing. Very good and strongly devotional.

Stalker, James. *The Life of St. Paul.* Old Tappan: Fleming H. Revell, 1950 edition. Popular as a biography and textbook. Very helpful.

Tenney, M.C. *Galatians: The Charter of Christian Liberty.* Grand Rapids: Eerdmans, 1954. Excellent use of various methods of Bible study.

Thomas, W.H. Griffith. *St. Paul's Epistle to the Romans.* Grand Rapids: Eerdmans, 1956. A very thorough exegetical and devotional study.

White, Reginald E.O. *Apostle Extraordinary: A Modern Portrait of St. Paul.* Grand Rapids: Eerdmans, 1962. Excellent insight into Paul's character and message.

Textbooks for the Course

Your Bible is the main textbook for this course. To help you interpret and apply its teachings, you will use this course.

Unit One: Paul Explains His Gospel

You have finished your study of Galatians and are about to begin studying Romans. Martin Luther, the great leader of the Reformation, called it the chief book of the New Testament, and the purest Gospel. He said that it could never be read or studied too much. In fact, the more it is handled, the more precious it becomes and the better it tastes.

In Galatians, Paul defended his gospel against the legalism of the Judaizers, but he did not attempt to present a complete and systematic statement of his theology. In the epistle to the Romans, we find this kind of presentation.

In the five lessons of this unit, you will study Romans 1–8, in which Paul presents a detailed development of the doctrine of salvation.

Then in Unit 2, you will examine Romans 9–16 and discover ways that this doctrine applies to our daily walk as Christians.

Lesson 1: Introduction and Preview
(Rom 1:1-17; 15:14–16:27)

Lesson Introduction

As you begin your study of Romans, it is important that you be able to answer certain background questions. To whom was Paul writing? Where were they located? Where was Paul located? Why was he writing? What were his main topics or themes? By studying this lesson carefully, you will establish a good foundation that will make it easier to understand the message of each chapter of the epistle.

Lesson Objectives

Topic 1 presents background information about Paul's epistle to the Romans.

In Topic 1, you will observe…

- The theological, spiritual, and practical value of this letter
- The reasons why Paul wrote this letter
- Important characteristics of the church at Rome
- The principal topics that Paul addresses in this letter
- The development of Paul's thought in the letter

Topic 2 summarizes the main points in Paul's introduction to the epistle.

In Topic 2, you will discover…

- How Paul's greeting provides additional background information about this letter
- How Paul's proposed visit demonstrates characteristics of a good minister of the gospel
- How the theme of this letter can be identified by observing Paul's use of the term "faith"

Lesson Outline

Topic 1: Background Information

Value of the Epistle

Paul's Reasons for Writing (15:14-33)

The Church at Rome (16:1-16)

Message of the Epistle

Preview of the Epistle

Topic 2: Paul's Introduction to the Epistle (1:1-17)

Greetings (1:1-7)

Paul's Proposed Visit (1:8-15)

Theme of the Epistle (1:16-17)

Word List

We hope you will enjoy using the word study at the beginning of each lesson. Some of the words you already know, but they are used in a special sense in the lesson. Others are theological terms, and some are new words for many students. Please read the word study before starting each lesson. Refer back to it as necessary.

Polemic - an aggressive argument. In Romans and Galatians, Paul's polemic presents the doctrine of justification by faith and defends it against the teaching of the Judaizers.

Topic 1: Background Information

In this section you will begin to learn about the Christians in Rome and about Paul's concerns as he sat down to write his epistle to them. You will also receive a brief overview of the main concepts covered in Romans and observe step-by-step how Paul develops his argument in the epistle.

Value of the Epistle

Objective 1 – At the end of this topic, you will be able to list the theological, spiritual, and practical value of the epistle to the Romans and state your objectives in studying it.

If you have doctrinal questions that you cannot answer, look for their answers in Romans. If you have studied the Galatians course, you received a good foundation for studying this epistle. The similarity of theme and subject matter in Romans and Galatians will help you find the answers to most of your questions.

The theological value of Romans is great. It is the foundational document of the whole Pauline system of truth and teaching. This book of the Bible provides us with the most systematic and complete theological presentation of the gospel. You will have a much deeper understanding of Christ's redemptive work and appreciation for it when you finish this study.

The spiritual value is equally great. Romans sheds light on the Christian way of life in a way that will be of great personal value to you. The source of strength and the secret of victorious Christian living are important themes in this epistle.

The practical value of the epistle lies in the definite picture painted of what Christianity really is. The latter portion of the epistle gives many important principles for everyday Christian living.

As you study these lessons, pray that the Holy Spirit will make Romans a source of spiritual enrichment to your personal life and a powerful tool for use in your ministry.

QUESTION 1

In which book of the Bible will you find the most systematic and complete theological presentation of the gospel?

    A. Gospel of Luke

    B. Gospel of John

    C. Epistle to the Galatians

    D. Epistle to the Romans

QUESTION 2

In your Life Notebook, briefly state three values of Romans as labeled below.

Theological:

Spiritual:

Practical:

QUESTION 3

Romans and Galatians are quite different in their theme and subject matter. *True or False?*

QUESTION 4

Galatians is primarily a defense of the gospel, whereas Romans is primarily an exposition of the gospel. *True or False?*

Paul's Reasons for Writing (Rom 15:14-33)

Objective 2 – At the end of this topic, you will be able to state when, where, and why Paul wrote his epistle to the Romans.

Do you remember the three things that we really need to know in order to understand any letter? We need to know something about the writer, something about the person to whom the letter is written, and the reason why the letter was written. In the course on Galatians, we studied Paul, the apostle to the Gentiles. You have seen how God prepared him to write this important exposition of the Christian faith. Even the problem with the Judaizers and his letter to the Galatians helped him develop the clear presentation that we have in Romans.

Paul spent the ten years from AD 47 to 57 evangelizing the countries bordering the Aegean Sea. Notice on the accompanying map that this sea lies between the Black Sea and the Mediterranean. It separates Europe from Asia. On the European side (in what is now Greece) Paul and his companions were preaching the gospel and planting churches in the principal cities of the Roman provinces of Macedonia and Achaia. On the Asian side (in what is now Turkey), they carried out the same work in the provinces of Galatia and Asia. Paul planted churches in Iconium, Philippi, Thessalonica, Corinth, and Ephesus and left them in the care of spiritual leaders.

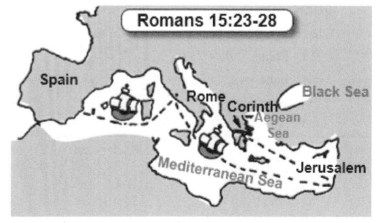

Paul spent the winter of AD 56-57 in Corinth at the home of his friend and convert Gaius (Acts 20:3; 1 Cor 16:16). His apostolic mission of taking the gospel to the Aegean lands was completed. Paul was looking for new fields to evangelize. He was a pioneer by choice (see Rom 15:18-24) and wanted to preach where people did not yet know Jesus Christ. He decided to go to Spain, the oldest Roman colony in the west and the center of Roman civilization in those parts.

The journey to Spain would give Paul the opportunity to visit Rome on the way. He did not plan to stay long or do much preaching in Rome because there was already a thriving church in that city. He was looking forward to fellowship with the Christians in Rome--encouraging them spiritually and being encouraged by them--before going on to Spain.

Paul had several good reasons for writing the epistle to the Romans. First, God inspired him to write it. Second, we know from Romans 16 that Paul had several personal friends and former fellow-workers who were now leaders of local congregations in Rome. He would naturally want to send them word that he planned to visit them. In addition, they would greatly appreciate a basic presentation of the gospel that they could teach to their congregations. You remember that the churches that Paul founded owed a great deal of their spiritual development to the teaching that he sent them in his letters.

Finally, there was always the possibility of problems with the Judaizers; they opposed Paul wherever he went. They also spread false reports about his teaching. Perhaps Paul wanted to be one step ahead of them on this occasion. The Lord led him to send the Roman Christians the full exposition of the gospel he preached. They could study this before he arrived. Then if they had any questions, he could answer them while he was there. If the Judaizers tried to stir up opposition or turn the Romans away from the true gospel, they would already be prepared to stand firmly for the faith.

So, during the early days of AD 57, eight years after writing Galatians, Paul dictated to his friend Tertius a letter for the Christians in Rome, the capital of the empire. In this epistle, he explained the reason for his proposed visit and provided the churches there with a full statement of the gospel as he understood it and proclaimed it.

QUESTION 5

Name four provinces Paul evangelized between AD 47 and 57. *(Select all that apply.)*

    A. Rome

    B. Macedonia

    C. Achaia

    D. Asia

    E. Galatia

    F. Bithynia

QUESTION 6

What new field did Paul plan to visit for pioneer evangelism?

    A. Rome

    B. Ephesus

    C. Jerusalem

    D. Spain

QUESTION 7

What was the relationship between Paul's choice of missionary field and his epistle to the Romans?

    A. Paul wrote to the Roman Christians to let them know he was coming to live and minister to them.

    B. Paul wrote to the Roman Christians to ask them to financially support his ministry in Jerusalem.

    C. Paul wrote to the Roman Christians to ask them to send helpers to assist him in his ministry.

    D. Paul wrote to the Roman Christians to let them know he would visit them on his way to Spain.

QUESTION 8

In what year and from what city did Paul write his letter to the Romans?

    A. AD 57 from Philippi

    B. AD 58 from Philippi

    C. AD 57 from Corinth

    D. AD 58 from Corinth

The Church at Rome (Rom 16:1-16)

> Objective 3 – At the end of this topic, you will be able to list three ways in which the church at Rome may have begun, and to identify in Romans 16 four observations about the church there.

We are not sure how the church at Rome began. We do know that some of the Christians living there accepted Christ before Paul was converted (see Rom 16:7). Wherever Christians went, they told people about Jesus. They met together in their homes for prayer, reading the Septuagint (Greek Old Testament), and fellowship. As more people accepted Christ, these home congregations multiplied all over the city.

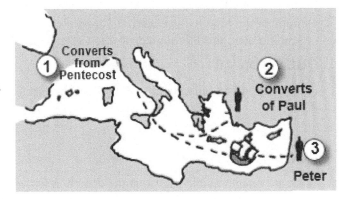

QUESTION 9

Read Acts 2:5-11. What idea does this give you as to who first took the gospel to Rome?

Many people believe that some of the pilgrims present in Jerusalem for the feast of Pentecost in AD 30 heard Peter preach the gospel, were converted and filled with the Holy Spirit, and took the good news back to Rome. You can learn about this by reading Acts 2:1-12.

Because Rome was the capital of the empire there were many opportunities for the gospel message to be brought to the people there. People frequently traveled between Rome and its provinces. In English, we still have the saying, "All roads lead to Rome." As Christian churches were established in such great population centers as Jerusalem, Antioch, Thessalonica, Philippi, Corinth, and Ephesus, many of the converts would visit the capital and tell their friends there about Christ.

You can see in Romans 16:3-16 that Paul had many friends in the church at Rome, although he had never been there. He sent greetings to people that he had met in different places. Some of them had been converted under his ministry but were now living in Rome.

Read Romans 16 and observe as many details as you can about the early Christian church.

Did you notice that the church met in the homes of the believers? The names inform us that the members were probably from many nationalities: Roman, Jewish, Greek, Asian, and Persian. Some of Paul's tribal kinsmen, who had been converted before he was, were there. The first convert from Achaia (or rather, the province of Greece) was there. Several women are mentioned as having an important part in God's work. Do you wish Paul had told us more about Phoebe when he recommended her so highly to the church? Some think she was a Christian businesswoman who took Paul's letter to Rome on one of her business trips. Some suggest she may have been a legal representative who defended the persecuted Christians in court.

Now read Romans 16:1-16 again in the light of these observations. A third possibility about the origin of the Christian church in Rome is the tradition that Peter went there and preached the gospel. Many people believe that he took the good news to the Jews living in Rome and founded the church.

The original group of believers in Rome most likely consisted of Jewish Christians. There was a Jewish community in Rome as early as the second century BC. The Roman government expelled the Jews from the city at least twice but later allowed them to return. Aquila and Priscilla (Paul's fellow workers in Corinth) were forced to leave Rome when the emperor Claudius ordered the Jews to leave (see Acts 18:2). It is possible that they were already Christians before they met Paul. Later, they returned to Rome and were among the church leaders to whom Paul sent his special greetings in this epistle (see Rom 16:3-5). Paul mentions also some of his Jewish kinsmen in Romans 16:7, 11.

In Romans 9; 10; 11, Paul's discussion about Israel leads us to believe that there were some Jews in the Roman church. However, by the time Paul wrote this epistle in AD 57, Gentile Christians seemed to outnumber the Jews in the church at Rome. Perhaps this was one reason why Paul felt the responsibility of sending them this thorough exposition of the gospel.

QUESTION 10

Paul seems to be writing mainly to the Jews in Romans 1:5-6, 13 and Romans 11:13, 25-30. *True or False?*

QUESTION 11

What are three possible ways that the church in Rome began? *(Select all that apply.)*

  A. By missionaries sent to Rome from the church in Jerusalem.

  B. By converts from Paul's ministry who went to Rome.

  C. By Jews reading Paul's earlier letters.

  D. By the ministry of Peter in Rome.

  E. By the testimony of Jews from Rome converted in Jerusalem during Pentecost.

When Paul finally reached Rome three years after writing this epistle, the circumstances were very different from those he had planned. While in Jerusalem, he had been accused of speaking against the temple and was put in prison. Paul finally appealed to have his case transferred to the jurisdiction of the emperor in Rome. On the way there as a prisoner, he was shipwrecked and spent a winter on the island of Malta. He reached Rome in AD 60.

The history of Paul's ministry in Acts ends abruptly after telling us that he spent two years in Rome under house arrest. In Acts 28:30-31, we see that during these two years Paul was preaching and teaching about Jesus Christ with all confidence.

What happened at the end of these two years is uncertain. From his letters, it seems that he was released after his trial and was able to travel again in the ministry for a short time. Soon afterwards, when a new persecution arose, it seems certain that he was arrested again and sentenced to death at Rome as a leader of the Christians. Paul was led out of the city and beheaded, but the persecution did not destroy Christianity in Rome. The church continued to grow and flourish in that great city.

Message of the Epistle

Objective 4 – At the end of this topic, you will be able to list at least five important topics that Paul discusses in both Galatians and Romans.

Romans was the last epistle Paul wrote before his imprisonment. Its theme and content are more similar to those of Galatians than to those of any other epistle. Galatians was written after Paul's first missionary journey; Romans was written after the third. During the intervening eight years of ministry, Paul had developed more thoroughly the truths that he had written so urgently to the Galatians. Now, at almost sixty years of age, Paul writes a systematic theological presentation of the teaching that he had given the Galatians.

The heart of Paul's gospel is the theme of justification by faith. We find in Romans an expanded teaching of this great doctrine of the Scriptures. In Galatians, the emphasis was on the fact that we are saved not by works of the law but by faith in Christ. In Romans, we see the doctrine of justification by faith from a different viewpoint and with a different emphasis--the righteousness of God. The same theme is discussed, but the emphasis is on faith as the way in which the righteousness of God is revealed.

QUESTION 12

What is the main theme of Romans?

    A. The place of the law

    B. God's holiness

    C. Justification by faith

    D. Paul's apostolic authority

Two Emphases:

Besides the main theme, you will find many subtopics or points of doctrine in Romans that you have already studied in Galatians. Faith is contrasted with works in Romans 3–4. Flesh (self-effort) is contrasted with the Spirit in Romans 7–8. Abraham is presented as a man of faith, and God's promise to Abraham is linked with the gospel. Paul discusses again the theme of divine love. The doctrine of the crucified Messiah and the significance of His work was mentioned briefly in Galatians and is presented more clearly in Romans. Both speak of circumcision and the Christian's relationship to the law.

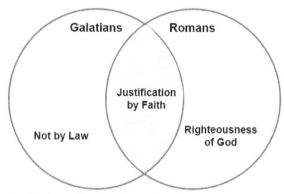

In Romans, Paul discusses some additional doctrines, too. Besides the question "How can a man be just with God?" he deals with such questions as: "What is the significance of Israel in history?" "What should the attitude of Gentile Christians be toward the Jews?" and "What are the practical evidences of Christian character?" Paul's answers to these questions provide us with a wealth of spiritual truth.

Chart of Topics

Galatians	Galatians and Romans	Romans
Defense of Apostleship	Justification by Faith	Origin of Sin
Testimony of Conversion	Faith versus Works	Universal Condemnation
Judaizers	Spirit versus Flesh	Scope of Salvation
Conflict with Peter	Failure of Self-effort	Israel's Destiny
Concern for Galatians	Promise to Abraham	Concern for Israel
Sarah and Hagar	Plan of Salvation	Jews and Gentiles
Servants and Sons	Divine Love	Government
	Union with Christ	Weak Christians
	Circumcision	Personal Plans
	Relationship to Law	Missions and Offerings
	Relationship to Others	Congratulations
	Water Baptism	Personal Greetings
	False Teachers	

Paul uses two sets of contrasts in both Romans and Galatians. They are: "by faith--not by works" and "by the Holy Spirit--not by flesh." He teaches that the Christian is justified by faith, not by anything he does (Rom 1:17). He goes on to teach that the Christian's life is to be controlled not by fleshly desires, but by the Holy Spirit (Rom 8:9).

QUESTION 13

Which expression describes how we are to live the Christian life?

    A. "By faith--not by works"

    B. "By the Holy Spirit--not by flesh"

    C. "By the Law--not by grace"

    D. "By our feelings--not by the Word of God"

QUESTION 14

Paul uses the expression "by faith--not by works" to describe how we are justified. *True or False?*

QUESTION 15

Which is NOT one of the doctrinal topics that Paul develops in both these epistles?

    A. The value of circumcision

    B. The promise of Abraham

    C. Abraham justified by faith

    D. The Second Coming

    E. The crucified Messiah

    F. Divine love

Preview of the Epistle

> Objective 5 – At the end of this topic, you will have an overall understanding of the development of Paul's thought in Romans by reading it straight through with the help of an outline.

In the Galatians course you were assigned preliminary readings with an outline. Now you are ready to follow the same steps with Romans. Doing this will help you see the epistle better as a whole and understand more clearly the development of Paul's thought, then you will be prepared for a detailed study of Romans.

First, read the outline of Romans.

Outline of Romans

Paul's Introduction to the Epistle	Romans 1:1-17
Greetings	1:1-7
Paul's Proposed Visit	1:8-15
Theme of the Epistle	1:16-17

Man's Need of Salvation	Romans 1:18-3:20
Wrath of God Revealed	**1:18**
Gentiles Condemned	**1:19-32**
• General Revelation of God	1:19-20
• Rejection of Truth	1:21-32
Self-righteous People Condemned	**2:1-16**
• Self-deceived and Self-condemned	2:1-6
• Principles of Judgment Revealed	2:7-16
Jews Condemned	**2:17 – 3:8**
• Advantages and Responsibility	2:17-29
• Questions and Conclusion	3:1-8
All the World Condemned	**3:9-20**

God's Provision for Salvation	Romans 3:21–5:21
Justification by Faith in Christ	**3:21-31**
• Revelation of God's Righteousness	3:21-26
• Justification Only by Faith	3:27-31
Justification in the Old Testament	**4:1-25**
• Abraham Justified by Faith	4:1-5
• Blessings of Imputed Righteousness	4:6-8
• Righteousness for Gentiles Too	4:9-25
Blessings Provided by Justification	**5:1-11**
Victory Over Sin and Death	**5:12-21**
• Sin and Death Through Adam	5:12-14
• Righteousness and Life in Christ	5:15-21

A New Life of Freedom	Romans 6-7
Freedom from Sin	**6:1-23**
• Death and Resurrection	6:1-10
• Victory Through Faith	6:11-14
• Choice of a New Master	6:15-23
Freedom from the Law	**7:1-13**
• Death and a New Marriage	7:1-6
• Functions of the Law	7:7-13
Freedom Not Reach by Self-effort	**7:14-25**

Life in the Spirit	Romans 8
Victory in the Spirit of Life	**8:1-13**
• Victory Over Sin and Death	8:1-4
• Victory Over the Flesh	8:4-9
• Resurrection Life	8:10-13
Spirit of Adoption for Sons of God	**8:14-16**
Suffering and Glory	**8:17-18**
Redemption of the Body	**8:19-25**
Help in Prayer	**8:26-27**
Perfection of Our Salvation	**8:28-39**
• Scope of the Father's Plan	8:28-30
• Security in the Father's Love	8:31-39

The Gospel for Jews and Gentiles	Romans 9–11
God's Chosen People	**9:1-29**
• Paul's Concern for Israel	9:1-5
• Chosen in God's Mercy	9:6-22
• Chosen from Jews and Gentiles	9:23-29
Salvation only by Faith	**9:30–10:11**
• Israel's Tragic Unbelief	9:30 – 10:3
• Man's Part in Salvation	10:4-11
God's Plan for Jews and Gentiles	**10:12 – 11:36**
• World Evangelism	10:12-21
• Not Total Rejection of Israel	11:1-16
• Gentiles Grafted In	11:17-25
• Israel Revived and Restored	11:25-31
• Riches of God's Wisdom	11:32-36

The Gospel and the Christian	Romans 12–13
Dedication and Transformation	**12:1-21**
• Attitude Toward God	12:1-2
• Attitude Toward Self	12:3-8
• Attitude Toward Others	12:9-21
Relationships with the World	**13:1-14**
• Good Citizenship	13:1-7
• Actions Determined by Love	13:8-10
• Wise Use of Time	13:11-14

The Gospel and the Church	Romans 14–16
Brotherly Love in the Church	**14:1–15:12**
• Not Judging and Quarreling	14:1-13
• Not Causing Others to Stumble	14:13-23
• Helping and Pleasing Others	15:1-6
• Accepting Others	15:7-12
Responsibilities of the Church	**15:13-33**
• Teaching and Spirituality	15:13-15
• World Evangelism	15:15-21
• Offerings	15:22-29
• Prayer	15:30-33
Christian Fellowship	**16:1-27**
• Recognition and Commendation	16:1-16
• Warning Against Divisions	16:17-20
• Fellowship Between Churches	16:21-24
• Glory to God	16:25-27

Next, imagine that you are a Roman soldier converted under Paul's ministry while you were stationed in Corinth, but you had to return to Rome before you could learn very much Christian doctrine. Now you are trying to tell your friends about God and salvation. They worship many gods. One philosopher friend is very interested, but you cannot answer his questions. Then one day Priscilla and Aquila tell you that they have received a letter from Paul and that he sends his greetings to the church in Rome. Priscilla and Aquila say that Paul wants them to share the letter with you and the others who meet in their home (Rom 16:3-5).

You are now ready to read the entire epistle, Romans 1–16. Refer to the outline of Romans as you read.

Topic 2: Paul's Introduction to the Epistle (Rom 1:1-17)

The first seventeen verses of Romans 1 provide additional background information about Paul and the subject, or theme, of his epistle. They also identify the persons to whom he is writing. In this section of Lesson 1, you will also encounter helpful ministry principles as you read Paul's discussion about his planned trip to Rome.

Greetings (Rom 1:1-7)

Objective 6 – At the end of this topic, you will be able to point out important information in Romans 1:1-7 about the writer, the subject of the epistle, and the persons to whom it is addressed.

The opening salutation in Romans is longer than that in any other Pauline epistle. The reason for this may be that Paul was not the founder of this church and, as far as we know, had never visited Rome. However, it is interesting to note that the Galatian epistle also has a very long salutation. The reason for this may be the nature of both these epistles. They both contain a strong polemic. In both letters, Paul uses a fairly long introduction to lay a foundation for the argument that is to follow.

The Writer

In most of his epistles, Paul begins with mention of his apostolic office, but here he starts with a different description of himself. Compare Romans 1:1 with 1 Corinthians 1:1; 2 Corinthians 1:1; Galatians 1:1; Ephesians 1:1; Colossians 1:1; 1 Timothy 1:1; 2 Timothy 1:1.

QUESTION 16

What title does Paul use for himself in Romans that is not found in the other Epistles?

Paul emphasizes here his commitment to Christ Jesus as Lord. The word *servant* in the Old Testament was used to describe Abraham, Moses, David, and the prophets. They were "servants of the Lord." Paul's use of this expression stresses the lordship of Jesus Christ. He does not hesitate to put Jesus in the position of the "Lord" of the Old Testament.

The word Paul uses for *servant* in the Greek language means "bondservant," or literally, "one who is bound." A bondservant is a slave. Paul was not a hired servant with a temporary contract. He had voluntarily given up his personal liberty and had committed his life freely and fully to his Master. Paul says that he is a servant of Jesus Christ set apart for the gospel of God. Paul is not only set apart or committed to the message, but he is also a "sent one," an apostle commissioned to proclaim this good news to the Gentiles.

The sense of the call of God and commitment to the gospel are both vitally important for a minister of the gospel. Can you testify to a similar call and sense of mission as Paul does in Romans 1:1?

Your commitment to Jesus Christ and separation to the gospel will be of prime importance in your ministry. Perhaps you would like to think and pray about this right now. Commit yourself wholly to the Lord Jesus Christ, to the gospel of God, and to the mission that He has for you.

The Subject

In Romans 1:1-4, we have a good definition of the gospel, the good news that Paul is writing about. Romans 1:1 gives us Paul's foundation for the gospel that he presents in this epistle. With the words *gospel of God* Paul announces two important truths. First, he tells us that the good news of the gospel is about God. Compare this with Romans 1:17. The gospel reveals the righteousness of God. Second, he says that the gospel has a divine origin; it is the gospel of *God*.

QUESTION 17

According to Romans 1:3, the theme of Paul's gospel is the holiness of the saints. *True or False?*

The good news is a person, not a formula. It is the Lord Jesus Christ. Paul was committed to a person, not to an ideal or philosophy. He was commissioned to preach about a person, not a religion. He declared the good news. Religion is not good news. The good news is that God, in the person of Jesus Christ, has come to men on a redemptive mission (see Jn 1:1 and Jn 1:14). God has visited this earth; this is the heart of the gospel message. This is why Paul fills these first seven verses of his epistle with a presentation of Jesus Christ as Lord. He is the gospel.

QUESTION 18

Read Romans 1:1-7, noting the titles given to Jesus which show His deity. Which of the following does not refer to His deity?

    A. His Son

    B. Christ our Lord

    C. Son of God

    D. Son of David

    E. Lord Jesus Christ

In the title the *Lord Jesus Christ* found in Romans 1:7, each word has its significance. *Jesus* is the Hebrew word meaning Savior. *Jesus* speaks of the humanity of Christ, the life and death of the man who came to earth at a certain point in history in order to save us from our sins. *Christ* means "the anointed one" (the Messiah). It speaks of Jesus' official work. He was anointed and commissioned to do a certain work. *Lord* speaks of Christ's sovereignty and deity. He is our Master, our Ruler, our King. All authority in heaven and earth has been given unto Him (see Mt 28:18).

QUESTION 19

In Romans 1:1-7 Paul offers a proof of the deity of Jesus Christ when he says, "...appointed the Son of God in power...by _____ from the dead."

QUESTION 20

Also in Romans 1:1-7 Paul refers to the humanity of Jesus when he calls Him, "..._____ of David with respect to the flesh."

Certain phrases in Romans 1:1-7 have great significance. "By the resurrection from the dead" is a statement that clearly presents a proof of the deity of Jesus Christ. "Descendant of David" is a clear reference to the humanity of Jesus.

In this opening salutation to the epistle Paul asserts that the gospel is centered in the person of Jesus Christ; it did not originate with the coming of Christ. His coming and the redemption of mankind had been promised long before that.

QUESTION 21

Read Romans 1:2. According to this verse, people heard the good news of the coming Savior in Old Testament times through _____ in the Holy Scriptures.

QUESTION 22

Read Romans 16:25-27. Paul describes the gospel as it was promised in the Old Testament as a mystery. What is the contrasting term he uses to describe his preaching of the gospel?

    A. Proclamation of Jesus Christ

    B. Revelation of the mystery

    C. Now is disclosed

    D. Prophetic Scriptures

One of those mysterious promises given to the prophets is found in 2 Samuel 7:12-16. There God promises David an eternal kingdom. This promise was fulfilled in the Messiah, who was a descendant of David and is often referred to as the Son of David. In Romans 1:3, Paul points out that Jesus was born of the royal line of David. His eternal reign will be the fulfillment of the promise made to David.

QUESTION 23

Now let's look again at Romans 1:4 and compare it with Romans 8:11. The miracle of Christ's resurrection took place by whose power?

    A. God the Father

    B. God the Son

    C. God the Holy Spirit

    D. All of the above

The word *appointed* in Romans 1:4 is better translated "established." The resurrection of Jesus did not make Him the Son of God, it merely established that fact, or made it evident.

QUESTION 24

According to Romans 1:5, God made Paul an apostle for the purpose of bringing obedience of faith from among _____.

    A. All Jews

    B. All Christians

    C. All Gentiles

    D. Only the Jews

QUESTION 25

What is produced by the kind of faith mentioned in Romans 1:5?

According to Romans 1:5, God made Paul an apostle to bring about the "obedience of faith" among the Gentiles. To what is Paul referring here? The best interpretation is that Paul was sent to the Gentiles to bring about a certain kind of faith that would result in obedience.

In other words, Paul's purpose was to bring the Gentiles to the same commitment to Jesus Christ that he had. He wanted them to become bondservants also, obedient to the Lord Jesus Christ and involved in His mission in the world. We find the principle of reproduction in this verse. Paul is committed to reproduce himself, to reproduce the same commitment to Jesus Christ in others. He is called to have "spiritual children."

This is a basic principle in God's plan to evangelize the nations. Let's examine two passages of Scripture on this subject.

QUESTION 26

What does Jesus tell us to do for all nations in Matthew 28:18-20?

    A. Go and make disciples.

    B. Go and evangelize.

    C. Evangelize and baptize.

    D. Baptize and circumcise.

QUESTION 27

One English translation says, "Make disciples of all nations." A disciple is a learner. What does Jesus say we are to teach people in order to make them the kind of disciples that He wants? (See Mt 28:20.)

Jesus' disciples were to reproduce themselves then and in every succeeding generation!

QUESTION 28

Now look at 2 Timothy 2:2. Paul tells Timothy to _____ to faithful men the things that Paul had taught him.

QUESTION 29

What kind of men is Timothy to teach these truths to? *(Select all that apply.)*

    A. Faithful men

    B. Men who will be able to teach others

    C. Men who are mature

    D. Men who are circumcised

This principle of reproduction is the key to the growth of your church. If you are the pastor of a local church, put this principle to work in your ministry and see what happens in your church! Train a faithful Christian to use the abilities and gifts that God has given him and give him responsibility and opportunities to serve. Help him become an effective servant of the Lord. You can also put this principle into practice by training people to witness for Christ. Inspire them to win the lost, then watch your church grow!

If you are not a pastor, this principle still applies to you. Jesus' command in Matthew 28:18-20 is for every Christian. Multiply yourself! Find someone and tell him about Christ. Consider him your spiritual child. Oversee his spiritual development and see how God will make you a blessing in your church. This is a ministry that every Christian can have and should have. Does 2 Timothy 2:2 apply to you? Of course it does.

Principles of Reproduction

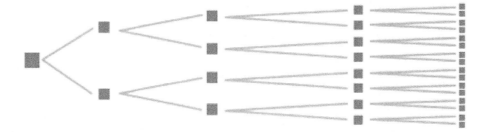

The Persons Addressed

You have already noticed from Romans 1:5-7 that Paul is writing chiefly to Gentile Christians in Rome.

QUESTION 30

Paul describes the people to whom he is writing with three phrases in Romans 1:7. What are they? *(Select all that apply.)*

    A. Called to belong to Jesus

    B. All who are in Rome

    C. Beloved of God

    D. Called to be saints

    E. All of the above

Saints are God's holy people, set apart for Himself.

QUESTION 31

In Romans 1:7, Paul's greeting to the Romans takes the form of a blessing or prayer. What two things does he wish for them? *(Select all that apply.)*

    A. Comfort

    B. Peace

    C. Freedom

    D. Grace

In Romans 1:7, Paul's greeting to the Romans takes the form of a blessing or prayer for them: "Grace and peace from God our Father and the Lord Jesus Christ." Grace is God's free love and unmerited favor to men which is given through Jesus Christ. The peace mentioned here refers to the well-being which such men enjoy through God's grace.

Paul's Proposed Visit (Rom 1:8-15)

> Objective 7 – At the end of this topic, you will be able to list at least five characteristics of a good minister of the gospel as you see them demonstrated by Paul in Romans 1:8-15 and apply these in your own life and teaching.

You have probably noticed as you read this passage that Romans 1:8 is a "bridge" verse that unites Paul's salutation in Romans 1:1-8 with the following message about his proposed visit. It tells us more about the people to whom the letter is addressed. It is clear that Paul introduces his new subject when he says, "First of all." In this verse, he follows his usual pattern of commending the church on one of its strong points.

QUESTION 32

What traits do we learn about the Roman church from Romans 1:8?

    A. Their faith

    B. Their works

    C. Their joy and enthusiasm

    D. Their adherence to the law

Paul was thankful that in the capital city of the empire there was a "missionary church." Notice that Paul prayed often for this church although he had never been to Rome. This is a good example for us. We should be concerned about the work of God in other areas and in other countries.

QUESTION 33

Paul longs to see these Christians to impart to them some _____ . (See Rom 1:11.)

Notice that the word *impart* in Romans 1:11 may be better translated "share." Paul uses the same Greek word in a similar statement in 1 Thessalonians 2:8. The idea is not that Paul distributes gifts, but that he shares with other Christians the gifts God has given him.

QUESTION 34

Paul wanted to minister to the Christians in Rome in order to rebuke them (Rom 1:11). *True or False?*

Does this verse bring you greater clarity on why Paul wrote his epistles, especially this one? Is this same desire a motivating force in your ministry?

Now notice an important principle for good leadership in Romans 1:12. Paul tells these Christians that they also may be a source of comfort and strength to him. There is a feeling of brotherhood between Paul and his readers, rather than a feeling of superiority on his part.

QUESTION 35

After you read Paul's description of an ideal Christian leader in Romans 1:8-15, see how many of those characteristics you can list in your Life Notebook. Pray over this list and indicate those you would like to cultivate. The first characteristic is listed for you.

Romans 1:8: He commends people when they deserve it.

Romans 1:9:

Romans 1:10:

Romans 1:11:

Romans 1:12:

Romans 1:13:

Romans 1:14:

Romans 1:15:

Theme of the Epistle (Rom 1:16-17)

> Objective 8 – At the end of this topic, you will be able to relate the theme of the epistle to the Romans to the use of the term *faith* throughout the epistle.

Romans 1:16-17 is a summary of the entire epistle. The theme of the book of Romans is the righteousness of God revealed.

Previously, we stated that religion is not good news. What does that mean? The righteousness of God has not been discovered by religion. Every religion has one basic characteristic: Its followers are trying to reach God, find God, and please God through their own efforts. *Religions* are systems of worship that reach up toward God. Is this the gospel? Is this "good news"? Would the righteousness of God be found in religion?

Paul tells us in Romans 1:17 that the righteousness of God is "revealed." The Greek word translated "revealed" in Romans 1:17 refers to uncovering something that has been hidden. The only way that men could know about how to have right standing with God (the righteousness of God) is for God to choose to make it known. We could not recognize the rightness of God or find a way to make our lives right without a revelation from God.

The righteousness of God is revealed in the gospel. The gospel is the story of God revealing Himself to man through His Son. The story concerns the life, death, and resurrection of Jesus. All of this originated with God and was accomplished through His Son Jesus Christ. How do we receive the revelation of the righteousness of God in the gospel? Entirely by faith.

QUESTION 36

We understand the righteousness of God in the gospel because ...

    A. We work hard and study diligently.

    B. We are taught by good teachers who help us understand.

    C. God chose to reveal the truth to us.

    D. The Gospels tell a consistent, truthful story.

In what sense is the gospel "to the Jew first"? This refers to the historic order in which the gospel was offered to mankind. While the opportunity to accept the gospel was offered to mankind it was first given to the Jews, God's chosen people (see Acts 3:25-26). When Paul says "and also to the Greek," he is using the term *Greek* loosely as the equivalent of Gentile or non-Jew. The message was first to the Jews and then to those of every nation.

You will want to use Romans 1:16-17 often in your ministry, and its summary will help you in your study of this epistle. We recommend that you memorize these two verses now.

QUESTION 37

According to Romans 1:16, what critical thing does the gospel provide us?

    A. Archeological information about the times of Christ

    B. Sociological insights into the times of Christ

    C. Cultural perspectives on Jesus' parables

    D. Power for salvation

QUESTION 38

What is the condition we must meet in order to receive the benefits of the gospel?

    A. Have faith in the gospel.

    B. Observe the Law.

    C. Agree with everything Paul taught.

    D. Be circumcised.

According to Romans 1:16, the gospel provides salvation. This salvation is available to everyone who believes. Here is a clear confirmation that the only condition a person must meet in order to receive the benefits of the gospel is faith.

QUESTION 39

According to Romans 1:16, why is Paul not ashamed of the gospel?

    A. Because he was a Jew

    B. Because he was chosen to preach to the Gentiles

    C. Because he believed

    D. Because it is the power of God for salvation

The righteousness of God that is revealed in the gospel, to men who have faith in Christ, is God's own righteousness. The term *righteousness* in Romans 1:17 speaks of a standing with God that a man receives when he believes. He is declared to be "in the right" before God. This condition conforms to God's law and His own personal righteousness.

As you have seen, the principle that brings this right standing with God is faith. The words "from faith to faith" mean that the first act of faith, which brings the right standing with God, will result in a life received by the same principle of faith. Paul quotes the Old Testament to emphasize this: "The righteous man shall live by faith" (Hab 2:4). This means that the man who is declared "righteous" by God is to live a righteous life. The ruling principle of the righteous man's life is faith.

QUESTION 40

What are the two uses of the term "faith" in Romans 1:17 in connection with the theme of the Roman epistle? *(Select all that apply.)*

    A. Right standing: the crisis act of faith that results in the righteousness of God.

    B. Right motives: the absolute personal commitment to do the right thing.

    C. Right living: the continuing, active faith or life principle that produces the righteousness of God.

    D. Right thinking: the clear understanding of righteousness and unrighteousness.

QUESTION 41

What is the meaning of "righteousness" as it refers to us in Romans 1:17?

    A. Conformity to God's law

    B. Conformity to conscience

    C. Right standing with God

    D. Correct in doctrine

QUESTION 42

Where do we find the revelation of the righteousness of God?

    A. In the sincere search for truth in any religion

    B. In the Christian church

    C. In worship

    D. In the gospel of Jesus Christ

QUESTION 43

Write from memory the verses that contain the theme and summary of the Epistle to the Romans.

Lesson 1 Self Check

QUESTION 1

What relationship did Paul's choice of missionary field have with his epistle to the Romans?

    A. Paul wrote to the Roman Christians to let them know he would visit them on his way to Spain.

    B. Paul wrote to the Roman Christians to ask them to financially support his ministry in Jerusalem.

    C. Paul wrote to the Roman Christians to let them know he was coming to live and minister to them.

    D. Paul wrote to the Roman Christians to ask them to send helpers to assist him in his ministry.

QUESTION 2

Paul's epistle to the Romans is most closely related to his epistle to the Philippians. *True or False?*

QUESTION 3

Who or what is the gospel?

    A. The Law

    B. Jesus Christ

    C. Paul

    D. Circumcision

QUESTION 4

Which is NOT one of the doctrinal topics that Paul develops in Romans and Galatians?

    A. The value of circumcision

    B. The promise of Abraham

    C. Abraham justified by faith

    D. The Second Coming

    E. The crucified Messiah

    F. Divine love

QUESTION 5

In Romans 1:1-7, Paul offers a proof of the deity of Jesus Christ when he says, "appointed the Son of God in power…by the resurrection from the dead." *True or False?*

QUESTION 6

According to Romans 1:16, why is Paul not ashamed of the gospel?

    A. Because he was a Jew

    B. Because he was chosen to preach to the Gentiles

    C. Because he believed

    D. Because it is the power of God for salvation

QUESTION 7

The book of Romans is primarily a book about the defense of the gospel. *True or False?*

QUESTION 8

Jews from Rome who converted to Christianity in Jerusalem during Pentecost were probably the first individuals to take the gospel to Rome. *True or False?*

QUESTION 9

According to Romans 1:11, Paul longs to see the Christians in Rome so that he might impart to them some spiritual gift. *True or False?*

QUESTION 10

In Romans 1:17, there are two usages of the term *faith* used in connection with the theme of the Roman epistle. The crisis act of faith which brings the righteousness of God is *right living. True or False?*

Lesson 1 Answers to Questions

QUESTION 1
    D. Epistle to the Romans

QUESTION 2: *Your answer*

QUESTION 3: False

QUESTION 4: True

QUESTION 5
    B. Macedonia
    C. Achaia
    D. Asia
    E. Galatia

QUESTION 6
    D. Spain

QUESTION 7
    D. Paul wrote to the Roman Christians to let them know he would visit them on his way to Spain.

QUESTION 8
    C. AD 57 from Corinth

QUESTION 9: *Your answer should be similar to the following:*
The gospel may have first been taken to Rome by Jews from Rome who were converted to Christ in Jerusalem at Pentecost.

QUESTION 10: False

QUESTION 11
    B. By converts from Paul's ministry who went to Rome.
    D. By the ministry of Peter in Rome.
    E. By the testimony of Jews from Rome converted in Jerusalem during Pentecost.

QUESTION 12
    C. Justification by faith

QUESTION 13
    B. "By the Holy Spirit--not by flesh"

QUESTION 14: True

QUESTION 15
    D. The Second Coming

QUESTION 16: *Your answer should be one of the following:*
A slave of Jesus Christ, Slave, Servant

QUESTION 17: False

QUESTION 18
    D. Son of David

QUESTION 19: Resurrection

QUESTION 20: *Your answer should be one of the following:*
Son, Descendant, Seed

QUESTION 21: *Your answer should be one of the following:*
God's prophets, His prophets, Prophets

QUESTION 22
    B. Revelation of the mystery

QUESTION 23
    C. God the Holy Spirit

QUESTION 24
    C. All Gentiles

QUESTION 25: Obedience

QUESTION 26

    A. Go and make disciples.

QUESTION 27: *Your answer should be one of the following:*

    Teach them to obey., Obedience

QUESTION 28: *Your answer should be one of the following:*

    Entrust, Commit, Teach

QUESTION 29

    A. Faithful men

    B. Men who will be able to teach others

QUESTION 30

    B. All who are in Rome

    C. Beloved of God

    D. Called to be saints

QUESTION 31

    B. Peace

    D. Grace

QUESTION 32

    A. Their faith

QUESTION 33: Spiritual gift

QUESTION 34: False

QUESTION 35: *Your answer*

QUESTION 36

    C. God chose to reveal the truth to us.

QUESTION 37

    D. Power for salvation

QUESTION 38

    A. Have faith in the gospel.

QUESTION 39

    D. Because it is the power of God for salvation

QUESTION 40

    A. Right standing: the crisis act of faith that results in the righteousness of God.

    C. Right living: the continuing, active faith or life principle that produces the righteousness of God.

QUESTION 41

    C. Right standing with God

QUESTION 42

    D. In the gospel of Jesus Christ

QUESTION 43: *Your answer should be similar to the following:*

For I am not ashamed of the gospel, for it is God's power for salvation to everyone who believes, to the Jew first and also to the Greek. For the righteousness of God is revealed in the gospel from faith to faith, just as it is written, "The righteous by faith will live."

Lesson 1 Self Check Answers

QUESTION 1
    A. Paul wrote to the Roman Christians to let them know he would visit them on his way to Spain.

QUESTION 2: False

QUESTION 3
    B. Jesus Christ

QUESTION 4
    D. The Second Coming

QUESTION 5: True

QUESTION 6
    D. Because it is the power of God for salvation

QUESTION 7: False

QUESTION 8: True

QUESTION 9: True

QUESTION 10: False

Lesson 2: Man's Need of Salvation (Rom 1:18–3:20)

Lesson Introduction

Paul begins his explanation of the gospel by showing our need of salvation. We must recognize our need before we can understand the good news that Christ will save us. Once we realize our own helplessness we can turn our lives over to the Savior.

Lesson Objectives

Topic 1 describes the wrath of God, which is the starting point for understanding man's need of salvation.

In Topic 1, you will discover…

- Basic characteristics of God's wrath
- What people of all kinds do that makes them objects of God's wrath

Topic 2 explains why the Gentiles are condemned.

In Topic 2, you will learn…

- How God has revealed Himself to all mankind through nature
- How rejection of this revealed truth has led Gentiles into false religions and sinful practices

Topic 3 explains why self-righteous people are condemned.

In Topic 3, you will learn…

- How the hypocrisy of the self-righteous leads to self-condemnation
- Why the self-righteous are condemned and can only be justified by faith.

Topic 4 explains why the Jews are condemned.

In Topic 4, you will discover…

- The advantages and responsibilities of the Jews
- The particular failure that led to their condemnation
- Three important questions that arise in light of God's condemnation of the Jews

Topic 5 confirms that all the world is condemned.

In Topic 5, you will consider how the condemnation of the world should motivate you to minister more effectively.

Lesson Outline

Topic 1: Wrath of God Revealed (1:18)

Nature of God's Wrath

Objects of God's Wrath

Topic 2: Gentiles Condemned (1:19-32)

Word List

We hope you will enjoy using the word study at the beginning of each lesson. Some of the words you already know, but they are used in a special sense in the lesson. Others are theological terms, and some are new words for many students. Please read the word study each time before starting the lesson. Refer back to it as necessary.

Blasphemed (Rom 2:24) - spoken against irreverently.

Covetousness, etc. (Rom 1:29) - desire for what belongs to another; *Malice* - desire to harm others; *Hostility* - evil, ill will.

No partiality (Rom 2:11) - no favoritism.

Retribution - repayment, reward, recompense.

Revelation - act of God in which He makes Himself known or reveals truth.

Throats are open graves (Rom 3:13) - words like an open grave, dangerous, and corrupt.

Wrath (Rom 1:18) - strong anger.

Topic 1: Wrath of God Revealed (Rom 1:18)

In the first chapter of Romans, Paul tells us that there are two revelations from heaven. In Romans 1:16-17, you saw that the *righteousness* of God is revealed in the gospel. Now in Romans 1:18 Paul speaks of a revelation of God's *wrath*. Before we can understand the righteousness of God in His work of redemption, we must understand the wrath of God revealed from heaven.

Nature of God's Wrath (Rom 1:18)

Objective 1 – At the end of this topic, you will be able to describe the nature of God's wrath and the way in which it is expressed.

Romans 1:18 introduces the theme of this whole lesson: the need to be saved from the wrath of God and the power of sin.

Let us look now at two aspects or descriptions of God's wrath. The first describes its basic nature. The second tells us how it is expressed.

Reaction of Holiness to Sin

First, let's look at the wrath of God as the response of His holiness to wickedness and rebellion. Some people find it hard to believe that God can be wrathful or angry. They think that anger does not agree with the character of God. This is because they think of wrath in terms of human anger, which so often includes sinful passion. God's anger is not unreasonable or unjust.

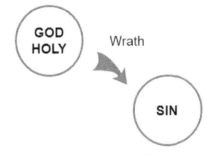

Since God is holy, He is against all kinds of sin. He is good, so He opposes evil. Suppose a dog attacked your child. What emotion would you feel toward the dog? Would you stand there with a smile and watch the dog kill the child that you loved? Would it be right or wrong of you to become angry with the dog and fight against it to rescue your child? Sin destroys the sinner. God, who loves us all, does not want sin to destroy us. His very goodness makes Him react against those things that destroy His children.

You can see, then, that God's wrath is His personal response toward sin. God is holy and it is in accord with His nature to respond to sin and wickedness by manifesting His wrath. This response does not come from sinful passion, but rather from the very character of God, from His holiness.

The more we think of God's wrath as the natural reaction of His holiness toward sin, the better we can understand why no sinners will be allowed to enter His eternal home. What kind of heaven would it be if we entered there with our sins and became the constant objects of God's wrath?

Principle of Retribution

A good and just God gives people the reward they deserve for what they do. This is the principle of retribution that must operate in a moral universe. Good deeds are rewarded. Evil deeds are punished. Did you notice this principle in Galatians (Gal 6:8)? In Romans, we see God's wrath manifested as the just payment that sinners deserve for their wickedness and rebellion. Death is the just payment for sin. Those who reject God, the source of life, face death. This is the just reward and natural consequence of rejecting life. The punishment fits the offense. Men reap what they sow. "The wages of sin is death" (Rom 6:23).

The wrath of God is the response of His holiness to sin, but we see it manifested in the principle of retribution, His just punishment of sinners. Watch for this principle in the rest of this chapter. Three times you will find it expressed in the words *God gave them up*.

QUESTION 1

The nature of God's wrath is the response of His holiness to sin. *True or False?*

QUESTION 2

How would you describe the principle of retribution?

    A. The way God expresses His wrath.

    B. The way God encourages diversity in the body of Christ.

    C. The way Christians should relate to one another.

    D. The way people respond when they are under God's wrath.

QUESTION 3

How is God's anger different from man's? *(Select all that apply.)*

    A. Not emotional

    B. Always righteous

    C. Not part of His character

    D. Free from sinful passion

QUESTION 4

Which term best describes divine retribution?

    A. Revenge

    B. Repayment

    C. Discipline

    D. Correction

Objects of God's Wrath (Rom 1:18)

Objective 2 – At the end of this topic, you will be able to state a principle found in Romans 1:18 about the results of rejecting God's truth.

In Romans 1:18, Paul talks about the revelation of the wrath of God. A person's response to God determines whether or not he will experience this wrath. Just as the righteousness of God is revealed to those who respond with faith to God's truth, so is the wrath of God revealed to the person who responds without faith (unbelief) to God's truth.

QUESTION 5

To respond in faith to God's revelation is to accept it. To respond in unbelief is to reject it. Which of the following are included in Paul's Romans 1:18 description of this rejection?

    A. Ungodliness

    B. Unrighteousness

    C. Suppressing the truth

    D. Hypocrisy

QUESTION 6

Look at Romans 1:18 and in your Life Notebook write a basic principle showing the results of rejecting God's truth. Give an example that you have seen of this principle.

The Living Bible paraphrase of Romans 1:18 says:

> "But God shows His anger from heaven against all sinful, evil men who push away the truth from them."

The Good News Translation says:

> "God's anger is revealed from heaven against all the sin and evil of people whose evil ways prevent the truth from being known."

The meaning of Romans 1:18 is that men were suppressing or holding back the truth by refusing to live by it. You will read more about that later in the lesson. In fact, the rest of this part of Romans is the development of the statement in Romans 1:18. It shows us how everyone is guilty of "holding the truth in unrighteousness" or how we have all sinned and have become the objects of God's wrath.

Topic 2: Gentiles Condemned (Rom 1:19-32)

Paul speaks in Romans 1:18 about the ungodliness and unrighteousness of those who reject God's revelation. In the following verses, he shows how rejection of God leads to ungodly living that becomes worse and worse. He shows us the origin of idolatry and moral corruption. He points out how one sin leads to another; the whole human race has become hopelessly lost without God.

General Revelation of God (Rom 1:19-20)

Objective 3 –At the end of this topic, you will be able to describe the general revelation of God, two sources through which people receive it, and its importance in the judgment.

In these verses, was Paul talking about the history of the human race? Or was he talking about the Gentiles of his day? Apparently he was talking about both. As a result of his knowledge of the Law, Paul was undoubtedly thinking about how man deliberately turned away from the original revelation of God until the world became so corrupt that God sent the flood. The human race made a fresh start with a new revelation of God, but most of Noah's descendants rejected the truth and chose the downward path of sin. At the same time, Paul was also describing the Gentile world of his day and pointing out that they too had had a revelation of God but had rejected it.

QUESTION 7

Which of the following verses in the first chapter of Romans tell us that the Gentiles had been given some kind of revelation of God?

    A. Romans 1:7-8

    B. Romans 1:16-17

    C. Romans 1:19-20

    D. Romans 1:24-25

Romans 1:19-20 makes it clear that the Gentiles have received enough of a revelation of God that they are without excuse for rejecting Him. Now read these other verses that show that they had some knowledge of God and understood that they were doing wrong when they deliberately turned away from it: Romans 1:21-23, 25, 28, 32.

QUESTION 8

What things did the Gentiles know about God according to Romans 1:20, 23, 25, 32? *(Select all that apply.)*

    A. His Son, Jesus

    B. His Holy Spirit

    C. His glory

    D. His righteous judgment

    E. His eternal power and divine nature

    F. His truth

Paul is writing here about people who did not have the Scriptures and had not heard the gospel message. Would they be condemned? This is an important question because we face it today.

QUESTION 9

This passage clearly shows that the revelation God gave to the Gentiles told them about redemption. *True or False?*

Two sources of knowledge about God have been given to the whole human race: conscience and nature. Some of the invisible things of God are "manifest" in us by the inner voice of God speaking to the conscience (see Rom 2:14-15). Others are revealed to our reason through the wonders of God's creation in the natural world (see Rom 1:19-20). This knowledge of God that is given to all men everywhere is called the general revelation of God. Creation tells us that a higher power made us and the world that we live in. If this is so, we should try to find Him. We should do what He wants us to do. He speaks to our conscience and lets us know right from wrong. If we accept His revelation, we will obey Him to the best of our ability.

Revelation

CREATOR and JUDGE revealed in:	GOD and HIS TRUTH revealed in:
Nature	Bible
History	Prophesy
Providence	Miracles
Conscience	Jesus Christ
	Experience

Unfortunately, the response of men to this general revelation of God has been rejection. There is evidence of an inward impulse to "push away the truth." This impulse is sin in the human heart.

Rejection of Truth (Rom 1:21-32)

Objective 4 – - At the end of this topic, you will be able to state the origin of false religions and sinful practices and describe the progressive nature of sin.

Origin of False Religions

What is the natural consequence of rejecting the truth? Believing what is not true. If we refuse to believe what God tells us about the origin of the world and the power that controls it, then God gives us up to our own ideas about these things. In Romans 1:19-23, we see that the Gentiles became guilty of idolatry after rejecting the revelation of God. They rejected the Creator and found themselves worshipping things that He had created! This seems unthinkable, but as it has often been said, man is incurably religious. If he rejects God, he will always find some other object or ideal to worship.

QUESTION 10

Can you think of some objects that people worship (or give first place to in their lives) instead of worshipping the true God? List them in your Life Notebook, then reflect on and interact with the following statement: "Sin in the life of the believer reveals that he or she is not fully satisfied in God." Do you agree or disagree? In what ways can Christians be guilty of idolatry?

Origin of Sinful Practices

In Romans 1:24, we see that men's idolatry causes God to give them up to immorality. Turning away from God and His holiness, they do what is unholy. Having rejected the revelation of God in nature, they become involved in sinful acts that are against nature (Rom 1:26-27). In this we see how the wrath of God continues to operate as the principle of retribution. Man makes his choice and takes the consequences. The words *God gave them up* are terrible words indeed! The worst judgment God can give sinful men is to lift His restraining hand and let them do as they please.

Progressive Nature of Sin

The picture that Paul paints in Romans 1:18-32 explains why there is so much sin in the world today. We learn an important lesson here about the nature of sin: it is progressive. It grows stronger, increases, spreads, and becomes worse and worse. One sin leads to another and on to others. Can you see the progressive, corrupting influence of sin in Romans 1:18-32? The rejection of God's truth is the starting point for this progressive immorality.

In order to help you remember the steps in the downward path of sin and the results, you can write the verses on a piece of paper, distinguishing between the steps and the results with different colors of ink. You can keep this paper with your Bible.

Romans 1:18--They held the truth of God in unrighteousness (pushed away the truth). Result - The wrath of God is revealed.

Romans 1:21--When they knew God they did not honor Him as God; were not thankful; became vain in their imaginations. Result - Their foolish hearts were darkened.

Romans 1:22--They boasted of their own wisdom. Result - They became fools.

Romans 1:23-24--They changed the glory of God into worship of created things, which is idolatry. Notice the degeneration: from God to man, birds, beasts, creeping things. Result - God gave them up to their own lusts and impurity.

Romans 1:25-26--They changed the truth of God into a lie. They worshipped and served the creature more than the Creator. Result - God gave them up to vile affections and their sexual perversion.

Romans 1:27--They practiced homosexuality. Result - They suffered physical consequences from their depravity.

Romans 1:28--They did not want to acknowledge God or even think about Him. Result - God gave them over to a depraved mind so they could follow their sinful ways.

Romans 1:29-- They were filled with unrighteousness, fornication, wickedness, covetousness, maliciousness, envy, murder, fighting, deceit, malice, gossip.

Romans 1:30They spoke evil of one another, hatred God, were disrespectful, proud, boasters, inventors of evil things, disobedient to parents.

Romans 1:31They were without understanding, covenant-breakers, without natural affection, implacable, unmerciful.

Romans 1:32--Knowing the judgment of God, that those who do such things are worthy of death, they continued to do them and took pleasure in those who practiced them. Result - They were worthy of death.

We see in Romans 1:32 the terrible final results of rejecting God's truth as the sinner becomes completely defiant toward God and is glad to see others rebel against Him and His laws. Have you ever seen anyone like this?

Can you understand better now the seriousness of rejecting the revelation of God's truth? In light of this passage, what do you feel about the importance of evangelism among children and youth? Does your preaching and teaching help people see the deadliness of sin?

QUESTION 11

According to Romans 1:18, the basic reason the wrath of God is revealed against men is because they have rejected His truth. In Romans 1:21-32, what is the consequence of this rejection?

    A. God chose to forgive them.

    B. God gave them up to their sin.

    C. God gave them a second chance.

    D. God decided to ignore their sins.

QUESTION 12

Read James 1:21-22, 26; Matthew 7:24-27. Is the rejection of truth described as the refusal to agree with it intellectually or the failure to live according to what it teaches?

    A. Neither

    B. Failure to live according to what it teaches

    C. Refusal to agree with it intellectually

    D. Both

QUESTION 13

In Romans 1:20 and Romans 1:32, what does God say about the guilt of those who have rejected His truth and the sentence that they deserve?

    A. They are guilty, but God is merciful.

    B. They acted on what they knew and will not be condemned.

    C. They are without excuse and deserve to die.

    D. Some are guiltier than others and they will be judged individually.

God has used this passage many times to convince people of the basic sinfulness of human nature and to show them their need of salvation. Do you plan to use it sometime in your preaching or teaching?

QUESTION 14

Based on the list of sins in Romans 1:24-32, our world is better than the pagan world of Paul's day. *True or False?*

QUESTION 15

Suppose someone says, "I live a good, clean life and don't harm my fellow man. Why do I need God or religion?" How could you use what you have just studied about the nature of sin to answer him? In your Life Notebook, write a two- or three-paragraph response to this person.

Paul has shown us in this chapter that apart from God we cannot resist sin's corrupting and degenerating influence. Only by faith in God's revelation, the gospel, can men be delivered from sin's power. We need the righteousness that only God can give us. The Gentile world needs the good news of a Savior because it has been tried, found guilty, and pronounced worthy of death.

Topic 3: Self-righteous People Condemned (Rom 2:1-16)

At the beginning of Romans 2, Paul turns his attention to the "good" man according to human standards. He might be either Jew or Gentile. Many Gentiles were strongly opposed to most of the sins listed in Romans 1:24-32. Good, moral people considered these sins very evil. In fact, they strongly condemned people who did such things. He may have had in mind the Jewish critics of his day. These men were proud of being a part of God's chosen people. They looked down on people of other nations and condemned them for their sins. Is it fair to say that these "good" people are condemned by God?

Self-deceived and Self-condemned (Rom 2:1-5)

Objective 5 – At the end of this topic, you will be able to explain how the sins of self-righteousness and hypocrisy can be recognized and apply this knowledge in your spiritual life and ministry.

What is God's evaluation of people who have a high moral standard and criticize those who do not measure up to it? Paul tells people of this type that they are guilty of some of the very things that they condemn in others.

Did you ever see a man who sometimes tells lies but punishes his son for lying to him? Or someone who would criticize a preacher for using the kind of language that he himself uses? Or who condemns a murderer but has an enemy that he hates? In reality, our critical attitude toward others is often an unconscious cover-up for the same faults in our own lives. Harsh criticism is usually a signal that something is wrong in the one that criticizes. And pretending that we are better than others is a form of hypocrisy. See the teaching of Jesus in Matthew 7:1-5.

QUESTION 16

What does Paul say about the guilt of those who condemn others for things that they themselves do (Rom 2:1)? *(Select all that apply.)*

    A. Minimal since all are sinners

    B. Inexcusable

    C. Less serious than some other kinds of sin

    D. Brings them under condemnation

QUESTION 17

According to Romans 2:3, "good, moral people" sometimes have the mistaken idea that they will escape God's judgment. *True or False?*

QUESTION 18

On what basis will God judge these people (Rom 2:2)?

    A. By their superiority over bad people

    B. By their moral standards

    C. By their concept of how good they are

    D. By the truth of what they really are

QUESTION 19

Some people trust in their own goodness and refuse to repent and ask God for His forgiveness. Of what sins are such people guilty (Rom 2:4-5)? *(Select all that apply.)*

    A. Stubbornness

    B. Contempt for God's forbearance and patience

    C. A lying spirit

    D. An unrepentant heart

    E. Contempt for God's kindness

    F. Bitterness

QUESTION 20

According to Romans 2:5, these "good, moral people" who refuse to seek God are storing up _____ for themselves.

Paul's argument in Romans 2:1-6 is that moral people who trust in their own goodness and harshly criticize others are deceiving themselves. Their very attitude shows that they are full of the sins of pride, harshness, and lack of love. It is perfectly fair for God to condemn them.

QUESTION 21

Suppose you are trying to persuade people to leave their sins and consecrate themselves fully to God. A member of your church says, "You say that telling lies and cheating in business is sin and that God punishes sin. But look at how God blesses me. He must not think there is anything wrong with lying or cheating. He knows I have to do it to stay in business. If it were so bad, he would surely punish me. And you can see how He has prospered me and how He blesses me at church. That proves I'm fine." How could you use this passage to explain God's dealings with him? In your Life Notebook, give a concise two-three paragraph statement of what you would say to him.

Principles of Judgment Revealed (Rom 2:6-16)

Objective 6 – At the end of this topic, you will be able explain why the self-righteous are condemned and can only be justified by faith.

Beginning in Romans 2:1, Paul addresses the case of the Jewish "moralist" who had the Law, was self-righteous, and condemned others as being unrighteous. In reality, however, this person was condemned, because He had not placed his faith in the Lord Jesus and therefore relied only on his own righteousness. In Romans 2:5, Paul confronted such a person: he was "stubborn" (a hardened heart) and "unrepentant." As such, he would be in store for God's wrath in the future day of judgment. Drawing upon Psalm 62:12 and Proverbs 24:12, Paul reminded the "moralist" that God will take into account each person's deeds and recompense him accordingly, and for this he must be prepared.

QUESTION 22

Those who do evil receive wrath, anger, affliction, and distress according to Romans 2:8-9. *True or False?*

QUESTION 23

Those who do good will receive what (Rom 2:10)?

    A. Glory and honor

    B. Honor and peace

    C. Peace and glory

    D. Glory, honor, and peace

In Romans 2:7-10, Paul takes up the case of men being recompensed for their deeds. He contrasts a positive outcome in vv. 7 and 10 with a negative outcome in vv. 8 and 9. Scholars have struggled to understand some of Paul's statements, especially v. 7 that God would grant "eternal life to those who by perseverance in good works seek glory and honor and immortality." Three primary interpretations have been suggested:

1. The life of a true believer will be evidenced by "perseverance in good works."
2. For faithful believers who "persevere in good works," they will be rewarded with an enhanced experience of life now (Jn 10:10) and a richer experience of eternal life in heaven—a reward at the Judgment Seat of Christ (1 Cor 3:12-15; 2 Cor 5:10-11).
3. Paul is only speaking hypothetically to help the "moralist" realize the impossibility of his philosophy, for in reality no one can gain eternal life by "persevering in good works."

The third view has several factors in its favor. First, the whole context of Romans 2:1-29 is aimed at the Jewish "moralist" who relies upon the Law, not the experience of believers in Christ. Second, Paul is very clear elsewhere in Romans (see 5:21 and 6:22-23) that eternal life only comes as the gift of God to those in Christ Jesus, not to those who "persevere in good works." Third, Paul speaks hypothetically again in Romans 2:13 when he says, "those who do the law will be declared righteous," that is, justified. Paul quite obviously does not mean to say that some actually will be justified in this way, for to do so would be a clear contradiction of what he had taught in Galatians 2:16: "by the works of the law no one will be justified." So, it seems that Paul is saying what he does in Romans 2:7-10 to wake the "moralist" up to the fact that it is hopeless trying to be justified and gain eternal life as a result of living up to the Law.

Paul now turns in Romans 2:11 to the problem that some have received revelation from God (the Law) and some have not. The Jews have received it, but Gentiles have not. How will God treat this situation?

The Jews believed that to be saved, one must possess the law of God and be circumcised. Yet Paul's ministry was to the Gentiles who neither received revelation of the law of God nor were circumcised. He now must meet the objection from the Jews that Gentiles without ever receiving the Old Testament Law can still be saved even if they have not received this special revelation from God.

Please read Romans 2:11-16. The word "for" (v. 11) usually tells us that what follows is connected to what occurred immediately before and will explain it.

QUESTION 24

How do verses 12-16 explain verse 11?

  A. They show that both Jewish and Gentile Christians will be rewarded, not just Jewish Christians.

  B. They show that one must be a doer of the law in order to be justified.

  C. They show that those non-believers who do not have special revelation from God (the Law) will be judged only by their conscience.

  D. They show that Gentile non-believers do not need the law because they are a law unto themselves.

Perhaps the biggest problem in interpreting these verses is Paul's statement in Romans 2:13. Please read Romans 2:13 and Romans 3:28.

QUESTION 25

Based on a comparison between these two verses, what can we conclude?

  A. Justification can only be secured by works.

  B. Justification can only be secured by faith alone

  C. Justification can only be secure by faith plus works.

  D. Although we know that Paul does not contradict himself, these verses do appear to be contradictory even though they are not.

QUESTION 26

Based upon Jeremiah 31:33, we are justified in understanding that Gentiles who have the law "written on their hearts" are probably believing, born again Gentiles. *True or False?*

QUESTION 27

We must consider more carefully the meaning of the word "justification" in the New Testament. While we know that the word refers to the legal imputation of Christ's righteousness to the believer at the moment he believes, in some contexts another well-established meaning appears. Please read Matthew 5:19-20; 12:37; Luke 7:35; 16:15; Romans 3:4; James 2:24, 25. Open your Life Notebook and summarize this alternative meaning. What are the conditions for obtaining justification in these verses and what kind of justification is in view? After you have done this, read the author's conclusion.

Justification

One explanation of the appearance of contradiction between Romans 2:13 and 3:28 is that in Romans 2:13 Paul is using the word "to justify" in the same sense he uses it in Romans 3:4. In that passage "justified" means "be vindicated," or "to demonstrate to be morally right, *prove to be right*." This is a common meaning of the verb in the New Testament (Mt 11:19, 12:37; Lk 7:35, 10:29, 16:15; 1 Cor 4:4; 1 Tim 3:16). They have already been justified in the forensic sense, acquitted once and for all by a God's declaration, Romans 5:1, in the sense they will never experience eternal damnation. But it is clear that there is a justification by works in the New Testament that means to be vindicated as morally right. This is the justification James spoke of (Jas 2:14). In this case Paul and James both mean that the "doer" is proven to have lived. He will be vindicated by his works before Christ in the sense that Christ will says, "Well done." He will then be rewarded in the future kingdom (2 Cor 5:10-11).

The more common justification is by faith alone and is a judicial act (Rom 5:1) whereby Christ's righteousness is imputed to us (2 Cor 5:21). Since one is by works the other is by faith, context determines which is meant. If works are the condition of justification in Romans 2:13, obviously it cannot refer to a forensic declaration that is obtained via faith alone apart from works.

The other possible explanation suggested by many bible scholars is that in Romans 2:16 Paul is speaking hypothetically. In other words, when Paul says that only "the doers of the law will be justified" this is absolute truth. The problem, however, is that there are no doers because Paul later says, "there is none righteous, not even one." God requires perfect obedience, perfect righteousness and no one has met that standard. Thus, man's only hope is the perfect righteousness offered by faith in Christ (see 2 Cor 5:21; Rom 3:28).

Topic 4: Jews Condemned (Rom 2:17 - 3:8)

Beginning in Romans 1:19, Paul presents clear evidence that the Gentiles are condemned to experience God's wrath because of their sin. Then, starting in Romans 2:1, he demonstrates that "good, moral people" are also condemned to experience God's wrath because of their sin. Now in Romans 2:17 he turns his attention to the Jews. The Jews had been privileged to receive God's Law and had developed an elaborate, detailed system for keeping it. Surely they were not condemned before God, were they? If that was the case, then of what value had there been to be God's chosen people?

Advantages and Responsibility (Rom 2:17-29)

> Objective 7 – At the end of this topic, you will be able to summarize the advantages and responsibilities of the Jews and explain how they came under condemnation.

Paul is talking directly to the Jews in Romans 2:17-29. Why? Because the Jews were always boasting of their privileges and advantages, but their lives did not measure up to their boasts. In Romans 2:17-18, we find six claims of their advantages:

1. They are called Jews.
2. They rely upon the Law.
3. They boast in their relationship to God.
4. They know God's will.
5. They approve the superior things (They have the right standard of values).
6. They receive instruction from the Law.

In Romans 2:19-20, we find five more claims. These show us how the Jews saw themselves with relation to the heathen or Gentiles:

1. A guide to the blind
2. A light to those who are in darkness
3. An educator of the senseless
4. A teacher of little children (young or immature)
5. Guardians of the form of knowledge and truth in the Law

Paul points out to these Jews who have been given such great advantages and privileges that privilege brings with it the responsibility to live according to the revelation they have received. The greater the knowledge of God and His will we possess, the greater our accountability to Him. The problem with the boasting Jew was that he did not live according to what he claimed to be.

QUESTION 28

What word best describes the sin of the Jews regarding their boasts and their lives in Romans 2:17-24?

 A. Hypocrisy

 B. Pride

 C. Adultery

 D. Murder

The Jews were God's chosen people. They were to be a missionary nation to tell others about God. The purpose for their existence was to receive and share with others the revelation of the true God. God called them His witnesses. The very name Jew means "praise." Their lives were to bring praise to God.

QUESTION 29

How did the Jews of Paul's day measure up to their boast of relying on the law, knowing God's will, having the right standard of values, and being instructed by the law (Rom 2:18, 23)? *(Select all that apply.)*

 A. The Jews were to praise God, but their boast in the law detracted from His glory.

 B. The Jews were a shining light to the nations.

 C. Their lives caused the Gentiles to blaspheme God.

 D. The Jews were to lead others to praise God, but they dishonored Him.

 E. The Jews led others to God by their devoted lives.

QUESTION 30

Romans 2:17 and Romans 2:23-24 point to the conflict between the claims and the actions of the Jews: though they claim to be Jews and rely on the Law, they actually _____ the law.

A. Obey

B. Break

C. Curse

D. Forget

QUESTION 31

How did breaking the law affect their rights and privileges as Jews according to Romans 2:25-29?

A. They were now subject to the laws of chance.

B. They were no longer real Jews.

C. They now needed to get their privileges reinstated in their local synagogue.

D. They were no longer saved.

Just as the Gentiles are judged and condemned for having rejected the revelation that they received of God, the Jews in this passage are judged according to what they do with their higher revelation and responsibility.

QUESTION 32

Examine the five claims of Romans 2:19-20 and how the Jews taught in Romans 2:21-23. What was wrong with their teaching?

A. They tried to impress people with their knowledge.

B. They were experts at making the lessons hard to understand.

C. They had a very shallow understanding of the Law.

D. They taught one thing with their mouths and another with their examples.

QUESTION 33

Compare the hypocrisy of these people and their privileges with the sins of the Gentiles. Which group would deserve greater punishment? *(Select all that apply.)*

A. The ones with more direct revelation

B. The ones with more moral issues in their background

C. The ones with a higher level of income

D. The ones with the greater knowledge of the truth

Keep in mind that while Paul is talking about the Jews of his day, there is a much wider application for his words. Do you know people who think of themselves as these Jews did? Paul's description fits many religious people of our times. They may be nominal Christians in name only or followers of another religion. Have you ever faced this problem in your church? Have you ever met people who refuse to believe the gospel because they have seen hypocrites in the church? This passage lets us know that God judges the hypocrites.

Some people call religion "the opiate of the people." Of course, this is not true of the true religion that brings a person into contact with the living God, but in one sense this statement is true. If a man trusts in his religion (his association with a church) but his life is ungodly, religion to him is like a drug. It is a false security. This is the type of person that Paul describes in Romans 2:17-29.

QUESTION 34

Which statement best expresses the theme of Romans 2:17-29?

    A. Jews should not boast.

    B. Religious people are all hypocrites.

    C. Greater privilege brings greater accountability.

    D. Gentiles have displaced the Jews.

Paul tells us in Romans 2:25-29 that to be a Jew is good if a person keeps the Law of God. But a Jew who breaks the Law is no better off than the Gentile. Circumcision, which Paul discusses here, was a sign of God's covenant with the Israelites. As you have seen in Galatians, this was the sign of the Jew's obligation to keep the whole Law. But if the person did not love and worship God in his heart, he disobeyed God's commands, the covenant was broken, and the outward sign of the covenant was meaningless. Some of the people in other nations also practiced circumcision. The Israelites who did not obey God from the heart were no better than the circumcised pagans.

In our study of Galatians, we saw that water baptism for the Christian can be seen as the New Testament equivalent to circumcision. Both are religious rites ordered by the Lord as outward signs of an inward commitment to Him. Today, some people trust in their water baptism and are proud of it, just as the Jews were of circumcision. But both are meaningless if they are not accompanied by the inward commitment that they symbolize.

QUESTION 35

In order to apply the lesson of this passage in your own life and ministry, read Romans 2:25-29 again, substituting the word *baptism* or *baptized* for *circumcision* or *circumcised*. In your Life Notebook, give a two- or three-paragraph teaching that applies these issues of false security in religion to your community.

Questions and Conclusion (Rom 3:1-8)

> Objective 8 – At the end of this topic, you will be able to state three common questions that arise in light of God's condemnation of the Jews and briefly summarize Paul's answer to each.

In Romans 3:1-8, Paul answers several questions that would naturally arise in the minds of the Jews to whom he is speaking.

QUESTION 36

Look in Romans 3:1, 3, 5. What are three sets of questions that the Jews might ask after reading about the Jews' failure?

Paul answers the questions of Romans 3:1 more thoroughly in Romans 9. Here he simply states that the most important advantage of the Jews is the special revelation of Himself that God has given them in the Scriptures.

The questions in Romans 3:3 are answered fully in Romans 10–11. Paul has shown us Israel's failure to be the missionary nation that God had chosen them to be. Their hypocrisy turned people away from the truth that they taught. They had broken the covenant and could no longer be considered real Jews and heirs of God's promise. Now they ask what this means. Have God's promises failed? Are His covenants no longer valid? Has God's plan failed? Paul answers that this could never be (Rom 3:4)! The lack of faith in men does not affect the faithfulness of God (see 2 Tim 2:13).

In Romans 3:5, Paul quotes questions that some people raise about the justice of God's judgment. Why does God allow us to sin and then punish us for it? If our sin displays His goodness by contrast, why should we be condemned for it? To Paul, such an idea was unthinkable and he does not answer it directly. This should be a lesson to us when people criticize Christianity and God Himself. Sometimes the questions of critics simply indicate a hardness of heart and an unwillingness to listen to reason. We should be led by the Spirit so that we will know when to speak and when not to speak. Instead of entering into an argument here, Paul lets us know emphatically that God is righteous in His judgment and that He will punish all those who do evil. Even though a person may have good motives, if he does wrong to try to accomplish his purpose, God justly condemns him for it.

QUESTION 37

Can you think of an example when you might be tempted to do something wrong in order for good to come from it? According to Romans 3:7, what would God call an evangelist who intentionally exaggerated the number of conversions in his meetings?

QUESTION 38

Which verse or verses in Romans 3:1-8 prove that the end does not justify the means?

    A. All of them

    B. Verses 7 and 8

    C. Verses 3 and 4

    D. Verse 8 only

Topic 5: All the World Condemned (Rom 3:9-20)

Just as you learned from your study of Galatians, you have also seen in the first part of Romans that everyone has broken God's laws at one time or another and is therefore guilty and condemned. In this section of Romans 3, Paul uses a familiar quotation from the Old Testament to summarize the detailed argument he presented in previous chapters.

> Objective 9 – At the end of this topic, you will be able to explain, using Scripture, the condition of mankind(both Jew and Gentile) as to their relationship with God.

The phrase "Jews and Greeks alike are all under sin" in Romans 3:9 is our key for this section. Remember that to the Jew the world consisted of only two groups of people: Jews and Gentiles. In Romans 1:18-32, Paul has shown us that the Gentiles are sinners and therefore under the judgment of God. In Romans 2:1-3:8, he shows that the Jews are likewise sinners and under the judgment of God.

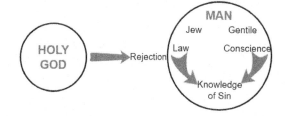

Now in Romans 3:10-18, Paul quotes the psalmist and the prophets to give us the scriptural picture of the human heart. We notice two aspects of the condition of the whole human race:

---

1. Romans 3:9-12: A universal condemnation.

2. Romans 3:13-18: An intensive and personal sin both in speech and action.

Beginning with Romans 3:9, notice the repetition of the words *both, all, no one, not even one, and together*. By noting these words, you will better see Paul's conclusion; he is emphasizing that the need for salvation is universal and without exception.

After Paul has shown how extensive sin is, he points out how intensive it is. It affects every part of man, from head to toe. Read Romans 3:13-18. Picture the terrible sickness of the human race that it describes. Paul proves his argument from the Scriptures. (He quotes from Ps 5:9; 10:7; 14:1-4; 36:1; Isa 59:7; Eccl 7:20.) Paul does not mean that every member of the human race practices all the sins listed here. He uses these Old Testament passages to illustrate the general and personal sinfulness of mankind.

QUESTION 39

Which verse or verses from Romans 3:9-18 express the underlying reason for the sins listed here?

    A. Verse 3:9--"All are under sin."

    B. Verse 3:10--"There is no one righteous, not even one."

    C. Verse 3:12--"All have turned away."

    D. All of the above

QUESTION 40

To whom is Paul speaking in Romans 3:19-20?

Paul uses the term "law" in Romans 3:19, referring to all the Old Testament Scriptures, not just the books of the Law. The Jews who were trusting in the Law to justify them (see Rom 2:17) cannot deny the verdict of "guilty" that the Law has passed on them. Read this verdict now in Romans 3:10-18.

QUESTION 41

What conclusion does Romans 3:20 state about the possibility of being saved by the Law? *(Select all that apply.)*

    A. No one can be justified by the Law.

    B. The Law helps us fulfill God's righteous requirements.

    C. The Law only lets us know what sin is.

    D. It gives us the power to free ourselves from sin.

    E. It does not give us the power to free ourselves from sin.

As you saw in your study of Galatians, it was never the purpose of the Law to provide justification. To the man who was dirty with sin, the Law was a mirror, not soap. Its purpose was to show him his need of cleansing, not to make him clean.

It has been said that after you look at the picture of mankind in the Scriptures, the thing that surprises you most is not that anyone should be *lost* but that anyone should be *saved*! Certainly this is true when we read Romans 1–3. In this epistle and throughout the Scriptures, the exceeding wickedness of men stands in clear contrast to the mercy of God. We are saved by grace, unmerited favor.

"For by grace you are saved through faith, and this is not from yourselves, it is the gift of God; it is not from works, so that no one can boast" (Eph 2:8-9).

In the first three chapters of Romans, we see that all men everywhere need two things: pardon from the death sentence that their guilt has brought upon them and freedom from the power of sin that dominates their lives. This is what God offers them in the gospel. This is the good news that we are to take them.

Paul clearly saw that everyone everywhere needed the gospel. Their need drove him on in his labors and caused him to become the great missionary that he was. He speaks of this inner constraint as the love of Christ in him. One translation of 2 Corinthians 5:14 says, "For the love of Christ puts us into action." You too should let this knowledge that all men need the gospel move you to action in taking them the good news. This is the mission of the church. This is your mission. Pray that God will help you do your part as a witness for Him.

QUESTION 42

Now think briefly about the need of the people in your area and their attitude toward sin. Do they think of sin as you have seen it described in Romans? In your Life Notebook, outline some preliminary plans for how you will teach the message of God's judgment as seen in Romans. Do sinners seem conscious of their guilt and need for salvation? What kind of preaching is needed on these subjects? Which verses from Romans 1:18-3:20 would make good sermon texts? While you are thinking about it, write down the references of these texts and the subject of the message you would like to teach from each one.

Lesson 2 Self Check

QUESTION 1

Which term best describes divine retribution?

    A. Revenge

    B. Repayment

    C. Discipline

    D. Correction

QUESTION 2

Romans 1:18 tells us that God's wrath will come on those who persistently reject what?

    A. His love

    B. His truth

    C. His law

    D. His goodness

QUESTION 3

God has revealed Himself to all mankind in two ways. According to Romans 2:14-15, one way is through conscience. According to Romans 1:19-20, what is the other way?

    A. Divination

    B. Judgment

    C. Nature

    D. Law

QUESTION 4

Based on Romans 1:21-32, which phrase would you use to describe the wrath of God toward those who have rejected His truth?

    A. God sent the flood to destroy mankind.

    B. God "brought down" the offending nations.

    C. God promised destruction at the end of the age.

    D. God gave them over "to idolatry and increasing sin."

QUESTION 5

Romans 2:2 tells us that God will judge the self-righteous according to His mercy. *True or False?*

QUESTION 6

All men, believers and unbelievers, will be judged by their works (Rom 2:6). *True or False?*

QUESTION 7

God gave the Jews privileges and with that came the responsibility of sharing who He is with others. *True or False?*

QUESTION 8

Part of God's plan was for the Jews to teach the Gentiles about Him. The principal reason the Jews failed was that they had a very shallow understanding of the Law. *True or False?*

QUESTION 9

Three common questions arise in light of God's condemnation of the Jews (Rom 3:1, 3, 5). Which one of the following is one of those questions?

    A. Is it better to serve ourselves instead of God?

    B. The God who inflicts wrath is not unrighteous, is He?

    C. If God loves His people, why does He judge them?

    D. Does baptism count for nothing?

QUESTION 10

In Romans 3:9, Paul states that "they are all under sin." This is the basic reason for all the sins listed in Romans 3:9-18 and is also a summary of the main message of Romans 1:18–3:20. *True or False?*

Lesson 2 Answers to Questions

QUESTION 1: True

QUESTION 2

    A. The way God expresses His wrath.

QUESTION 3

    B. Always righteous

    D. Free from sinful passion

QUESTION 4

    B. Repayment

QUESTION 5:

    A. Ungodliness

    B. Unrighteousness

    C. Suppressing the truth

QUESTION 6: *Your answer*

QUESTION 7

    C. Romans 1:19-20

QUESTION 8

    C. His glory

    D. His righteous judgment

    E. His eternal power and divine nature

    F. His truth

QUESTION 9: False

QUESTION 10: *Your answer*

QUESTION 11

    B. God gave them up to their sin.

QUESTION 12

    B. Failure to live according to what it teaches

QUESTION 13

    C. They are without excuse and deserve to die.

QUESTION 14: False

QUESTION 15: *Your answer*

QUESTION 16

    B. Inexcusable

    D. Brings them under condemnation

QUESTION 17: True

QUESTION 18

    D. By the truth of what they really are

QUESTION 19

    A. Stubbornness

    B. Contempt for God's forbearance and patience

    D. An unrepentant heart

    E. Contempt for God's kindness

QUESTION 20: *Your answer should be one of the following:*

Wrath, Judgment

QUESTION 21: *Your answer*

QUESTION 22: True

QUESTION 23

    D. Glory, honor, and peace

QUESTION 24

    A. They show that both Jewish and Gentile Christians will be rewarded, not just Jewish Christians. [The Gentiles in view are those who have the law written on their hearts. This indicates they are born again and are recipients of the new covenant (Jer 31:33).]

QUESTION 25

    D. Although we know that Paul does not contradict himself, these verses do appear to be contradictory even though they are not.

QUESTION 26: True [We cannot be sure, but it appears that if one has the law written on one's heart, this means he is a saved member of the new Covenant.]

QUESTION 27: *Your answer*

QUESTION 28

    A. Hypocrisy

QUESTION 29

    A. The Jews were to praise God, but their boast in the law detracted from His glory.

    C. Their lives caused the Gentiles to blaspheme God.

    D. The Jews were to lead others to praise God, but they dishonored Him.

QUESTION 30

    B. Break

QUESTION 31

    B. They were no longer real Jews.

QUESTION 32

    D. They taught one thing with their mouths and another with their examples.

QUESTION 33

    A. The ones with more direct revelation

    D. The ones with the greater knowledge of the truth

QUESTION 34

    C. Greater privilege brings greater accountability.

QUESTION 35: *Your answer*

QUESTION 36: *Your answer should be similar to the following:*

(a) Therefore what advantage does the Jew have, or what is the value of circumcision? (b) If some did not believe, does their unbelief nullify the faithfulness of God? (c) The God who inflicts wrath is not unrighteous, is he?

QUESTION 37: *Your answer should be one of the following:*

A sinner, Sinner

QUESTION 38

    B. Verses 7 and 8

QUESTION 39

    D. All of the above

QUESTION 40: *Your answer should be one of the following:*

The Jews, Jews

QUESTION 41

    A. No one can be justified by the Law.

    C. The Law only lets us know what sin is.

    E. It does not give us the power to free ourselves from sin.

QUESTION 42: *Your answer*

Lesson 2 Self Check Answers

QUESTION 1
  B. Repayment

QUESTION 2
  B. His truth

QUESTION 3
  C. Nature

QUESTION 4
  D. God gave them over "to idolatry and increasing sin."

QUESTION 5: False

QUESTION 6: True

QUESTION 7: True

QUESTION 8: False

QUESTION 9
  B. The God who inflicts wrath is not unrighteous, is He?

QUESTION 10: True

Lesson 3: God's Provision for Salvation (Rom 3:21-5:21)

Lesson Introduction

In Romans 1:18–3:20, you have seen how Paul proves the universal need for the righteousness of God. From the Gentile idol worshipper to the enlightened Jew, Paul proves that all are sinners and under God's condemnation. Lesson 2 ended with the truth that all men are guilty before God. Paul has painted a dark picture for us, but it is an accurate one.

It has been said that men will not value the gospel until they see their need of it. Certainly, an awareness of the seriousness of sin causes men to look for a savior! After Paul presents man's condition, the need for a savior cannot be denied. Men desperately need pardon for their guilt, deliverance from the power of sin, and a new nature that will make it possible for them to live the right kind of life. This is the righteousness that only God can give. This is our only hope because we have seen that we are powerless in ourselves to live up to God's standard of righteousness.

Lesson Objectives

Topic 1 presents a detailed description of God's provision, which is justification by faith in Christ.

In Topic 1, you will learn…

- Three ways God reveals His righteousness to mankind
- Why the Law is incapable of making men right with God
- Why God's provision for salvation is the same for both Jews and Gentiles
- How the words *redemption* and *propitiation* clarify the nature of God's salvation
- Answers to three common questions about justification by faith

Topic 2 defends justification by faith in Christ by examining justification in the Old Testament.

In Topic 2, you will discover…

- Two examples of Old Testament men who were justified by faith
- Evidence that Abraham was justified by faith
- Not by circumcision
- Not by obedience to the Law

Topic 3 defends justification by faith in Christ by describing blessings provided by justification.

In Topic 3, you will identify…

- The nature of the blessings that accompany justification
- How God's love transforms our lives through the work of the Holy Spirit

Topic 4 focuses on one of the blessings of justification, which is victory over sin and death.

In Topic 4, you will learn how the principle of grace has overcome the principle of sin.

Lesson Outline

Topic 1: Justification by Faith in Christ (Rom 3:21-31)

Revelation of God's Righteousness (3:21-26)

Word List

We hope you will enjoy using the word study at the beginning of each lesson. Some of the words you already know, but they are used in a special sense in the lesson. Others are theological terms, and some are new words for many students. Please read the word study each time before starting the lesson. Refer back to it as necessary.

Acquittal - deliverance from the charge of an offense, verdict of not guilty.

Reconciled (Rom 5:10) - brought back to friendship after estrangement or enmity.

Reconciliation (Rom 5:11) - peace with God that comes from Christ's satisfaction for sin.

Sanctification - separation from sin and dedication to God.

Satisfaction, etc. (Rom 3:25) - propitiation, appeasement, conciliation, causing a person to be favorable. *By His blood* - in His death as our Substitute. *Forbearance* - exercise of patience, long-suffering, refraining from enforcing what is due.

Topic 1: Justification by Faith in Christ (Rom 3:21-31)

The words "but now" in Romans 3:21 turn our eyes from the terrible condition of mankind to the provision that God has made for our salvation. In this section of Romans, Paul shows us how the gospel uniquely meets the sinner's need of righteousness.

The relationship between the first part of Romans and this part is well-illustrated in these lines:

> "Do this and live, the law commands, but gives me neither feet nor hands.

> A better word the Gospel brings. It bids me fly and gives me wings."

> --Kenneth Wuest

Revelation of God's Righteousness (Rom 3:21-26)

> Objective 1 – At the end of this topic, you will be able to recognize three aspects of the revelation of God's righteousness in Romans 3 and their application to God's justice in His dealings with sinners.

Romans 3:21-22 introduces the second main theological section of Romans and restates the theme of the epistle. Compare Romans 3:21-22 with Romans 1:16-18.

QUESTION 1

What is revealed in Romans 1:18?

    A. The grace of God

    B. The wrath of God

    C. The sinfulness of man

    D. The righteousness of God

QUESTION 2

What is revealed in Romans 1:17 and Romans 3:21?

    A. The grace of God

    B. The wrath of God

    C. The sinfulness of man

    D. The righteousness of God

QUESTION 3

In Romans 1:17, where does Paul say the righteousness of God is revealed?

    A. In the Bible

    B. In the epistles

    C. In the gospel

    D. In Jesus Christ

In Romans 3:21-31 Paul shows how the gospel reveals three aspects of God's righteousness:

1. The righteousness that God gives to men is revealed in personal experience as they trust in Christ.
2. The righteousness that God gives is offered to all without distinction, since according to God's standard all have sinned and need salvation.
3. The righteousness of God Himself is revealed in redemption. He is just and right in all of His dealings with men.

Righteousness by Faith, Apart From Law

> Objective 2 – At the end of this topic, you will be able to defend the assertion that the works of the Law have absolutely nothing to do with how God puts men right with Himself.

In Romans 3:21-22, Paul compares "depending on the Law for righteousness" and "depending on faith for righteousness." He says that the righteousness of God has been revealed. These words by themselves shed no light on the dark picture of sin. But Paul adds the words "without the law." Now a ray of light and hope breaks through! God's righteousness had been seen in His written commandments but no one could keep them. The Law was good and right, but it could not change the sinful nature of men. As you have seen in Galatians, the Law could only show men their need. Now Paul presents the theme that you have already studied in Galatians: God's way of righteousness for men is apart from the Law.

In the first three chapters of Romans, we have seen Paul explaining to both Gentiles and Jews that they all are condemned and need to be made right with God. Now his statement that this righteousness can be theirs "apart from the Law" brings hope to the Gentiles but puzzles the Jews. Apart from the Law! How could this be? Paul carefully shows that the way in which God reveals His righteousness here is in accord with the Old Testament Scriptures. The Law and the prophets witnessed to this way of righteousness (Rom 3:21).

QUESTION 4

According to Romans 3:21, what is disclosed apart from the works of the Law?

    A. The righteousness of God

    B. The salvation for all who believe

    C. The love of God toward all men

    D. The hope for heavenly rewards

In Romans 3:21, Paul means that God's righteousness is revealed apart from the works of the Law. He emphasizes here an important truth about justification: the works of the Law have absolutely nothing to do with how God puts men right with Himself. This truth is basic to a correct understanding of the gospel. Paul carries this theme throughout both Galatians and Romans. He says that the Law is not how God gives us His righteousness or right standing with Him.

QUESTION 5

According to Romans 3:22, how can we receive the righteousness of God ?

    A. Obeying the Law

    B. Obeying the teachings of Paul

    C. Obeying the church leaders

    D. By faith in Christ, believing in Him

In Romans 3:22, we begin to see the righteousness of God as He provides a way of salvation that is within the reach of all. Sinful men, although condemned and spiritually helpless, can have *faith* in Jesus Christ. Here the little ray of light that we saw in Romans 3:21 becomes brighter and brighter until it totally dispels the darkness of Romans 1:18-3:20. Righteousness comes through *faith* in Jesus Christ! This is good news!

QUESTION 6

Compare Romans 1:16-17 with Romans 3:21-22. These passages both talk of God's righteousness being revealed to those who believe in Jesus Christ. *True or False?*

God's Way of Righteousness	
Romans 3:21-22	
Source	God
Relation to the Law	Apart from the Law
	Witnessed by the Law
Chief Characteristic	Faith in Jesus Christ
Condition	Belief in Christ
Extent	Unto all
Reason for the extent	No difference
Gift	The righteousness of God

Paul restates the faith-to-faith principle of Romans 1:17 in the words "through faith in Jesus Christ to all who believe" (Rom 3:22, NIV). When we believe the gospel and put our trust in Christ, He gives us the faith that we need for salvation and the right kind of life. The faith which brings righteousness to a sinner's life becomes the principle by which he can live a life of victory over sin. The initial response of faith to God becomes a day-by-day response to Him. Theologically speaking, the first act of faith has to do with justification. The life of faith which follows has to do with sanctification. Here we see the groundwork for Paul's teaching in this epistle on sanctification. The life of faith, responding daily to God's Word, progressively sets the believer apart from sin. Faith, Paul is saying, is the way to holiness.

Righteousness for Jew and Gentile Alike

> Objective 3 – At the end of this topic, you will be able to explain why God has only one way of salvation for Jews and Gentiles.

In Romans 3:22-23, we see that God has only one way of salvation for Jews and Gentiles. All are guilty. And all the guilty ones must approach God in the same way in order to receive salvation. How? By faith. No man is closer to God than another. God makes no distinction between race, nationality, or personal merit. There is no difference.

QUESTION 7

Who may receive the righteousness of God?

  A. The Jews
  B. The Gentiles
  C. The Greeks
  D. All who believe

QUESTION 8

The words "there is no distinction" in Romans 3:22 would be especially good news to which group?

  A. The Jews
  B. The Gentiles
  C. The Greeks
  D. All who believe

QUESTION 9

"All have sinned and fall short of the glory of God" is the reason given in Romans 3:23 for God's provision of only one way of salvation. *True or False?*

Romans 3:23 is a summary of the first main section of the epistle. All men have been proven sinners. This verse states that as individuals all have sinned. The verb tenses in the original Greek also present sin as a definite act in the past with a continuing result in the present, as seen in this translation: "For all sinned and are falling short of the glory of God." We see a similar idea in Romans 5:12. Paul speaks there of **how sin entered the world through Adam's sin and since then all have sinned.**

The reason for such a statement here in Chapter 3 may be because of a parallel between Romans 3:22-23. Both speak of a crisis act and a continuing experience. In Romans 3:22, the single act of faith brings righteousness which is to be followed by the continuous response to God in believing (see Isa 1:17). In Romans 3:23, the single act of sin brought death. The continuing result was that all men continued to come short of the glory of God.

Parallel in Romans 3:22-23

Crisis Act		Continuing result
Righteousness by faith	⇒	Believing
Sin	⇒	Short of God's glory

"Falling short of the glory of God" means that ever since Adam's time everyone has failed to reach the glorious ideal that God had in view when He created man. You have already seen in Romans 1:18-32 how sin resulted in a continuing spiritual weakness. Its corrupting influence took men farther and farther into sin.

Righteousness Revealed in Redemption and Propitiation

> Objective 4 – At the end of this topic, you will be able to describe the dilemmas faced by both God and man and how God solved both of them.

The Dilemma

Justification is a legal term. It brings to our mind a courtroom scene. A man is on trial. His innocence is proven and the judge declares him not guilty. But our problem is that we are all guilty of breaking God's laws. How, then, can we be declared not guilty and be free from punishment for our sins?

Because God is holy, He must condemn sin and judge the sinner. But God is also loving and kind. How could God be righteous and just in His judgment of sinful men and still treat them with mercy and love? Justice demanded their death. Love demanded their pardon. This was the dilemma that God faced.

Paul has shown us how God puts men right with Himself through faith in Jesus Christ. But what about sin? What does God do with the sin that stands as a barrier between Him, a holy God, and sinful men? Can God remain just and at the same time justify sinful men? How can He forgive sinners when justice demands their punishment? How does God solve the dilemma? We now come to one of the most important theological passages in all the New Testament, Romans 3:24-26. Here Paul explains God's solution to the dilemma. He describes for us God's provision for the salvation of man.

Grace

First, notice the manner of God's provision, being justified "freely by his grace." This can also be translated as a "gift by his grace." Paul begins by emphasizing that God's justifying act is not in any degree based on anything men do. Justification is a completely unmerited gift. The reason why God justifies sinners is because of His love for them (Eph 2:4-5). Before Paul became a Christian, he hoped that if he followed God's Law throughout his life, at the end God would pronounce him righteous. But in God's way of righteousness the procedure is reversed. God pronounces a man righteous at the beginning of his spiritual life, not at the end. Therefore, the source of man's righteousness cannot possibly be anything that he has done. Rather, it is the grace of God.

It is important to understand that God pronounces a person righteous the moment he believes in Christ as his Savior. In some churches, people are told that they can never know whether or not they are in the right relationship with God. They have no assurance of salvation. They think they must wait until they die to know if God looks on them as righteous. As you continue your study of the gospel in Romans, notice the assurance we can have that we are justified.

Redemption

Two words in Romans 3:24-25 show us how God settled the problem of sin. They are "redemption" and "propitiation." The term "redemption" speaks of a slave market. Redemption is the act of buying a slave out of bondage and setting him free. Why is there redemption in Jesus? Because He bought us in the slave market of sin, He gave His own blood, His life, as the price of our freedom. By His death He delivered us from the bondage of sin.

Paul also may have had in mind another picture of redemption: the deliverance of the Israelites from their bondage in Egypt. The sacrifice of the Passover lamb and its blood over the door and on the lintels protected each home from the angel of death. God's power in the plagues and in opening up the Red Sea freed them from the bondage of Egypt. From then on, the whole nation that had been redeemed was to be a holy people, set apart for the Lord, servants of the Lord.

QUESTION 10

According to Matthew 20:28; Romans 3:24-25; 1 Peter 1:18-19, why did Jesus die?

    A. Without the shedding of blood, it is impossible for sins to be forgiven.

    B. Jesus died as an example for us as to how we should live our lives.

    C. Jesus gave His life as a ransom to redeem us.

    D. Jesus died because the Jews failed to obey and follow Him.

Propitiation

Now let's look at this word "propitiation" (which can also be translated as satisfaction for sin). It carries the idea both of a covering and an appeasement or satisfaction for a wrong that has been done. It reminds us that God's just wrath is directed against sinful men. Justice demands the death sentence for all. How can its demands be satisfied? How is God's wrath (the reaction of His holiness against sin) to be appeased? God Himself took our punishment and satisfied justice. God the Son died in our place. His righteousness was placed to the account of all who accept Him as their Savior. His blood covers our sins and all the accusations of the Law. God's love and grace have provided the propitiation that frees us from the death sentence and gives us peace with God.

QUESTION 11

According to Romans 3:25, what did God set Jesus forth to do?

    A. Share God's love with all humankind.

    B. Instruct the disciples to share the gospel.

    C. Satisfy the debt of our sin.

    D. Heal the sick.

QUESTION 12

For what purpose did God send Jesus to earth according to 1 John 4:10?

    A. Prophet to the world

    B. Priest to the world

    C. King of the world

    D. A propitiation, or atoning sacrifice, for our sins

QUESTION 13

According to 1 John 4:10, God's righteousness is what caused Him to send His Son as a propitiation for our sins. *True or False?*

QUESTION 14

In your Life Notebook, answer the following questions:

Is 1 John 2:2 a perfect answer to the problem of Romans 1:18 and Romans 3:23? Why or why not?

Salvation Past and Present

The word *propitiation* reminds us of the whole system of sacrifices in the Old Testament and especially of the mercy seat that covered the Ark of the Covenant in the holiest place of the tabernacle. In fact, the same word that is translated *propitiation* here is translated "mercy seat" in Hebrews 9:5. The book of Hebrews tells us that what occurred at the mercy seat is a picture of how we can meet with God and find His mercy because of Jesus' death.

Inside the Ark of the Covenant were the Ten Commandments, the law of God. The presence of God was above the mercy seat. On the Day of Atonement each year, the high priest entered the most holy place and sprinkled the sacrificial blood on the mercy seat. He did this as a representative of the whole nation to ask God's forgiveness for the sins of the people. The law demanded death for the sinners, but the blood of the sacrifice covered the law with its demands. There at the mercy seat, by faith in the sacrifice, the people were pardoned. Their sins were covered by the blood of the sacrifice. God met with the representative of His people at the blood-sprinkled mercy seat and blessed the whole nation with His presence.

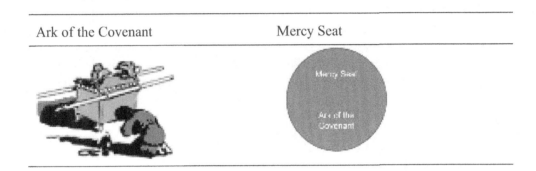

Ark of the Covenant	Mercy Seat

QUESTION 15

In your Life Notebook, answer the following questions:

Compare Exodus 25:21-22 with Hebrews 9:5. What meaning do you find if you read "mercy seat" instead of "propitiation" in Romans 3:25 and 1 John 2:2? How does this impact your personal life?

In Romans 3:25, Paul speaks of the revelation of the righteousness of God in forgiving the sins of His people in Old Testament times. Everyone knew that the life of an animal was not worth the life of a man. The blood of animals could not possibly take away sin! But now, the death of the Son of God wholly covers all the demands of the Law. All the former sacrifices offered in faith were just a temporary measure pointing to the sacrifice of the Lamb of God who takes away the sin of the world. God dealt with sin fully at the cross (see Heb 10:14 and Heb 9:11-12). Only the cross of Christ could bridge the gap between a holy God and sinful men. We can see now that the way in which men received the gift of God's righteousness has always been by faith. They offered their sacrifices in response to God's Word, trusting in His promise. Before Calvary, men could not see that this arrangement was just. But Calvary settled the whole account.

In Romans 3:26, we see that not only in the past but in the present, too, God's righteousness is declared by forgiving sinners on the basis of faith in Christ. The dilemma is solved through redemption and propitiation. God is the justifier; He declares right in His sight those who trust in Jesus. God is also right in doing this--He is just.

The Dilemma of Salvation Solved

SALVATION IN ROMANS 3:24-26

How?	Through redemption in Christ Jesus' propitiation
How received?	Freely through faith in His blood
Why?	Because of His grace
What result?	Justified

QUESTION 16

At what point in the Christian's life does God pronounce him righteous?

A. When he accepts Christ as his Savior

B. When he is baptized in water

C. When he is baptized in the Holy Spirit

D. When he dies trusting Christ

QUESTION 17

Of what Old Testament event does the word "redemption" remind us?

A. Adam and Eve's removal from the Garden of Eden

B. Joseph's rise to power in Egypt

C. Israel's deliverance from bondage in Egypt

D. Jesus' death on the cross

QUESTION 18

To what object in the Old Testament is the word "propitiation" related?

A. The cross

B. The temple

C. The altar

D. The mercy seat

QUESTION 19

What word describes Jesus' death as a sacrifice to satisfy the demands of the law and appease God's wrath?

A. Grace

B. Redemption

C. Propitiation

D. Salvation

QUESTION 20

What word describes Jesus' death as a price paid to set the sinners free from sin?

A. Grace

B. Redemption

C. Propitiation

D. Salvation

Defense of Justification by Faith (Rom 3:27-31)

> Objective 5 – At the end of this topic, you will be able to explain three positive features of the salvation that God has provided mankind through Christ.

In Romans 3:27-31, we find Paul's logical conclusion to all that he has presented up to this point in Romans. He makes three key statements about justification by faith, each introduced by one or more questions:

     1. A man is justified by faith apart from works of the law (Rom 3:27-28).

     2. God will justify both the circumcised and the uncircumcised by faith (Rom 3:29-30).

     3. Through faith we uphold the law (Rom 3:31).

QUESTION 21

According to Romans 3:27, if people could be justified by their good works they would have a right to…

    A. Boast

    B. Complain

    C. Save others

    D. Witness

QUESTION 22

Compare Ephesians 2:8-9 with Romans 3:27. We have no right to boast about our goodness or relationship with God because our salvation comes as a _____ through faith.

QUESTION 23

In the first part of Romans, Paul spoke about two groups who criticized others and boasted of their own goodness or standing with God. Name those groups. *(Select all that apply.)*

    A. Sadducees

    B. Self-righteous critics

    C. Pharisees

    D. Jews

QUESTION 24

According to Romans 3:30, what is the only way possible for anyone to be made right with God?

    A. Obeying the Law

    B. Being baptized

    C. Going to church

    D. Having faith in Jesus Christ

QUESTION 25

Compare Romans 1:16 with Romans 3:22-23 and Romans 3:29-30. Give two reasons why there is only one way of salvation for both Jews and Gentiles. *(Select all that apply.)*

    A. All have the same need since all have sinned.

    B. The same God provides righteousness for all.

    C. Because the Law did not work.

    D. Because God is one.

QUESTION 26

Compare Romans 3:20 and Romans 3:31. In your Life Notebook, answer the following question: In what way do we uphold the law when we go to Jesus Christ for salvation?

Topic 2: Justification in the Old Testament (Rom 4:1-25)

You have already studied in Galatians Paul's reference to Abraham as a scriptural example of justification by faith (see Gal 3). Paul follows again a principle that is very important in law courts. A lawyer looks for precedents--cases similar to the one he is presenting where the argument or the decision can be an example for his case. The basis of this chapter is clearly given in Romans 4:3. Memorize this verse.

Important Examples of Justification by Faith (Rom 4:1-8)

> Objective 6 – At the end of this topic, you will be able to give two examples that Paul cites from the Old Testament of men who were justified by faith.

Abraham Justified by Faith, Not Works

First, Paul points to Abraham, the father of the Jewish nation and shows that he was justified by faith and not by works. You have already seen in Galatians that Abraham is the "father of the faithful" and a pattern of the way in which both Jews and Gentiles are justified before God.

QUESTION 27

According to Romans 4:1, to whom was Paul writing in this chapter?

    A. Jews

    B. Gentiles

    C. Jews and Gentiles

    D. Greeks

QUESTION 28

Write from memory the Bible verse that Paul quotes as a basis for all of Romans 4 (Rom 4:3).

QUESTION 29

Which of the following key words do you see repeated in this chapter? *(Select all that apply.)*

    A. Credited

    B. Righteousness

    C. Abraham

    D. Father

    E. Believe

    F. Faith

The term "credited to" is the key of the chapter. It is a bookkeeping term that means "to give credit for" or "to put to the account of."

QUESTION 30

Which of the following in Romans 4:3-11 and Romans 4:22-24 are counted as righteousness? *(Select all that apply.)*

    A. Obedience

    B. Faith

    C. Believing God

    D. Transformed

QUESTION 31

Compare Romans 4:5 with Romans 4:4. What is Paul emphasizing here about God's method of justifying the ungodly? *(Select all that apply.)*

    A. Salvation is by faith through grace.

    B. Salvation is by grace through faith.

    C. Salvation is a gift.

    D. Salvation is not by works.

QUESTION 32

Compare Romans 4:5 with Romans 3:26. In order to become children of God, what must we do? *(Select all that apply.)*

    A. We must believe in Jesus.

    B. We must obey the law.

    C. We must receive God's forgiveness by trusting in Jesus.

    D. We must receive Jesus as our Savior.

David Praised God for Imputed Righteousness

Abraham was not the only Old Testament character to experience justification by grace. Beginning at Romans 4:6, Paul presents the testimony of David by quoting from Psalm 32:1-2.

QUESTION 33

David's testimony in Psalm 32:1 reminds us of propitiation when he declared that his "sins are pardoned." *True or False?*

Not imputing sin (Rom 4:8) is the same as counting a person righteous! This negative form of describing justification reminds us that the word justification is a legal term. It carries the idea of acquittal, or being declared not guilty. God treats the sinner who believes in Christ as if he had never sinned. Christ's righteousness is put to our account.

In these verses, Paul introduces the subject of the blessedness of the person who is justified by faith without trying to earn God's favor with his own efforts. What a release from guilt! What peace in knowing that he is forgiven! We will study more about the blessings of justification in Romans 5.

Abraham Justified While Uncircumcised (Rom 4:9-12)

Objective 7 – At the end of this topic, you will be able to explain the significance to Gentiles of Abraham's justification prior to being circumcised.

Paul asks a question in Romans 4:9 and then takes the rest of the chapter to answer it. Who can have this blessedness that God's righteousness brings? Just the Jews or the Gentiles too? You are already acquainted with Paul's answer as he gives it in Galatians and repeats it here.

QUESTION 34

What would you say circumcision means in Romans 4:9?

- A. The Jewish, male population
- B. The Jewish, male and female population
- C. The religious, Jewish population
- D. Those people, Jews and Gentiles, who have been circumcised

QUESTION 35

What is meant by uncircumcision? (Rom 4:9)

- A. The Gentile, male population
- B. The Gentile, male and female population
- C. The non-religious, Jewish population
- D. Those people, Jews and Gentiles, who have not been circumcised

QUESTION 36

Which statement is true about Abraham?

- A. His obedience was the result of his faith.
- B. His good works, together with his faith, justified him before God.
- C. His circumcision and faith were counted as righteousness.
- D. His good works were the basis for God's offer of justification.

QUESTION 37

According to Romans 4:9-10, was Abraham a Jew or a Gentile at the time he was justified?

QUESTION 38

According to Romans 4:12, who can claim Abraham as their spiritual father?

    A. Only Jews

    B. Only Jewish believers

    C. Only Gentiles

    D. All who follow his example of faith, Jews and Gentiles

Because Abraham was justified before he was circumcised, this makes him the spiritual father of all the uncircumcised (the Gentiles) who have the same kind of faith. But because he was circumcised later, he is the spiritual father of all the circumcised (the Jews) who believe in the same manner that he did. Whether a person is circumcised or not, then, is of no importance as far as justification is concerned. Justification and all its blessings come to us through faith (see Rom 4:16).

Abraham Justified Apart From the Law (Rom 4:13-25)

Objective 8 – At the end of this topic, you will be able to, based on the life of Abraham, describe the kind of faith that results in salvation.

Romans 4:13-18 speaks of the promises made to Abraham and his seed (descendants). Romans 4:13 mentions God's promise that Abraham would be heir of the world. Romans 4:17-18 refers to God's promise that he would be a father of many nations.

From Romans 4:11 on, we begin to see another major aspect of salvation. It is more than acquittal. Paul begins to describe it in terms of life. We are the spiritual children of Abraham (Rom 4:11-12) and inherit the promises made to him because he is our spiritual father (Rom 4:13, 16).

Does Romans 4:14 remind you of Galatians? There you saw that the Law, given 400 years after the promise to Abraham, could not annul God's promise or change the terms of His will. Romans 4:15 reminds us of the first main section of Romans. The Law cannot justify us or make us good. It can only make our sinfulness more serious as we deliberately break God's laws and face His wrath. Compare this with Romans 3:20.

QUESTION 39

Romans 4:17 tells us that the God in whom Abraham believed does what two things? *(Select all that apply.)*

    A. He gives life to the dead.

    B. He calls things that are not as though they were.

    C. He seeks those who are lost.

    D. He cleans those who are sinful.

Notice the relationship between the first part of Romans 4:17 and the last part. God said: "I *have made* you the father of many nations" (emphasis added) when these nations were not yet in existence and Abraham did not even have a son. God was calling those things that He had promised accomplished facts. Abraham simply believed what God said.

Let's look at Abraham's faith in Romans 4:17-21. First of all, he believed in God as the Life-giver and Creator. God would have to give Abraham and Sarah new life so that they could have the son He had promised them. They were "as good as dead" (Rom 4:19 and Heb 11:11-12) because of their advanced age. Abraham recognized this fact, but in verse 18 we see that when there was no hope, humanly speaking, Abraham believed and looked forward to the fulfillment of God's promise. Romans 4:19-20 gives us some important principles of faith. He did not look at the difficulties, he looked at the promise.

QUESTION 40

What are three things about Abraham's faith that we see in Romans 4:20? *(Select all that apply.)*

    A. He gave glory to God.

    B. He believed God even though there was no evidence to do so.

    C. He did not waver in unbelief about the promise of God.

    D. He was strong in faith.

Here we learn that a person's faith is strengthened when it receives a challenge. Faith grows strong as it rests on God's promises, considering His nature, His power, and His ability to do what He has promised. One English translation says in Romans 4:20-21: "His faith filled him with power, and he gave praise to God. He was absolutely sure that God would be able to do what he had promised" (GNT). Notice in these verses the attitude of praise and confidence that Abraham had toward God.

In Romans 4:22-25, Paul applies the illustration of Abraham's faith to our relationship with Jesus Christ. Abraham's faith was put to his account as righteousness (Rom 4:22). God had this statement written in the Scriptures (Rom 4:23) for our benefit (Rom 4:24). We too must believe in God as the Life-giver and Creator. He raised Jesus from the dead (Rom 4:24) and gives spiritual life to all those who believe.

Romans 4:24-25 shows us three things that our faith in God must include: **1)** We accept Jesus as our Lord. **2)** We believe that God sent Jesus to be crucified for our sins. **3)** We believe that God raised Jesus from the dead to give us new life (a life of righteousness and right standing with God) in Him.

Topic 3: Blessings Provided by Justification (Rom 5:1-11)

Paul has established God's way of righteousness. So far in this third major section of Romans 3:21-5:21 he has shown this way to be faith. God's provision in the cross of Jesus Christ was seen to be the answer to the "dilemma" which God faced. Paul also established that this way was supported by Old Testament Scripture.

Romans 5 is a transitional passage in Paul's development of his theme *the righteousness of God revealed*. Up to this point, his treatment concerned the righteousness of God and its imputation to men-- justification. Now Paul turns to another treatment of the theme: the righteousness of God in its day-by-day outworking in the behavior of the Christian--sanctification.

For those who have trusted in Jesus Christ for their salvation, this first half of Romans 5 begins to answer the question, "What happens now?" Again the faith-to-faith principle emerges. Justification concerned the first crisis act of faith. Now Paul turns to the continuous, living faith by which men are delivered from sin's power. The following chapters (Rom 6–8) will deal in-depth with the power of sin which indwells the hearts of men.

Blessings for Those Who Believe (Rom 5:1-4)

Objective 9 – At the end of this topic, you will be able to describe the nature of the blessings that accompany justification.

In Romans 5, Paul begins to talk about the positive implications in daily life of the salvation that God has provided through Jesus Christ. He starts out Romans 5:1 with the phrase, "*Therefore* having been justified by faith…" (emphasis added). This is an obvious reference to the salvation he has presented in previous chapters.

One might say that up to this point Paul has proven that by faith we have a right standing before God. Now in Romans 5:2 he expands on that concept by referring to our new standing as being in the grace of God. In other words, the door to the unmerited favor of God has been opened by faith. This is a reference to what happens after we are justified by faith.

The point Paul is making at the beginning of Romans 5 is that there are blessings which accompany those who are justified!

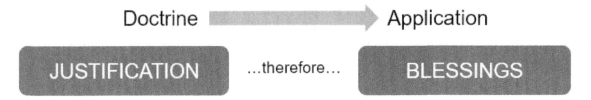

At least three blessings are mentioned in the Bible passage before you--peace, joy, and hope. The important question here is: Are these blessings part of your Christian experience? Paul has proven that they are available to those who are justified. Do you have peace? Joy? Hope?

Potential Blessings

There are many Christians who have been justified and who have standing or position in the grace of God but are not experiencing these blessings. Why not?

For the answer, let's look once more at the faith-to-faith principle that is so important in this epistle. Remember it in our key verse (Rom 1:17)? Then we see it again in Romans 3:22: The faith that brings us into the grace of God is to become the principle by which we live. The initial act of faith is to continue in the believer's life. "The righteous man shall live by faith" (Rom 1:17, NASB). In light of this principle, we can understand Romans 5:1-11 better. The blessings of justification are not automatic, although they belong to us. Faith must claim the blessings that God's grace has provided for us. The door is open to all the peace, joy, and hope that we need. Let's believe so and claim them!

Several translations of Romans 5:1-3 bring out our responsibility in appropriating the blessings of our justification. Here is an example from *The New Testament: A Translation in the Language of the People* by Charles B. Williams:

> "Since we have been given right standing with God through faith, then *let us* continue enjoying peace with God through our Lord Jesus Christ, by whom we have an introduction through faith into this state of God's favor, in which we safely stand, and *let us* continue exulting in the hope of enjoying the glorious presence of God. And not only that, but this too *let us* continue exulting in our sufferings…." (Rom 5:1-3, emphasis added).

The following chart is an analysis of Romans 5:1-4.

Romans 1-4

POSITION

1. We have been justified through faith – Romans 5:1
2. We stand in the sphere of God's grace – Romans 5:2

POTENTIAL

Three appeals to the believer
1. Let us continue at peace with God – Romans 5:1
2. Let us exult in the hope of the divine splendor that is ours – Romans 5:2
3. Let us exult in our sufferings – Romans 5:3-4

Note that faith has been the instrument or means by which we are in the position illustrated in the chart below. The blessings of justification, or our position, are listed in the chart under the word *Potential*. Paul appeals to believers to have these things.

The Challenge of Outer Conflict

The central truth here is that the blessings of justification are not automatic. They must be appropriated by faith. Our faith placed us in a position of being right before God. Faith also introduced us into the grace of God. The *same* faith will appropriate for us a continual enjoyment of the peace of God, a state of joy in which we can even rejoice in the troubles that come our way.

Experience agrees with what Paul is teaching in these verses. The wonderful state of peace with God can be disturbed. Satan can disturb it with his attacks and lies. A sense of guilt which comes from not believing that God has forgiven sin can disturb it. The daily battle with the flesh can disturb it. Our joy can be lost in the cares of life and the troubles that are part of every Christian's experience. Hope can grow dim in the midst of a trial. Peace, joy, and hope are not fixed, unchanging quantities in the Christian life! They require a living and vital faith! Paul says, "Since you have this position before God and standing in His grace, appropriate from God the blessings of such a position--by your faith!" (see Rom 5:1-4, paraphrased by author).

Paul explains, "Now you understand your position; believe it then!" When the conflicts, trials, and assaults from Satan come, with the eye of faith we should look to God for grace and help in our time of need. The most important thing is that we are at peace with God. Paul tells us to enjoy that fact no matter what the circumstances. Again in Romans 14 Paul tells us that righteousness, peace, and joy are our birthright in the kingdom of God (see Rom 14:17). The kingdom of God is the realm where God rules. Note the order of the words in Romans 14:17. Righteousness is mentioned first, then peace, and then joy in the Holy Spirit. This is also the order in Romans 5:1-2. The Holy Spirit is the One by whom we maintain our Christian joy. He is also referred to in Romans 5:5.

Paul wants the Roman Christians to live and serve Christ with joy in the Holy Spirit. The church at Rome was a persecuted church. The Jewish Christians in Rome were driven out of the city on three different occasions by the government. Christians in Rome were unpopular and reputed to be "enemies of the human race." In many cases, Christians became the "scapegoats" for social and political trouble. This persecution intensified to the point when the Roman Emperor Nero executed large numbers of Christians. According to tradition, Paul himself was martyred in the wake of this persecution.

We should not think that Paul is a theologian interested in theology but not in life. This is not true. Nor should we think that in his letter to this Roman church he presents theology which was unrelated to life. Before he even gets to what many call the "practical" section of the letter (Rom 12; 13; 14; 15; 16), there are many practical sections. The Bible passage before us is one of them. In this passage, Paul is calling on the Roman Christians to rejoice in their position as the justified children of God. To do this they must exercise their faith.

QUESTION 41

How does the Romans 5:1-3 faith-to-faith principle apply to your life situation today? Open your Life Notebook and record your answer.

The Reality of Inner Conflict

In Romans 5:1-11, Paul is giving the Roman Christians a principle that will help them in facing opposition and conflict. A living faith will sustain them in times of trial and persecution. But Paul has another dimension of opposition and conflict in mind here also. The phrase "the hope of the glory of God" directs our attention to an inward conflict.

In Romans 3:23, the phrase "glory of God" referred to the standard which God required men to live up to. There Paul said that men came short of what God intended them to be. Man was created in the image of God to live for God's glory. The primary reason why men are unable to live up to God's standard or His glory is sin. Men have an inward problem which makes them fall short of the glory of God. The principle of sin marred the image that God had created in men.

In Romans 5:2, the phrase "hope of the glory of God" refers not only to a future glory to be revealed at the coming of Christ--but also to the restoration of the image of God in the believer now. Paul focuses our attention on the great battlefield of conflict--the inward conflict with the power of sin. In Galatians, this warfare was described as the conflict of the flesh and the Spirit. Here in Romans, Paul is telling the church that they should not let this inner conflict rob them of their enjoyment of peace with God.

When Christians are engaged in this conflict with the flesh, Satan often takes advantage. He tells them that the fact that there is a conflict means that they are not right with God. Of course this is not true. Satan may say, "You were tempted, therefore you have sinned; you have failed God, and you are not a Christian at all." This is an example of the lies of Satan. Temptation is not sin. Yielding to temptation is sin. If a Christian sins, God is faithful to forgive him (see 1 Jn 1:9).

Paul is saying here: "Rejoice in the hope of the glory of God." In other words, rejoice that God assuredly *will* accomplish what He has intended in your life. In spite of the conflict, there is hope that God is restoring in us the image of God by the ministry of His Spirit. The glory of God is a reality in the Christian's life now. Paul deals with this inward conflict extensively in Romans 6-8. Here we are introduced to it.

In Romans 5:3, Paul also says, "Since you know that you are at peace with God, you may also rejoice in tribulations!" In other words, Paul tells them not to let the outer battle, tribulations, and conflict of life disturb their enjoyment of the peace of God either. It takes faith to rejoice in tribulations, but it is possible for the Christian whose life is not left to chance or fate. All of the events in a Christian's life are known by God. It is possible to rejoice in tribulations because they come in the will of God. If they are encountered in faith, the very things that destroy and cause bitterness in other lives will work to the good of the Christian. The tribulations will serve to cultivate endurance and steadfastness of character (Rom 5:3-4). These in turn will stimulate hope.

Transforming Power of God's Love (Rom 5:5-11)

Objective 10 – At the end of this topic, you will be able to explain how the Holy Spirit helps us appropriate God's blessings.

It is important to understand that the word "hope," as it is used in the New Testament, does not imply uncertainty about the future. On the contrary, it is an attitude that expresses complete confidence that God will accomplish what He has promised.

The argument we find here is similar to the one that Paul uses in Romans 8. There he says, "And we know that God causes all things to work together for good to those who love God, to those who are called according to His purpose" (Rom 8:28). He goes on to say, "If God is for us, who is against us" (Rom 8:31). He uses the same argument in Romans 5:5-11, reminding the Romans that God is for them!

In Romans 5:5, Paul says that this hope is not disappointing. It is not disappointing because there is strong evidence for it. The presence of the Holy Spirit in the lives of Christians is able to communicate the love of God to them (Rom 5:5). The Holy Spirit also plays an important role in Paul's similar argument in Romans 8.

You saw in a previous section of this lesson that the kingdom of God is righteousness, peace, and joy in the Holy Spirit. The Holy Spirit is the one who helps us in living a righteous life, maintains our peace of mind and heart, and also is the source of our joy. Here we see that He is also the one who assures us of the love of God. He also makes it possible for us to rejoice in the midst of inner and outer conflict. You will learn more of the ministry of the Holy Spirit in Romans 8.

QUESTION 42

Paul says, "Take heart, God is for you." According to Romans 5:6-11, God demonstrated His love to mankind by sending Christ to die for us while we were still sinners. *True or False?*

QUESTION 43

How does Paul reason that God will help Christians now that they have been justified? (See Rom 5:10.)

- A. God helped sinners because they could not do it by themselves, but He expects believers to walk in a worthy manner.
- B. Since He sent Jesus to die for us while we were still sinners, He will continue to help us after we become believers.
- C. Since sinners are dead and believers are alive, believers do not need God's help in their normal day-to-day walk.
- D. God will only help those who call upon His name.

"Rejoice in God!" Paul says in Romans 5:11. Our joy is not just in a hope of the future or in knowing that our troubles will make us better. We rejoice in God Himself and enjoy fellowship with Him (Rom 5:11). Through Jesus Christ we have been reconciled with Him.. We are no longer enemies of God but friends. God is for us. He will take care of us to the end. We can trust Him and use our faith to overcome inner conflicts and outer tribulation. Let us rejoice in the conflict. It is developing our Christian character. God knows all about our troubles. Let's keep on rejoicing in the peace of God.

QUESTION 44

What is the key phrase in the section Romans 5:1-11?

- A. Once dead, now alive
- B. Blessed among all men
- C. Through our Lord Jesus Christ
- D. Sons of the Most High

Topic 4: Victory Over Sin and Death (Rom 5:12-21)

All the blessings of a victorious Christian life come to us through our relationship with Jesus as our Lord and Savior. Romans 5:12-21 tells us more about the transforming power of this relationship.

> Objective 11 – At the end of this topic, you will be able to compare the two principles Paul discusses in Romans 5:12-21.

Paul begins Romans 5:12 with the word "therefore." This word points back to Romans 5:1-11. There Paul pointed out the necessity of using faith to implement the blessings and benefits of our standing in the grace of God. He now wants to explain more about this position or standing in the grace of God. Progressively, Paul is bringing us from the doctrinal and theoretical to the practical and realistic.

In these verses (Rom 5:12-21), Paul contrasts Adam and Christ. But the comparison here is not just between Adam and Christ. What is in focus here are two relationships that the Christian has--one with Adam and the other with Christ.

In order to understand the passage before you, it is necessary to make a distinction between "sins" and "sin." Sin is both an act and a power or principle. Up to this point in his epistle, Paul has dealt primarily with the "sins" of men, their acts of transgression. Now in the transitional passage he explains how "sin," the powerful principle residing in the hearts of men, came into the experience of mankind through Adam.

Because of our relationship to Adam, the presence of the power of sin in us is a reality which must be dealt with. Paul does not deny the reality of the presence of sin. Adam's disobedience caused great damage to the human race. He does not underestimate this. We can call this the principle of sin.

However, Paul is saying here that the Christian's relationship with Christ has introduced a new principle into the arena of our conflict with the principle of sin. It is the principle of grace (Rom 5:15; Rom 5:17; Rom 5:20-21). The emphasis of this passage is that God's provision in Jesus Christ is *more* than enough to take care of the problems related to our relationship with Adam.

QUESTION 45

Read again the verses in which the words "grace" or "grace of God" are mentioned. What other words are repeated in connection with grace or grace of God? *(Select all that apply.)*

    A. More

    B. Much more

    C. Gifts

    D. Love

The comparison of Christ and Adam here shows the triumph of grace over sin. The benefits of the relationship with Christ are more than enough to overcome sin. This is the main emphasis of the passage. This is Paul's encouragement to the Romans: The position that they were in was a winning position! Paul said where sin increases, grace increases much more (Rom 5:20)!

The following chart is an analysis of Romans 5:12-21.

Principles of Adam and Christ Compared

Verse	Adam – Relationship PRINCIPLE OF SIN	Christ – Leadership PRINCIPLE OF GRACE
12	Sin entered into the world and death through sin. Adam, the representative man, sinned. Because of this, death passed on to all men, because all sinned.	
15	By the one transgression (Adam's) man died.	Much more did the grace of God and the gift by the grace of the one man Jesus Christ abound to many.
16	Judgment and condemnation were the result of Adam's act.	In spite of many transgressions the free gift resulted in justification.
17	Death reigned in the human race through Adam's act.	Much more those who receive the abundance of grace and the gift of righteousness will reign in life through the One (Christ).
18	All men were condemned through one act of sin.	Through the act of righteousness there resulted justification of life to all men.
19	Through one man's disobedience the many were made sinners.	Through the obedience of one the many will be made righteous.
20	The Law came so that the transgression might increase. Sin increased.	Grace abounded all the more.
21	Sin reigned in death	Grace reigns through righteousness to eternal life through Jesus Christ our Lord.

QUESTION 46

Respond to the following questions in your Life Notebook: How does Paul's faith-to-faith principle relate to Romans 5:12-21 and how you live your life?

It is important to note that there is a difference of opinion as to how much effect Adam's act of disobedience has on men today. The approach taken in this course is that Paul is teaching solidarity with both Adam and Christ in this passage. The difficulty with the passage arises not out of the concept of our relationship or solidarity with Christ, but out of the concept of our solidarity with Adam.

The idea of participating with someone who acts as a representative for a group is a concept familiar to the Eastern mind. The name Adam in the Hebrew language means "mankind." Paul speaks of Adam acting as the representative of mankind when he sinned. He views all men as having collectively participated with Adam (Rom 5:12, 18-19). The idea is not unfamiliar in Scripture; Levi is said to have paid tithes in the person of Abraham even before Levi was born. The representative act of Abraham is said to have been shared by Levi (Heb 7:9).

Paul is saying that from the Hebrew viewpoint not only are men guilty because of sins, but they are also guilty because of what they are. They are sinners; the power of sin resides in their nature (see also Eph

2:3; Job 14:4; 15:14; Ps 51:5). Paul shows here that sin is more than just an act of the will of man. It is defined also as a principle or law at work in the human heart (Rom 7:21, 23 and Rom 8:2).

Not only in this section of Romans (Rom 5:12-21) but also in 1 Corinthians 15:22, 45-49, Paul draws a parallel between Adam and Christ. Christ is even referred to as the "last Adam" (1 Cor 15:45). These two passages are evidence for the view that Adam was representing the human race when he sinned. However you should notice that the analogy between Adam and Christ is not parallel in all points. Paul points this out in several places (Rom 5:15-16). The relationship with Adam is a necessary union; it is by birth not by choice. But the relationship with Christ is a potential union, depending upon a person's response of faith in the redeeming work of Christ.

QUESTION 47

In your Life Notebook, explain the source and effect of the two principles that Paul discusses on your life. Use Romans 5:12-21 to help explain the principle of sin and the principle of grace.

Lesson 3 Self Check

QUESTION 1

What does "apart from the law" mean in Romans 3:21?

    A. Apart from the works of the law

    B. Apart from the effects of the law

    C. Apart from the result of the law

    D. The law is totally unnecessary.

QUESTION 2

God has a different way of salvation for the Jew than for the Gentile. *True or False?*

QUESTION 3

To which object in the Old Testament is the word "propitiation" related?

    A. Sacrificial lamb

    B. Scroll of the Law

    C. Altar

    D. Mercy seat

QUESTION 4

According to Romans 3:27, if people could be justified by their good works they would have a right to …

    A. Boast

    B. Complain

    C. Look down on others

    D. Persecute Christians

QUESTION 5

Which Old Testament character reminds us of propitiation in Psalm 32 by declaring that his "sins are pardoned"?

    A. Abraham

    B. David

    C. Jesus

    D. Asaph

QUESTION 6

According to Romans 4:12, who can claim Abraham as their spiritual father?

    A. Only Jews

    B. Only Jewish believers

    C. Only Gentiles

    D. All who follow his example of faith, Jews and Gentiles

QUESTION 7

One facet of Abraham's faith that we see in Romans 4:20 is that he believed God even though there was no evidence to do so. *True or False?*

QUESTION 8

Paul says, "Take heart, God is for you." According to Romans 5:6-11, God demonstrated His love to mankind by sending Christ to die for us while we were still sinners. *True or False?*

QUESTION 9

Paul reasons in Romans 5:10 that since God sent Jesus to die for us while we were still sinners, He will continue to help us after we are believers. *True or False?*

QUESTION 10

The main emphasis of Romans 5:12-21 is that the benefits of the Christ-relationship are more than enough to overcome sin. *True or False?*

Lesson 3 Answers to Questions

QUESTION 1
    B. The wrath of God

QUESTION 2
    D. The righteousness of God

QUESTION 3
    C. In the gospel

QUESTION 4
    A. The righteousness of God

QUESTION 5
    D. By faith in Christ, believing in Him

QUESTION 6: True

QUESTION 7
    D. All who believe

QUESTION 8
    B. The Gentiles

QUESTION 9: True

QUESTION 10
    C. Jesus gave His life as a ransom to redeem us.

QUESTION 11
    C. Satisfy the debt of our sin.

QUESTION 12
    D. A propitiation, or atoning sacrifice, for our sins

QUESTION 13: False

QUESTION 14: *Your answer*

QUESTION 15: *Your answer*

QUESTION 16
    A. When he accepts Christ as his Savior

QUESTION 17
    C. Israel's deliverance from bondage in Egypt

QUESTION 18
    D. The mercy seat

QUESTION 19
    C. Propitiation

QUESTION 20
    B. Redemption

QUESTION 21
    A. Boast

QUESTION 22: Gift

QUESTION 23
    B. Self-righteous critics
    D. Jews

QUESTION 24
    D. Having faith in Jesus Christ

QUESTION 25
    A. All have the same need since all have sinned.
    B. The same God provides righteousness for all.

QUESTION 26: *Your answer*

QUESTION 27
    A. Jews

QUESTION 28: *Your answer should be similar to the following:*
Abraham believed God and it was credited to him as righteousness.

QUESTION 29
    A. Credited
    B. Righteousness
    C. Abraham
    D. Father
    E. Believe
    F. Faith

QUESTION 30
    B. Faith
    C. Believing God

QUESTION 31
    B. Salvation is by grace through faith.
    D. Salvation is not by works.

QUESTION 32
    A. We must believe in Jesus.
    C. We must receive God's forgiveness by trusting in Jesus.
    D. We must receive Jesus as our Savior.

QUESTION 33: True

QUESTION 34
    C. The religious, Jewish population

QUESTION 35
    B. The Gentile, male and female population

QUESTION 36
    A. His obedience was the result of his faith.

QUESTION 37: *Your answer should be similar to the following:*
Gentile--When he was justified he was not yet circumcised.

QUESTION 38
    D. All who follow his example of faith, Jews and Gentiles

QUESTION 39
    A. He gives life to the dead.
    B. He calls things that are not as though they were.

QUESTION 40
    A. He gave glory to God.
    C. He did not waver in unbelief about the promise of God.
    D. He was strong in faith.

QUESTION 41: *Your answer*

QUESTION 42: True

QUESTION 43
    B. Since He sent Jesus to die for us while we were still sinners, He will continue to help us after we become believers.

QUESTION 44
    C. Through our Lord Jesus Christ

QUESTION 45
    A. More
    B. Much more
    C. Gifts

QUESTION 46: *Your answer*
QUESTION 47: *Your answer*

Lesson 3 Self Check Answers

QUESTION 1
    A. Apart from the works of the law

QUESTION 2: False

QUESTION 3
    D. Mercy seat

QUESTION 4
    A. Boast

QUESTION 5
    B. David

QUESTION 6
    D. All who follow his example of faith, Jews and Gentiles

QUESTION 7: False

QUESTION 8: True

QUESTION 9: True

QUESTION 10: True

Lesson 4: A New Life of Freedom (Rom 6–7)

Lesson Introduction

In this lesson, we begin the third major division of the theological part of Romans. We can summarize these first three divisions in three words:

1. **Condemnation** in Romans 1:18–3:20

2. **Justification** in Romans 3:21–5:21

3. **Sanctification** in Romans 6:1–8:39

The first division spoke of universal condemnation. We saw the whole world guilty of sin and sentenced to death. The second division showed us God's provision for salvation--justification through faith in Jesus Christ our substitute. Here we find pardon, removal of guilt, and right standing before God. Now in the third division we have the theme of sanctification--a new life in Christ. These chapters show us how we can experience a life of victory over sin.

In Romans 6 and 7, we see the provision for our sanctification and our need for sanctification. We see, too, how the Law and self-effort are completely powerless to separate us from sin. Then in Romans 8 we will see how the Holy Spirit works in our lives to give us victory over every obstacle.

Lesson Objectives

Topic 1 describes our freedom from sin.

In Topic 1, you will learn...

- The meaning of the word *sanctification* and how it applies to our lives as Christians
- How water baptism illustrates our spiritual death and resurrection
- How faith enables us to experience victory in daily life
- The importance of choosing a new master

Topic 2 describes our freedom from the Law.

In Topic 2, you will discover...

- Six uses of the word "law" in the Scriptures
- How death of a spouse and re-marriage illustrate our freedom from the Law
- Four reasons why God originally instituted the Law

Topic 3 demonstrates that our freedom is not reached by self-effort.

In Topic 3, you will learn why Christians don't always experience a life of freedom.

Lesson Outline

Topic 1: Freedom from Sin (Rom 6:1-23)

Death and Resurrection (6:1-10)

Victory through Faith (6:11-14)

Choice of a New Master (6:15-23)

Word List

We hope you will enjoy using the word study at the beginning of each lesson. Some of the words you already know, but they are used in a special sense in the lesson. Others are theological terms, and some are new words for many students. Please read the word study each time before starting the lesson. Refer back to it as necessary.

Baptized (Rom 6:3) - placed in, immersed in. To immerse is to plunge into or to baptize by submerging in water.

Dominion (Rom 6:9) - rule, authority, power to govern.

Old man (Rom 6:6) - old nature, sinful self.

Reckon (Rom 6:11) – to consider, to calculate by adding up the facts.

Temporal - relating to existence in this world, limited by time and other natural laws, not eternal.

Topic 1: Freedom from Sin (Rom 6:1-23)

A saint is a holy person, one who belongs to God. In Romans 6, we see that the gospel is a way of holiness. It makes saints out of sinners!

> Objective 1 – At the end of this topic, you will be able to give the basic meaning of sanctification, describe two of its aspects, and place it into the context of the first three main divisions of Romans.

Holiness is the condition of a life that is set apart for God. It includes separation from sin and freedom from the power of sin. Sanctification is the act or process by which a person becomes holy.

It is important that we understand the structure of Romans 6. It is divided into two sections, each of which presents sanctification from a different viewpoint. The first section (Rom 6:1-10) shows us sanctification from God's viewpoint. He has freed us from sin, accepted us as His children, and set us apart for Himself. The second section (Rom 6:11-23) gives us man's viewpoint of sanctification. It is not just an initial experience but also a progressive, day-by-day giving of himself to God.

In the table to the right, you can see a comparison between these two aspects of sanctification. Here we have one of the paradoxes of the Christian life. The Christian is called a saint, but in practice he is still in the process of being sanctified. Strange as it sounds, Christians are to become what God says they already are! You have already seen this idea in the doctrine of justification. In Romans 1:17, you saw that men are declared righteous when they have faith. But they are also to use their faith to live a righteous life. God declares men righteous; He says, "Now be righteous in the way you live."

Sanctification

God's Viewpoint	Man's Viewpoint
Positional	Experiential
Instantaneous	Progressive
Ideal	Practical
Complete	Partial

QUESTION 1

Identify the **three** major theological divisions of Romans. *(Select all that apply.)*

    A. Romans 1:18–3:20--Man's depravity (sinfulness)

    B. Romans 1:18–3:20--Man's need (condemnation)

    C. Romans 3:21–5:21--God's provision (justification)

    D. Romans 3:21–5:21--God's gift (grace)

    E. Romans 6:1–8:39--New hope (promise of heaven)

    F. Romans 6:1–8:39--New life (sanctification)

QUESTION 2

Romans 6:1-10 teaches that our sanctification from God's viewpoint is positional, instantaneous, perfect, and complete. *True or False?*

Death and Resurrection (Rom 6:1-10)

Objective 2 – At the end of this topic, you will be able to appreciate the meaning of water baptism and use this illustration to explain important truths about our relationship to sin.

In Romans 5, Paul described the principle of grace operating in the life of the believer. He pointed out that God's grace was sufficient to deal with sin in the Christian's life. He said that where sin increased, grace increased more. This message would greatly encourage the believers in Rome. But right away Paul realized that some people might interpret it incorrectly. Some, such as the Judaizers, might say that Paul's teaching encouraged careless or sinful living. And others, such as the anti-law party, might say: "If we continue to sin, God's grace will take care of it, so why worry? If grace always abounds in the presence of sin, let's keep on sinning so that grace will increase. The more we sin, the more we let people see how great God's grace is in forgiving us." Paul gave an emphatic answer to those who would pervert the doctrine of grace in this way. He had already pointed out that grace produces righteousness, not sin. Now in Romans 6 he shows us how the death and resurrection of Christ frees the believer from sin and gives him a new life.

QUESTION 3

Read Romans 5:20-21 with Romans 6:1-2. Through which of the following does grace reign?

    A. Mercy

    B. Love

    C. Righteousness

    D. Sacrifice

QUESTION 4

Romans 6:2 is the key verse for this chapter. A true Christian can no longer live in sin because he is _____ to sin.

Paul explains in the following verses how a believer is dead to sin. In Romans 6:3, he tells us that we have been baptized into union with Jesus Christ--into His death. God identifies us so completely with our substitute that He counts us as having died with Christ on the cross and having risen again with Him to live a new life. Our position in Christ means that we are dead to sin. In God's sight, we have been separated from sin and are now saints, His own people. We occupy this position of holy people, even though in practice we still have to fight against sin. In fact, Paul called the Corinthian believers saints although they were involved in some very serious sins (1 Cor 1:2).

Paul speaks of the experience and meaning of water baptism as a powerful reason why we should no longer live in sin. Water baptism is the Lord's command for those who have accepted Christ (Mt 28:19-20). Obedience to this command, the confession of our faith in Christ, is a great help to us spiritually. It is important to teach Christians what baptism means. If we understand its meaning, the very act of baptism strengthens our resolve to live for Christ. It is like our oath of allegiance to Him.

At times it is hard to know if a passage of Scripture refers to the outward experience of water baptism or the spiritual experience of being baptized into the body of Christ (see 1 Cor 12:13). In Romans 6:3, Paul speaks of the spiritual experience and our identification with Christ. Therefore, the word in Romans 6:4 points back to the spiritual experience in Romans 6:3 and forward to water baptism which symbolizes it in Romans 6:4. This passage gives us the meaning of water baptism. It is a public testimony that we have died to sin and have begun a new life in Christ.

The words "buried with him by baptism into death" show how baptism officially recognizes our position with relation to sin. Baptism is the seal on our death certificate. It is our burial to the life we once lived in sin. We have accepted Christ's death for sin as ours, so how can we live in sin any longer? This is Paul's answer in Romans 6:2.

QUESTION 5

Water baptism only serves as a public announcement of our decision to follow Christ. *True or False?*

QUESTION 6

Romans 6:5 tells us that we are united with Christ not only in His death but also in his _____.

Romans 6:6 tells us that the power of sin in a Christian's life has been broken. Our old, rebellious sinful nature is crucified with Christ so that the law of sin is annulled. The body that was once given over to sin and was under its rule has been freed from that law by death (Rom 6:7). We need not obey sin any longer!

QUESTION 7

Have you found that water baptism helps people recognize more clearly their union with Christ? Do you refer often to the importance of water baptism in your preaching or teaching? Should you? Enter your thoughts in your Life Notebook.

Several forms of water baptism are used by different Christian churches. Some immerse the believer in water. Some pour water on the head. Others sprinkle water on the believer. Whatever the form, baptism symbolizes cleansing and separation from sin and dedication to God through our union with Christ in His death and resurrection.

QUESTION 8

Which form of baptism most clearly symbolizes the spiritual experience of a Christian according to Romans 6:3-5?

    A. Pouring

    B. Immersion

    C. Sprinkling

    D. None

QUESTION 9

Romans 6:10 suggests that water baptism symbolizes two things. What are they? *(Select all that apply.)*

    A. Separation from sin

    B. Dedication to life

    C. Separation from death

    D. Dedication to God

Read Romans 6:4-10. Notice that in these verses our life is in Christ, His victory. That is what God says. We accept it as the truth, and it becomes a fact in our daily lives. Paul goes on to tell us how this takes place in the following verses.

Victory through Faith (Rom 6:11-14)

> Objective 3 – At the end of this topic, you will discover how faith enables us to experience victory over sin in daily life.

We have seen that Romans 6:1-10 describes our position before God. In Christ we are dead to sin and resurrected to a new life of victory over sin. But now notice what happens beginning with Romans 6:11. We must believe what God says and let that faith govern our actions. We are commanded to reckon ourselves to be dead indeed to sin but alive to God.

The Greek word translated *reckon* is the same one that is translated *impute* in Romans 4. There it is a key word speaking of God's act of imputing righteousness. Here, too, it is a key word in the life of faith and of the Christian's victory over sin. God reckons our justification, but we are to reckon our sanctification!

The practical aspect of sanctification (holiness in daily life) depends on our willingness to count on what God has already provided for us.

Notice in Romans 6:11-12 that faith converts knowledge into action. Look back at the mental acceptance of truth in Romans 6:3-9. We know that Christ died for us and rose again to free us from sin. We understand and believe the doctrine of identification with Christ. But faith applies this

Romans 6:12

truth to life in obedience to the will of God. Just as Paul encouraged us to claim by faith the blessings and benefits of justification, he now tells us to accept by faith what God says about our sanctification. By recognizing that Christ has broken the power of sin over us, we experience deliverance from it.

QUESTION 10

The word "therefore" in Romans 6:12 refers back to Romans 6:4-11 and our position in Christ: dead to sin and alive to God. *True or False?*

QUESTION 11

What does the word "therefore" point forward to in Romans 6:12-13? *(Select all that apply.)*

    A. Not letting sin reign in us

    B. Presenting or yielding ourselves to God

    C. Not being under the Law

    D. Letting God have His way in our lives

We sometimes speak of the negative and positive aspects of sanctification. Separation from sin is the negative side. Dedication to God is the positive side. Death to sin and new life in Christ. Both are important.

QUESTION 12

How is the positive side of sanctification expressed in Romans 6:13? *(Select all that apply.)*

    A. We are now under grace.

    B. Present or yield ourselves to God.

    C. We are alive from the dead.

    D. We can be used by God for righteousness.

In Romans 6:14, Paul says that the Christian is to be free from the power of sin because of the standing that he has in the grace of God. God's grace is sufficient to make him victorious.

In Galatians 2:20, we have Paul's personal testimony that illustrates perfectly what he has said in Romans 6:4-14. Compare these passages before answering the following question.

QUESTION 13

In which two ways does Paul express his position in Christ and his secret of victory over sin in daily life? *(Select all that apply.)*

    A. Through the law I died to the law so that I may live to God.

    B. I have been crucified with Christ; and it is no longer I who live, but Christ lives in me.

    C. The life I now live in the body, I live because of the faithfulness of the Son of God, who loved me and gave Himself for me.

    D. We are raised with Christ to walk in newness of life.

Choice of a New Master (Rom 6:15-23)

> Objective 4 – At the end of this topic, you will be able to use the illustration of the relationship of a slave to his master to explain our relationship to sin.

Romans 6:15 is almost an echo of Romans 6:1 as Paul introduces another part of his answer to the criticism of the gospel put forth by his opponents.

In Romans 6:2-10, Paul answered the question of Romans 6:1 by pointing to our position in Christ. We are dead to sin, so how can we live in it any longer? Next, in Romans 6:11-14 he told us we must reckon this to be so and apply it in our daily life. Then in Romans 6:15-23, he goes on to show us that in practice our sanctification depends on our own choice. Paul illustrates this point with the relationship of a slave to his master.

QUESTION 14

A slave is compelled to obey his master. *True or False?*

QUESTION 15

According to Romans 6:17, what were we slaves to at one time?

QUESTION 16

What wages were we working for? Compare Romans 6:17 with Romans 6:23.

We were slaves to sin, but through our union with Christ we have died to our old life. Our old master has no more claim on us. You have also seen that Christ has redeemed us from the bondage of sin (Rom 3:24). Now that we have been set free, what shall we do? Our redemption does not automatically make us obedient Christians. We are not robots. God does not force us to serve Him. If we are going to serve God, it will be because we want to. The choice is ours.

QUESTION 17

What are the two choices of masters to serve that Paul mentions in Romans 6:16? *(Select all that apply.)*

    A. Death
    B. Sin
    C. Obedience
    D. Righteousness

QUESTION 18

What does it mean "to present yourselves" a slave to of either of these two masters? (See Rom 6:16.)

    A. To make a deal with the master
    B. To yield in complete obedience to the master
    C. To resist the master
    D. All of the above

QUESTION 19

What does Romans 6:16 say is the result of service to each master? *(Select all that apply.)*

    A. Obedience brings righteousness.
    B. Yielding brings slavery.
    C. Sin brings death.
    D. Sin brings immediate pleasure.

In this passage, Paul is emphasizing obedience. Notice in Romans 6:17 the kind of obedience that produces righteousness. It is from the heart--sincere, voluntary--the obedience of faith. This obedience is based on the teaching that is given to us in the gospel.

QUESTION 20

Compare Romans 6:19 with Romans 6:22. What term does Paul use to describe the result of becoming a servant of righteousness, or being made free from sin and becoming servants to God?

Throughout the latter part of this chapter, the emphasis is on the progressive sanctification of the believer. Each day he must continue to reckon himself dead to sin (Rom 6:11) and give himself completely to his new life as a servant of God. In Romans 6:19, we see a contrast in progression. The sinner goes from bad to worse. The believer goes from right standing to right living. The person with a wrong standing before God goes to wrong living. This is the principle that Paul points out in his defense of the gospel both in Romans and Galatians. The believer is able to live the right kind of life, because he is in right standing with God and is dead to sin's power over him.

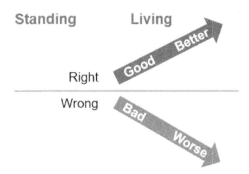

This chapter closes with a sharp contrast in Romans 6:23; a life lived in sin results in death, but eternal life is the gift of God. It gives us a strong reminder that any teaching that says we can earn eternal life by our obedience is not true.

The important truth to understand about Romans 6 is that the power of sin has been broken in the believer's life. Sin is now rendered powerless in the believer's life because he is now dead to sin; brought about through his union with Jesus Christ in his death, burial, and resurrection. He is to reckon it true for his life…to add up the facts in Romans 6:1-10 and act upon them!

What does this mean for the believer? It simply means he has the power through Christ to resist **every** temptation to sin, whether in thought, word, or deed. Now that is really good news!

QUESTION 21

Answer the following in your Life Notebook. Read through Romans 6:1-23 once again. In your own words, write several paragraphs describing what you understand this passage is expressing and what the practical implications are for your daily life. Read again Romans 6:11-13. Now consider areas of your life where you continue to struggle with sin; then prayerfully apply what you have learned in this passage.

Topic 2: Freedom from the Law (Rom 7:1-13)

Paul has already proven that justification is by faith apart from the law (see Rom 3:21-26). Now he is proving that our sanctification is also apart from the Law.

In Romans 6, we saw that we are sanctified instantaneously by our union with Christ and then progressively by reckoning ourselves dead to sin and yielding ourselves to obey and serve God. In Romans 7, we will see that the believer is dead to the law too. The law demanded death for the sinner. Christ suffered that death for us. In union with Christ, the believer died to both sin and the law. The law ends at death. It now has no more claim on us.

> Objective 5 – At the end of this topic, you will be able to list six basic uses of the word "law" in the Scriptures.

What you have learned in Galatians about the law and its purpose and limitations will help you understand Romans 7. The Scriptures use the word "law" with these six meanings:

1. Mosaic law: moral law in Ten Commandments

2. Mosaic law: moral, civil, and ceremonial laws

3. Mosaic law: the first five books of the Bible, called the Pentateuch or the Torah

4. The Old Testament as a whole

5. Inner law of conscience

6. Rules made and enforced by government

Paul's references to the law and its functions and limitations generally relate to the first two meanings.

QUESTION 22

Which of the six meanings or uses of law listed above does Paul refer to as the law?

    A. 1, 2, and 3

    B. 4

    C. 1 and 2

    D. All six

Death and a New Marriage (Rom 7:1-6)

> Objective 6 – At the end of this topic, you will be able to use the illustration of marriage to explain our relationship to the law.

Paul follows a familiar pattern by stating the main truth of a section in an opening sentence. Then he goes on to develop that truth. Romans 7:1 is the key verse as Paul introduces the subject of our relationship to the Law of Moses. He develops this truth with the illustration of marriage. The bride and groom promise to be faithful to each other until death parts them. The death of one of the partners ends that relationship. Death cancels the marriage bond.

Let us remember an important principle in biblical interpretation: Illustrations are usually given to make or prove only one point. We are likely to misinterpret the Scriptures if we try to see a meaning in every detail of the illustration.

QUESTION 23

The main point that Paul is applying from the illustration of marriage in Romans 7:1-2 is that death cancels the marriage bond. *True or False?*

QUESTION 24

In Romans 7:4, Paul refers to two marriages of the believer. The first is marriage to the _____.

QUESTION 25

The result, or fruit, of the first marriage is _____ (Rom 7:5).

We see again in Romans 7:5 what Paul has explained already. The prohibitions and commandments of the Law stir up our rebellious nature. This reaction against God's authority is sin that leads to death. The Law can only condemn the sinner, not save him (see Rom 7:7-8).

QUESTION 26

What is the new marriage in Romans 7:4? How is it possible if we have died (compare with Rom 6:4-5)? *(Select all that apply.)*

    A. We have risen with Christ to a new life.

    B. We are now married to Christ.

    C. We are married to both the law and to Christ.

    D. We are married to Christ as long as we obey the law.

QUESTION 27

The purpose of the second marriage (Rom 7:4) is to bear _____ to God.

Romans 7:6 contrasts the old, outward motivation for serving God with the new, inward motivation. The first was the letter of the Law. But now, the Spirit of God has brought us new life, which is lived in His power.

The first marriage to the Law was fruitless with regard to righteousness. The death of Christ ended the marriage for all those who are united with Him by faith. The second marriage is to the risen Christ. This marriage is so that we may bear the fruit of righteousness resulting in actions that please and honor God.

QUESTION 28

Which is a more effective way to get a congregation to live right and work for God: rules or revival?

Functions of the Law (Rom 7:7-13)

Objective 7 – At the end of this topic, you will be able to list four functions of the Mosaic law and show how they are fulfilled.

Romans 7 shows us just what Paul showed the Galatians: It is impossible for the Law to save anyone from sin. The Mosaic law can neither justify us nor give us the power to live a holy life. This was never its purpose. Let's review the purposes for which the Law was given by God:

1. **Revelation**: The Law reveals God--His character and His will for man.

2. **Health**: The sanitary, moral, and civil laws have protected and preserved man. They have served as a basis for many nations in the development of their law.

3. **Conviction**: The standards of the Law have convinced us of our sinfulness and our need of salvation.

4. **Guidance**: The standards of right and wrong in the Law are repeated and explained in the New Testament as practical guidance for everyday life.

QUESTION 29

As you look over Romans 7:7-13, what is the function of the Law? *(Select all that apply.)*

A. To reveal sin.

B. To keep us from specific sins such as coveting.

C. To show the believer that he is not alive.

D. To make sin alive.

E. To show what is good.

F. To make sin utterly sinful.

QUESTION 30

How did the Law incite Paul to sin as revealed in Romans 7:7-8?

A. The Law introduced Paul to sin.

B. The Law made it clear how to sin.

C. The Law produced all kinds of wrong desires.

D. Forbidding a certain action encourages people to do it.

QUESTION 31

What is true of the Law, even though it led to death (Rom 7:7-13)? *(Select all that apply.)*

A. The Law is deceptive.

B. The Law is holy, righteous, and good.

C. The Law produces wrong desires.

D. The Law achieved its purpose of making people recognize their sinfulness and need of help.

The Law is like a thermometer. It shows the patient his condition but cannot take away his fever. The Law succeeds in showing us our sinful condition, but we must turn to the Savior for deliverance.

QUESTION 32

If the Law is not to blame for making people sin, what is? (Rom 7:8-13)

    A. The interpretation of the Law

    B. The gods

    C. The Pharisees

    D. The sinful nature

If Paul says the Law is holy, just, and good (Rom 7:12), why does he emphasize the fact that we are free from the Law and dead to it? Why is he opposed to a person's attempts to keep the Law?

Think back to the whole message of Galatians. The Judaizers were trying to get the Gentile Christians to accept the Mosaic law in order to be saved. The Christian life would then be a matter of keeping rules. We learned in Galatians that saving people was not one of the functions of the Law.

Paul told the Galatians the same truths that he gives us here in Romans 7 and Romans 8:

1. We are free from the Law and its demands because of our position in Christ.
2. Self-effort ends only in failure and the works of the flesh. Victory over sin comes only as the fruit of the Spirit.

Topic 3: Freedom Not Reached by Self-effort (Rom 7:14-25)

In this section of Romans 7, Paul shows us the absolute impossibility of meeting God's standards of righteousness by our own self-efforts. This is the reason for death to the Law and resurrection to a new life of freedom in Christ.

> Objective 8 – At the end of this topic, you will be able to better understand your own spiritual conflicts and those of other Christians. You will also be able to summarize the principles given in Romans 6 and 7 for a life of victory over sin.

You may have noticed that beginning with Romans 7:7, Paul changes from the pronoun *we* to *I* in describing this very personal battle against a sinful nature. There is a great deal of speculation about what period in Paul's life he was referring to in this passage. It is important to interpret the passage in the light of its context.

In these verses, Paul describes his own inner conflict with the flesh and the principle of sin. Nevertheless, we see here not only Paul's experience, but also yours and mine. The Christian lives in both the temporal world and the spiritual world at the same time. Both of these worlds are in conflict with each other. We have already studied about this conflict as a war between the flesh and the spirit.

As sons of Adam, we live in a temporal world in a body of flesh. We have inherited a sinful human nature which rebels against the laws of God. Paul points out that the desires of our own selfish nature are constantly at war with the Spirit of God. In Romans 7:15, Paul points out his own helplessness to obey the voice of his conscience. Knowing what was right was not enough. Even accepting the right standards for his life was not enough.

QUESTION 33

Paul says the principle at work in him keeping him from doing what he wanted to do is the law of
_____ (Rom 7:21-23).

QUESTION 34

The New English Bible reads in Romans 7:21, "When I want to do the right, only the wrong is within my reach." Have you ever experienced an inner battle such as this? Have you ever seen Christians who never got beyond this stage of constant conflict? Do you know anyone now who has this problem? Enter your responses in your Life Notebook.

QUESTION 35

We sometimes assume that telling new converts what they should do is enough to make them do right if they are sincere. What else do they need?

    A. They need a more complete knowledge of the Law.

    B. They need deliverance from sin.

    C. They need a time of serious prayer and fasting.

    D. They need additional counsel from wise men.

QUESTION 36

This gloomy, discouraging passage reaches its climax in Romans 7:24 with Paul's cry of despair, "Who will rescue me?" What is the implied truth behind these words?

    A. Paul has given up any hope that he, or any human, can be saved from sin.

    B. Paul hopes that his wretchedness does not disgust God.

    C. Paul believes that a recognition of his own helplessness makes it possible for him to accept the help God offers.

    D. Paul believes that the Law serves to make us so aware of our sin that we may become discouraged.

Even before Paul sums up his argument of our own helplessness and need in Romans 7:25, he bursts out in praise to God that there is an answer to that desperate cry! Christ will deliver! Then, in the following chapter, he tells us how the Holy Spirit works in us to give us this victory.

Let's look at a few practical suggestions about this passage before going on to the next lesson.

First, do not isolate it from its context. Remember that it demonstrates why the only help for us is dying to sin and receiving a new life in Christ. Above all, do not view this as the normal Christian experience of conflict and defeat. It is the dark background for the glorious picture of victory in the next chapter. This passage, together with Romans 8, develops the same argument that Paul uses in Galatians 5 by contrasting the works of the flesh and the fruit of the Spirit.

Second, it should make us more concerned for those who are battling against sin. Remember that a person is justified when he believes in Christ as his Savior. He is also sanctified (set apart for God) at the same time. But the practical outworking of sanctification is progressive. We need to encourage one another to look to the Lord for deliverance and victory.

Third, we should remember that it is useless to look to self for the solution to any spiritual problem. The prominence of the personal pronouns *I*, *me*, and *my* in this passage remind us of the personal nature of the conflict and also of the fact that self is our chief enemy. The prominence of self in our lives is the main hindrance to our sanctification. Trusting in our strength leads to certain defeat. But continually focusing our attention on our weaknesses also leads to failure. The secret of victory lies in looking away from ourselves to the Lord Jesus Christ. We still have to fight against sin, but the victory is ours as we focus our attention on Christ and the victory He won for us at Calvary.

Finally, just as the apostle Paul admitted in another of his epistles, let us freely admit that we are not perfect. Let us thank God that our salvation does not depend on how good we are. But at the same time let us "press toward the mark for the prize of the high calling of God in Christ Jesus" (Phil 3:14).

QUESTION 37

Read and reflect upon the principles for living a victorious Christian life in Romans 6. You may want to use this as a Bible study as well as for your own benefit. Match the Scripture references with the corresponding principles that best fit.

Scripture References	*Principles*
Romans 6:1-2	Be baptized in water as a public testimony of my union with Christ--dead to sin and resurrected to a new life in Christ.
Romans 6:3-10	Think of the results of sinful acts--shame and death--and of the results of serving God--fruit of holiness and the gift of everlasting life.
Romans 6:4	Refuse to let sin control my body. Resist temptation. Recognize that I am no longer a servant of sin. Keep busy doing things that please God as a servant of God and righteousness.
Romans 6:11	Consider myself dead to sin and alive to God in Jesus. Remind myself of it. Count on it.
Romans 6:12-20	Be joined to Christ in His death and resurrection. Recognize that the purpose of Christ's death and resurrection was to give me a new way of life.
Romans 6:21-23	Recognize that God does not want me to go on sinning. My way of life must change.

Lesson 4 Self Check

QUESTION 1

Which aspect of sanctification does the first section of Romans deal with?

    A. Man's viewpoint

    B. Experiential

    C. Instantaneous

    D. Practical

QUESTION 2

Romans 6:2 is the key verse for this chapter. It tells us that a true Christian can no longer live in sin because he is _____ to sin.

    A. Enslaved

    B. Resistant

    C. Dead

    D. Indifferent

QUESTION 3

Romans 6:5 tells us that we are only united with Christ in His death. *True or False?*

QUESTION 4

How is the positive side of sanctification expressed in Romans 6:13?

    A. It separates us from sin.

    B. We are dead to sin.

    C. Through it, we present or yield ourselves to God.

    D. Because of it, we do not need to present or yield ourselves to God.

QUESTION 5

In Romans 6:16, Paul mentions that for the Christian there are two choices of masters to serve. They are sin and _____.

    A. Law

    B. Obedience

    C. Life

    D. Self

QUESTION 6

When Paul uses the term "law" what does he typically mean?

    A. The Old Testament

    B. The Mosaic law

    C. The inner law of conscience

    D. The rules made and enforced by government

QUESTION 7

In Romans 7:4, Paul refers to two marriages of the believer. The first marriage is the marriage to Christ. *True or False?*

QUESTION 8

The Law incited Paul to sin because it produced all kinds of wrong desires *True or False?*

QUESTION 9

Paul said that a principle was at work in him keeping him from doing what he wanted to do. That principle was the Law of _____.

    A. Moses

    B. Christ

    C. Selfishness

    D. Sin

QUESTION 10

Paul's gloomy statements come to a climax in Romans 7:24 with the exclamation "who will rescue me…?" The significance of this exclamation is that God's rescue comes from outside ourselves. *True or False?*

Lesson 4 Answers to Questions

QUESTION 1
 B. Romans 1:18–3:20--Man's need (condemnation)
 C. Romans 3:21–5:21--God's provision (justification)
 F. Romans 6:1–8:39--New life (sanctification)

QUESTION 2: True

QUESTION 3
 C. Righteousness

QUESTION 4: Dead

QUESTION 5: False

QUESTION 6: Resurrection

QUESTION 7: *Your answer*

QUESTION 8
 B. Immersion

QUESTION 9
 A. Separation from sin
 D. Dedication to God

QUESTION 10: True

QUESTION 11
 A. Not letting sin reign in us
 B. Presenting or yielding ourselves to God
 D. Letting God have His way in our lives

QUESTION 12
 B. Present or yield ourselves to God.
 C. We are alive from the dead.
 D. We can be used by God for righteousness.

QUESTION 13
 B. I have been crucified with Christ; and it is no longer I who live, but Christ lives in me.
 C. The life I now live in the body, I live because of the faithfulness of the Son of God, who loved me and gave Himself for me.

QUESTION 14: True

QUESTION 15: Sin

QUESTION 16: Death

QUESTION 17
 B. Sin
 C. Obedience

QUESTION 18
 B. To yield in complete obedience to the master

QUESTION 19
 A. Obedience brings righteousness.
 C. Sin brings death.

QUESTION 20: Sanctification

QUESTION 21: *Your answer*

QUESTION 22
 C. 1 and 2

QUESTION 23: True

QUESTION 24: Law

QUESTION 25: Death

QUESTION 26
   A. We have risen with Christ to a new life.
   B. We are now married to Christ.
QUESTION 27: Fruit
QUESTION 28: Revival
QUESTION 29
   A. To reveal sin.
   B. To keep us from specific sins such as coveting.
   D. To make sin alive.
   F. To make sin utterly sinful.
QUESTION 30
   C. The Law produced all kinds of wrong desires.
QUESTION 31
   B. The Law is holy, righteous, and good.
   D. The Law achieved its purpose of making people recognize their sinfulness and need of help.
QUESTION 32
   D. The sinful nature
QUESTION 33: Sin
QUESTION 34: *Your answer*
QUESTION 35
   B. They need deliverance from sin.
QUESTION 36
   C. Paul believes that a recognition of his own helplessness makes it possible for him to accept the help God offers.
QUESTION 37

Scripture References	Principles
Romans 6:1-2	Recognize that God does not want me to go on sinning. My way of life must change.
Romans 6:3-10	Be joined to Christ in His death and resurrection. Recognize that the purpose of Christ's death and resurrection was to give me a new way of life.
Romans 6:4	Be baptized in water as a public testimony of my union with Christ--dead to sin and resurrected to a new life in Christ.
Romans 6:11	Consider myself dead to sin and alive to God in Jesus. Remind myself of it. Count on it.
Romans 6:12-20	Refuse to let sin control my body. Resist temptation. Recognize that I am no longer a servant of sin. Keep busy doing things that please God as a servant of God and righteousness.
Romans 6:21-23	Think of the results of sinful acts--shame and death--and of the results of serving God--fruit of holiness and the gift of everlasting life.

Lesson 4 Self Check Answers

QUESTION 1
   C. Instantaneous
QUESTION 2
   C. Dead
QUESTION 3: False
QUESTION 4
   C. Through it, we present or yield ourselves to God.
QUESTION 5
   B. Obedience
QUESTION 6
   B. The Mosaic law
QUESTION 7: False
QUESTION 8: True
QUESTION 9
   D. Sin
QUESTION 10: True

Lesson 5: Life in the Spirit (Rom 8)

Lesson Introduction

Beginning with Chapter 3, Paul has been unfolding his gospel, the good news of the provision of God. He showed how a just and loving God solved the dilemma that faced Him and provided salvation for sinful men. Through faith in the redemptive work of Christ, guilty sinners could enter into the grace of God.

In Romans 6 and 7, we saw the Christian separated from sin and dedicated to God and identified with Christ in His death and resurrection. But his new life in Christ is not one of automatic victory over sin. His flesh is the battleground in his fight against sin. We saw the impossibility of victory in our own strength. And now in Romans 8 we find the power to live the new life that Christ gives us.

Romans 7 and 8 explain in much detail the concepts of conflict and victory that we studied earlier in Galatians 5:16-18. You may want to review those verses before beginning this lesson.

Lesson Objectives

Topic 1 confirms that victory is available through the Spirit of life.

In Topic 1, you will discover…

- Five ministries of the Holy Spirit described in Romans 8 and five more found in other parts of the epistle
- How Christ's work on the cross provides the basis for our victory over sin
- How the cultivation of our spiritual mind leads to victory over the flesh
- The true nature of the power that is available to us through the Holy Spirit

Topic 2 describes benefits available through the Spirit of adoption.

In Topic 2, you will learn…

- How the Holy Spirit influences Christians by providing redirection and assurance
- Why we Christians experience suffering as well as glory
- When Christians can expect the redemption of their bodies
- How the Holy Spirit helps us when we do not know what to pray

Topic 3 affirms the ultimate perfection of our salvation.

In Topic 3, you will be encouraged by…

- The promised completion of God's redemptive plan
- The daily certainty of God's perfect love.

Lesson Outline

Topic 1: Victory through the Spirit of Life (8:1-13)

Victory over Sin and Death (8:1-4)

Victory over the Flesh (8:4-9)

Resurrection Life (8:10-13)

Topic 2: Spirit of Adoption for Sons of God (8:14-27)

    Redirection and Assurance (8:14-16)

    Suffering and Glory (8:17-18)

    Redemption of the Body (8:19-25)

    Help in Prayer (8:26-27)

Topic 3: Perfection of Our Salvation (8:28-39)

    Fulfillment of the Father's Plan (8:28-30)

    Security in the Father's Love (8:31-39)

Word List

We hope you will enjoy using the word study at the beginning of each lesson. Some of the words you already know, but they are used in a special sense in the lesson. Others are theological terms, and some are new words for many students. Please read the word study each time before starting the lesson. Refer back to it as necessary.

Adoption (Rom 8:15) - receiving believers as sons of God with all the rights of sonship based on Christ's redeeming work.

Assurance - firm confidence, certainty.

Condemnation, etc. (Rom 8:1) - sentence of guilt, judgment of guilty for wrongdoing. *Walk not after the flesh* – do not let their own human desires rule their lives and actions.

Elect (Rom 8:33) - chosen ones.

Foreknow, etc. (Rom 8:29) - know beforehand. God is not limited by time. He knows the present and future as well as the past. *Predestined* - to be foreordained, chosen for a certain purpose. *Conformed to the image* - molded in the likeness of, become like. *Firstborn* – first child born to a mother and father.

Glorified (Rom 8:30) - exalted, honored, shared His glory with them, raised them to a new dignity and condition as children of God.

Saints (Rom 8:27) - those who belong to God. Paul uses this name for all Christians.

Sanctification - the process of being made holy, separation from sin and dedication to God.

Trinity - the triune God, three Persons united in one in the Godhead.

Topic 1: Victory through the Spirit of Life (Rom 8:1-13)

Romans 8 has been called the sunlit summit of Christian doctrine. It is the favorite chapter of many Christians. Reading it frequently has helped many to maintain a joyful life of victory over sin and confident communion with God. Here we find the secret of victorious life. It is life in the Spirit.

Objective 1 – At the end of this topic, you will be able to identify five works or ministries of the Holy Spirit in Romans 8 and five found in other parts of this epistle. You will use them to describe life in the Spirit.

The Holy Spirit comes to live in us to make us holy and to lead us in the way of holiness. The Spirit of life frees us from sin and death. As you study this wonderful chapter you may want to take note of the verses that are of special help to you.

QUESTION 1

Match the member of the Trinity with correct Scripture divisions.

Member of the Trinity	Scripture Division
God the Father	Romans 6–8
Jesus Christ the Son	Romans 1:18–3:20
The Holy Spirit	Romans 3:21–5:21

In the first part of Romans, we see God the Father and His righteous judgment of all mankind. In the second part, we see the Son taking our guilt and our death sentence, then rising again to give us a new life of freedom from the Law, sin, and death. Now in the third part, we find the Holy Spirit working out in us what the Father and the Son planned and provided for us. However, we should not think of the three members of the Trinity as working independently of one another. They all cooperate in the work of redemption, but the Scriptures show us that each one also carries out a definite part of the work.

QUESTION 2

What do these verses in Romans tell you about the work of the Holy Spirit? In your Life Notebook, record your response for each verse listed below.

Romans 1:4

Romans 5:5

Romans 8:2

Romans 8:4-5

Romans 8:9

Romans 8:11

Romans 8:14

Romans 8:15

Romans 8:16

Romans 8:26

Romans 8:27

Romans 9:1

Romans 14:17

Romans 15:13

Romans 15:16

Romans 15:18-19

Now look back over your list and place an "x" beside each of these ministries of the Holy Spirit that describes life in the Spirit.

Place a check mark, or other symbol, beside each work of the Spirit that you feel a definite need of in your own life or ministry. Talk with the Lord about it.

In your Life Notebook, lay out your preliminary plans for a series of sermons or Bible studies on the work of the Holy Spirit. You might think in terms of the initial work of the Spirit in leading us to Christ, the continuing or present work of the Spirit in the believer, and His future work in our glorification. With the overview of these verses in Romans, we are now better prepared to study the details of this chapter.

Victory over Sin and Death (Rom 8:1-4)

> Objective 2 – At the end of this topic, you will be able to point out the importance and nature of Christ's incarnation and work as they relate to our life in the Spirit.

"No condemnation for those who are in Christ Jesus!" What a wonderful statement! The guilt is all gone! The punishment has been canceled! We do not have to fear a future judgment! And this freedom from condemnation even releases us from slavery to sin! We are no longer servants of sin. The law of sin and death has been broken and we are free!

Romans 8:1 is the theme which is developed step by step in the rest of the chapter. Notice how the verses are interlinked, each one explaining or adding some detail to the one before it and then being more fully developed in the verse that follows. Glance down the page and see how many of the verses begin with *for* (meaning because), *because, and,* as well as *but*. With the verses so tightly interwoven, we find it hard to divide the chapter into sections. (For example, Rom 8:4 is an important bridge between this section and the next one and belongs to both.) Each verse becomes more meaningful as we see its relationship to the others.

QUESTION 3

Determine the words in Romans 8:1-4 that refer to the members of the Trinity. Which ones have some part in giving us this life free from condemnation? *(Select all that apply.)*

    A. Father

    B. Son

    C. Holy Spirit

    D. None

QUESTION 4

Through Christ we receive deliverance from sin and death. *True or False?*

The word *therefore* in Romans 8:1 reaches all the way back to Romans 1:17 and the theme of the epistle: "The just shall live by faith." More specifically, *therefore* refers back to Romans 7. There we saw that in Christ we have died to the Law and are freed from its sentence of death. Paul has convinced us that any other method of trying to live the right kind of life ends only in failure. Therefore, we are ready to turn from our own dismal failures and accept by faith the glorious provision of victory in Christ.

The word *therefore* also points ahead to the reason why we do not have to go through the frustrating struggle against the flesh that Paul describes in Romans 7. The law of the Spirit of life living within us is the solution to the conflict that we have seen in the previous two chapters.

QUESTION 5

There are three different laws mentioned in Romans 8:2-3. Which one of these produces a righteous life, according to Romans 8:2-4?

    A. The law of sin and death

    B. The law of the Spirit of life

    C. The Law of Moses

    D. None of them

QUESTION 6

According to Romans 8:2, the law of the Spirit of life has broken the power of the principle of sin and death working in us. *True or False?*

QUESTION 7

According to Romans 8:4, whose influence and power enables us to live a righteous life?

    A. Our own

    B. The church's

    C. The Spirit's

    D. Paul's

Before concluding this section, let's look for a moment at an expression in Romans 8:3 that may seem strange to you. It refers to the incarnation of Jesus.

QUESTION 8

According to Romans 8:3, how did God send His own Son to the earth?

    A. In humble circumstances

    B. In the fullness of time

    C. In the likeness of sinful flesh

    D. In newness of life

Paul's description of the incarnation here helps us see the error of two false doctrines. Docetism taught that Jesus did not have a real human body. The opposite emphasis produces the error that Jesus was simply a man, with a sinful human nature like other men. By using the words "in the likeness of sinful flesh" Paul lets us know that Jesus came in human flesh to be a sin offering for us, the sacrifice provided by God for us. But Jesus was not sinful. He had a body like ours, He came in the likeness of sinful flesh, but He gained the victory over sin. He condemned sin in the flesh, broke its power, and ordained that those who share His life would share His victory over sin.

Now the Holy Spirit has come to work out in us this victory that Christ has provided for us. It is only on the basis of Christ's sacrifice and victory that we can have victory over sin and death.

QUESTION 9

Do you know anyone who would like to enjoy the blessings that the Holy Spirit brings but has doubts about the incarnation of Christ? How important do you feel it is to show him the relationship between the incarnation of Christ and life in the Spirit? Why? In your Life Notebook, give your talking points on what you would share with this individual.

Victory over the Flesh (Rom 8:4-9)

> Objective 3 – At the end of this topic, you will be able to identify in Romans 8 three points of contrast between the carnal mind (life in the flesh) and the spiritual mind (life in the Spirit).

Although the believer stands in the grace of God and shares in Christ's victory over sin and death, he is still surrounded by temptations and fights a daily battle against sin. The outcome of each battle depends on his acceptance of the provision God offers him for victory. Whoever tries to fight the battle in his own willpower, strength, or effort fights a losing battle. Paul showed us clearly that he was no match for the principle of sin at work in him in Romans 7:21-24. This passage precedes Romans 8 as a warning to anyone who thinks he can live the Christian life apart from the power of the Holy Spirit.

However, there is no need for the believer to live in frustration and defeat. He has been pardoned and set free from the power of sin. The Holy Spirit has come to lead him in the way of holiness. The problem now is whether or not the Christian is willing to follow the leading of the Holy Spirit. You have seen in Romans 6:15-23 that a person is either a slave of sin or a servant of God, according to which one he yields himself. We can choose between a life of defeat or a life of victory.

QUESTION 10

According to Romans 8:4, a Christian who wants to enjoy a life of victory and righteousness has the responsibility to "not walk according to the flesh but according to the _____."

We are reminded of our studies in Galatians as we see the conflict here between the flesh and the Spirit. Compare Romans 8:4-9 with Galatians 5:16-24.

QUESTION 11

In the Bible, the term "flesh" has several meanings, all listed below. Which meaning does it have in Romans 8:4-9 and Galatians 5:16-24?

    A. The human body

    B. Base nature

    C. Mankind

    D. Natural human descent

When Paul talks about the warfare between flesh and spirit, he is definitely not speaking of the physical body and the mind. Some people believe that the body itself is sinful and must be punished. The Bible does not teach this.

QUESTION 12

According to Romans 6:13, we can make our bodies instruments for either righteousness or

_____.

We have already seen in Galatians that our conflict is with our selfish nature that wants to have its own way. This is the fleshly, carnal nature that can be conquered as we walk in the Spirit.

QUESTION 13

Again comparing Romans 8:4-9 with Galatians 5:16-24, what provision do you see for victory for every Christian in this conflict?

QUESTION 14

Look at Romans 8:1-14. Match the partial statements with the needed word(s).

Partial Statements	Needed Word(s)
The spiritual mind obeys the things of the _____.	After the spirit
The carnal mind obeys the things of the _____.	Death
The spiritual mind results in _____.	Spirit
The carnal mind results in _____.	Condemnation
The spiritual mind will walk _____.	Flesh
The spiritual mind receives no _____.	Life

QUESTION 15

Compare Romans 8:8 with Romans 8:9. How do we know that "in the flesh" is referring here to sinful human nature and not just to those who are alive in human bodies?

    A. For the Romans, "the flesh" was commonly understood as referring to sinful human nature.

    B. The Romans were only concerned about physical concepts, but Paul wanted to expand their understanding.

    C. The Romans were alive and in their bodies, but Paul tells them that they are not in the flesh.

    D. The Romans had prohibitions against speaking of the flesh figuratively, so Paul was vague.

Romans 8:8-9 are vital verses for us. What did Paul mean when he told the Christians at Rome that they were not in the flesh but in the Spirit? For Paul the phrase "in the flesh" meant to be under the control of the old sin nature. In contrast, "in the Spirit" meant that the Spirit of God lived within them to give them a new life. Prior to trusting in Christ as Savior they were in the flesh, but now they were in the Spirit.

QUESTION 16

What does Paul say about the person who does not have the Spirit of Christ (the Holy Spirit)? (Rom 8:9)

    A. This person hardly belongs to Him.

    B. This person is incapable of knowing Him.

    C. This person is closest to Him.

    D. This person does not belong to Him.

It is clear that the Holy Spirit comes to live in every person who accepts Jesus Christ as his Savior and Lord. Paul's message to *all* Christians in this passage is: "You do not have to be defeated by sin. You are justified. You have the Holy Spirit living within you. Walk in the Spirit."

Resurrection Life (Rom 8:10-13)

Objective 4 – At the end of this topic, you will be able to describe the reviving power of the Holy Spirit in Romans 8:11 and give several examples of a need for this power that you might experience in your life or ministry.

In Romans 8:11, Paul mentions that our bodies are mortal and subject to death, but the Spirit of life who lives in us will bring them back to life. What is Paul trying to say here? Is he suggesting that once we trust in Christ we will never die? It is clear from other writings of Paul that this is definitely not what he had in mind. For example, in 1 Thessalonians 4:13-18 Paul indicates that some Christians will be alive at the return of the Lord, but refers to many who have "fallen asleep" (a term he often uses to describe believers who have died).

A common interpretation of Romans 8:11 is that Paul is referring to the future physical resurrection of our mortal bodies. Paul describes this resurrection in detail in 1 Corinthians 15:12-58.

QUESTION 17

How does Paul describe the death and resurrection of our bodies in 1 Corinthians 15:42-54? *(Select all that apply.)*

    A. It is sown a perishable body and raised an imperishable body.

    B. It is given and taken away.

    C. It is sown in weakness and raised in power.

    D. It is sown a natural body and raised a spiritual body.

    E. It is sown in dishonor.

    F. It will never perish.

Although it is certainly possible that in Romans 8:11, Paul is speaking of the physical resurrection of our bodies in the future, it is more likely that he is referring to a spiritual resurrection of our bodies now, in the present. This becomes apparent when we look at other statements about the resurrection made by Paul in Romans.

QUESTION 18

Read Romans 6:4-5. When Paul refers to the resurrection in these verses, he is speaking of the physical resurrection of the believer. *True or False?*

QUESTION 19

Now read Romans 6:8-12. Paul is describing life "in the Spirit" in Romans 8:11. According to Romans 8:12, this means that we are not obligated to the _____.

Paul sums up his argument about resurrection life in Romans 8:12-13 by pointing out that victory over the flesh comes from the Spirit and is a life-or-death matter. These two verses expand on what Paul stated back in Romans 6:23. If we go ahead and live according to our natural desires and instincts, we will experience "death." If we try to gain victory over the flesh through self-punishment, we will most certainly fail. Victory only comes when we depend on the Holy Spirit for resurrection power and through that power put to death the sinful deeds of our bodies.

QUESTION 20

Compare Romans 8:11 and Romans 8:13. By the power of _____ a drug addict can be freed from his craving for drugs, an alcoholic from drink, or a sex addict from his lust.

QUESTION 21

Suppose a new Christian asked you what life in the Spirit means. How would you describe it and encourage him to have this kind of life? In your Life Notebook, prepare a simple outline of what you would share with this new Christian.

Topic 2: Spirit of Adoption for Sons of God (Rom 8:14-27)

We know from other Scripture verses that the Spirit of God leads sinners to repent of their sins. He has led us to the Savior. He gave us the faith to believe in Christ. He performed in us the miracle of the new birth that gave us a new nature. By following His leading, we have become children of God. The Christian life, however, is not just an initial experience of adoption or rebirth. It is a continuing, day-by-day walk.

Redirection and Assurance (Rom 8:14-16)

Objective 5 – At the end of this topic, you will be able to describe two important ways that the Holy Spirit has influence over every Christian.

The work of the Spirit is described in a variety of ways in Romans 8:14-16. In Romans 8:14, we are told that the Spirit leads us as sons of God. Romans 8:15 indicates that the Spirit confirms that God is our Father. Romans 8:16 says that the Spirit lets us know that we are children of God. Studying each of these verses will add to your understanding of life in the Spirit.

Redirection

First let's look at what it means to be led by the Spirit of God. This is an important concept, for Romans 8:14 indicates that the Spirit leads us into a special relationship with God as His sons.

QUESTION 22

Read Galatians 5:16-18. By comparing Galatians 5:16 and Galatians 5:18, what can we conclude about the phrases "live by the Spirit" and "led by the Spirit"?

    A. They refer to the same thing.

    B. They refer to nearly the same thing.

    C. They refer to opposite things.

    D. They refer to non-related things.

Comparing Romans 8:1, Romans 8:4, and Romans 8:14 leads to the same conclusion. The expressions "walk in the Spirit" and "led by the Spirit" are two different phrases that describe the same continual, habitual experience. They are two different ways to describe life in the Spirit. Each phrase reminds us of the progressive nature of our sanctification. The Spirit leads us step-by-step as we let Him direct us.

In the book of Acts, we read about the work of the Holy Spirit in what we might call crisis experiences. We see the Holy Spirit coming to the church suddenly with supernatural signs and great power on the day of Pentecost (Acts 2:14). Afterwards, we find the Holy Spirit filling individual believers who open their hearts to receive Him (Acts 10:44 and Acts 19:6). We see miracles take place, multitudes converted, the church multiplied, and the Gospel spreading from country to country as the sons of God are led by the Spirit of God.

Paul's emphasis in his epistles is more on the continuous work of the Spirit in Christians than on the crisis experiences. Such terms as *walk, fruit, life,* and *led* in the epistles help us understand what the words "filled with the Spirit" mean in the book of Acts.

QUESTION 23

Look at Romans 8:13-14, which describes what it means to be led by the Spirit. Romans 8:13 says that if we _____ the deeds of the body, we will live.

QUESTION 24

Now read Paul's description of certain men and women in 2 Timothy 3:1-7. According to 2 Timothy 3:6, these individuals were not led by the Spirit, but instead were "led along by various passions." What does this tell us about how to be led by the Spirit?

    A. It tells us that we need to be passionate about being led by the Spirit.

    B. It tells us that outward appearances are more important than inner realities.

    C. It tells us that religion without power is acceptable as long as one is being led by the Spirit.

    D. It tells us that we need to follow the inner promptings of the Spirit rather than give in to the desires of the flesh.

While it is true that every Christian has the Holy Spirit living in him (Rom 8:9), not all are allowing the Spirit to lead them. In other words, they are not walking in the Spirit. They are not listening to and responding to the still, small voice of God's Spirit. Their lives show very little of the fruit of the Spirit.

Have you ever felt that you were standing still spiritually, or moving backward instead of forward? Have you wished that you could walk in the Spirit more consistently? Or do you know another Christian who feels this way? Thank the Lord now for the positive influence that the Holy Spirit provides in the hearts of those who are children of God. Pray for those who need help in following His leading.

QUESTION 25

Think back over some of your experiences of the leading of the Holy Spirit. Has He sometimes made you feel sorry for something you had done wrong? Did you feel His urge to make it right? Is He currently speaking to you about some change that you need to make in your life? If so, what steps do you need to take? In your Life Notebook, write down the specific details of how the Holy Spirit has been speaking to you.

Assurance

To many people, the truth of Romans 8:15-16 is one of the most important of all those revealed in the Bible. You will have occasion to use these verses many times in preaching, teaching, or helping other Christians. And they will often be an encouragement to you. So we suggest you memorize them now and refer to them often.

QUESTION 26

Some people try to live right so that God will not punish them. They live in constant fear of offending God. Their religion is chiefly making sure that they do certain things and not others. In Romans 8:15, Paul describes their condition as having a spirit of _____.

QUESTION 27

In Romans 8:15, Paul refers to the spirit of slavery. What did he mean by this? *(Select all that apply.)*

    A. This was the condition of the Roman Christians before they knew Christ.

    B. Some were actually household slaves and had to contemplate more years of slavery.

    C. Some were in bondage to idols and afraid of them.

    D. Others were in bondage and fear under the Mosaic Law.

QUESTION 28

What title of the Spirit does Paul use to contrast with the spirit of fear? (Rom 8:15)

    A. Spirit of adoption

    B. Spirit of love

    C. Spirit of freedom

    D. Spirit of courage

Some translations of this verse use the term "spirit of sonship" as a more literal rendering of the Greek. Others say, "A Spirit that makes you God's sons," or something similar. We already know from Jesus' teaching that what He called the new birth, or to be born again, is the supernatural work of the Holy Spirit in the sinner who accepts Jesus as his Savior. The Holy Spirit makes such a change in the nature of the person that it is like being born again. He starts a new life as a child of God (Jn 3:3-8 and 2 Cor 5:17). Here in Romans 8:15, though, Paul is emphasizing the relationship, not our change in nature. A legal transaction has taken place in heaven. God has adopted us as His sons!

Abba is an Aramaic term for father. Jewish children in Paul's day used it in the home when they spoke to their fathers. However, the people did not use it in speaking to God. Jesus was the one who first taught His followers to address God as Father. And now Paul tells us that the Spirit of adoption brings us into this intimate family relationship with God, so that we can confidently come to Him and call Him Father. We are no longer slaves, but sons!

Paul in his writings uses the word *spirit* in several ways:

    1. The spirit or immortal part of man, especially the God-conscious element in man which is dead until it receives life from the Spirit of God

    2. The higher nature of a Christian as contrasted with his lower nature in the war between the flesh and the spirit

    3. A personal disposition or attitude

    4. The Spirit of God

    5. A spirit being, either good (angel) or evil (demon)

QUESTION 29

Which of the above meanings of *spirit* do you think Paul had in mind in Romans 8:15 for the spirit of slavery?

    A. The Spirit of God

    B. A personal disposition or attitude

    C. A spirit being, either good or evil

    D. The higher nature of a Christian

The Holy Spirit who has come into our lives is not a domineering tyrant who would produce in us the response of fearful, cringing slaves. The main point that Paul is making in Romans 8:15-16 is also stated in Galatians 4:6-7. He is emphasizing that we are no longer slaves but sons.

Practice reproducing the following chart until you can do so by memory. You could reproduce this chart to illustrate a sermon or lesson.

The Spirit We Have Received

Scripture Passage	NOT	BUT
1 Corinthians 2:12	Of the world	Of God
Romans 8:15	Slaves	Sons
2 Timothy 1:7	Of fear	Of power, love, a sound mind

QUESTION 30

Suppose someone tells you that you cannot be sure until after you die whether you are saved or not. Which verse from Chapter 8 would you show him? In your Life Notebook, give its meaning briefly in your own words.

These verses should move us to praise God for the assurance we have and to pray for those who lack the assurance of their salvation. Invest some time in praise and prayer to your Father.

Suffering and Glory (Rom 8:17-18)

Objective 6 – At the end of this topic, you will be able to explain the relationship between suffering and glory in the life of a Christian.

In Romans 8:14-25, Paul is talking about the continuing day-to-day walk of the Christian. Here, in Romans 8:17-18, we are reminded that many blessings are associated with being a child of God. However, being a child of God also means that suffering will come our way. It is important as a Christian to develop a balanced perspective concerning blessings and suffering.

QUESTION 31

As fellow heirs with Christ, what two things does Romans 8:17 say that we will do or share with Him? *(Select all that apply.)*

    A. We will be buried with Him.

    B. We will be glorified with Him.

    C. We will suffer with Him.

    D. We will be resurrected with Him.

Just as Satan fought Jesus with temptation and persecution, so he fights against those who follow the Lord. Sometimes we wonder, "Why does God let Christians suffer as they do?" But we know that everything we suffer for His sake here will bring us a greater degree of blessing in heaven. There is also much evidence in Scripture that God uses our suffering in this life to mold us and shape us in a positive way.

QUESTION 32

Compare Romans 1:17-18 with 2 Corinthians 4:16-18; Matthew 5:10-12; Acts 5:40-42. What should our attitude should be if we are slandered, criticized, threatened, or persecuted for following Christ? Why?

    A. We should rejoice since God will reward us in heaven because of our faithfulness.

    B. We should rejoice because it is an honor that God gives us to suffer with His Son and share in His reward.

    C. We should be angry because anger toward sin is the best response toward persecutors.

    D. We should be indifferent since it helps to shield us emotionally.

QUESTION 33

According to Hebrews 12:3-11, an immediate benefit we can expect from the sufferings of this life is that we will experience both greater holiness and the peaceful fruit of righteousness. *True or False?*

Redemption of the Body (Rom 8:19-25)

God created the earth to be a home for mankind. Man was to have dominion over the earth and all that was in it. As long as Adam followed God's instructions in relation to the earth, it was a perfect home for him. But the day he rebelled against God, his sin affected not only himself and his descendants but also the earth.

QUESTION 34

Compare Genesis 3:17-19 with Romans 8:19-23. Paul says that all creation is waiting for the revelation of the _____ of God.

QUESTION 35

In Romans 8:21, Paul describes the physical earth as being in bondage to decay. What change will come to the whole earth at the time of the redemption of the body or the revelation of the sons of God?

    A. It will be delivered from the bondage of decay into the glorious liberty of the children of God.

    B. It will be delivered from the bondage of decay into the suspension of the laws of nature.

    C. It will be delivered from the bondage of decay into a fundamental alteration of the elements.

    D. It will be delivered from the bondage of decay into the radiance of God's glory.

QUESTION 36

Romans 8:23 describes what the revelation of the sons of God is. What are the two things that Paul calls it? *(Select all that apply.)*

    A. The understanding of our calling

    B. The redemption of our bodies

    C. Recognition of the fellowship of believers

    D. Our adoption

Notice the word *adoption* in Romans 8:23. Back in Romans 8:15 Paul used the word adoption to speak of the initial state of the believer when he is adopted into the family of God. Here in Romans 8:23 Paul shows us the completion of the adoption, the manifestation of the sons of God, and the resurrection of the body.

While on this earth, the Spirit of adoption assures the believer of his new relationship and all of its rights. In addition, he has received the first fruits of the Spirit. But he lives in a world in rebellion against God. His physical environment and his body suffer the results of that rebellion. The believer is now a son of God, but in his suffering and limitations he does not look much like one.

QUESTION 37

Knowledge of the coming liberation of the earth and the manifestation of the sons of God fills a Christian with hope. This hope causes us to eagerly wait with _____. See Romans 8:23-25.

QUESTION 38

Read Isaiah 35:1-10; Isaiah 65:25; Revelation 21:4. In your Life Notebook, list briefly the solutions of physical or environmental problems that you find there. Note the verses that you can use to encourage or comfort yourself or others.

QUESTION 39

How often do you preach or teach about the approaching solution to all earth's problems? About the glorious future for a Christian? Do you think people around you need more conversation about it? Should we sing more songs about it? Would this have a stabilizing influence? Would it make you happier and more patient? Meditate on these questions. Talk with a friend about them when you have an opportunity. In your Life Notebook, write any suggestion you have for yourself as a result.

Help in Prayer (Rom 8:26-27)

> Objective 8 – At the end of this topic, you will be able to explain our need for the Holy Spirit's help in prayer and how He meets that need.

Now let's see how Romans 8:26-27 relates to the preceding verses. In Romans 8:17-18, Paul indicated that suffering is a normal part of our experience as Christians. In Romans 8:19-25, he explained how our suffering is linked to the fallen condition of the earth. The result is that the whole creation groans and suffers, waiting to be set free (Rom 8:22), and we also groan within ourselves as we wait for the redemption of our bodies (Rom 8:23).

Have suffering, grief, or the influence of your surroundings ever made you feel that God had abandoned you? Or that there was no solution to the problem? Do you sometimes wonder how to pray about a person's need? Do you want to pray effectively for God's plan to be worked out in lives around you? How do you pray for His kingdom to come and His will to be done on earth as it is in heaven? Here in Romans 8:26-27 Paul encourages us by revealing that, in the midst of our times of weakness, the Holy Spirit intercedes for us before the Father.

QUESTION 40

We need the help of the Holy Spirit in prayer because we are _____ and do not know how to pray (Rom 8:26).

QUESTION 41

What form does the Holy Spirit's intercession take? (Rom 8:26).

    A. He intercedes for us with groanings and meaningless words.

    B. He intercedes for us with groanings too deep for words.

    C. He intercedes for us with silence and sorrowful expressions.

    D. He intercedes for us with inner impressions within our spirits.

QUESTION 42

Even though the Holy Spirit's intercession does not take the form of words, God the Father hears and understands. Why? (Rom 8:27)

    A. The Spirit is able to pray for us before we think of what we need, so our prayers are not that essential.

    B. The mind of the Spirit makes our mental processes unimportant because the Father understands anyway.

    C. God knows the mind of the Spirit, the Spirit always intercedes according to the will of God.

    D. The Spirit hears our groans and interprets them to the Father.

Topic 3: Perfection of Our Salvation (Rom 8:28-39)

The main theme of Romans 8 is how to find power to live the new life that Christ gives us. The suffering that Paul has described in Romans 8:17-27 can easily discourage us in our pursuit of new life. In this final section of Chapter 8, Paul encourages Christians to never give up, for God is definitely at work in the world, has a perfect plan, and loves us with a perfect love.

Fulfillment of the Father's Plan (Rom 8:28-30)

> Objective 9 – At the end of this topic, you will be able to show the relationship between foreknowledge, predestination, calling, justification, and glorification.

Romans 8:28-30 presents salvation in one grand sweep from its beginnings in the eternal past to its completion in the eternal future. It is clear that salvation is more than a doctrine; it is an experience. The truths taught here should have an impact on our daily lives.

We have already rejoiced over the extent of redemption as we looked at the restoration of the earth and the manifestation of the sons of God in their glorious resurrected bodies (Rom 8:17-23). Now in Romans 8:28 we have a promise and an assurance that is enough to make us praise God and rejoice under any circumstances. God has called us to be His children, and we love Him. All things work together for our good! How can we ever be sad about our circumstances if we believe this?

Romans 8:28 reaches back to Romans 8:17-18. It points to the path of suffering with Christ that leads to glorification with Him. It is also linked with the verses that immediately precede it which describe the Holy Spirit's prayer for the will of God to be done, even with unutterable groans.

Now notice the word *for* (meaning *because*) that links Romans 8:29-30 to Romans 8:28. We know that all things are working together for our good because God is in control of our lives. Paul encourages suffering Christians by showing that God is working out His plan for His children. Our sanctification, being made like Christ, may sometimes be a painful process, but it is an essential part of our glorification. It is a part of God's redemptive work.

QUESTION 43

Suppose you are explaining Romans 8:29 to a child. What would you say "conformed to the image of His Son" means? In your Life Notebook, give a concise explanation as you would to a child.

QUESTION 44

Compare Romans 8:29 with Hebrews 2:9-11. Do you think that what God permits us to suffer is in order to develop Christ-like character, or so He can use us to lead others to Him? Or both? Have you seen this happen? In your Life Notebook, record the results of your comparison of these two passages.

How can we pray in our private Gethsemanes: "Nevertheless, not my will but Your will be done"? First, we can pray this prayer because the promise of Romans 8:28 sustains us. We know that God has a perfect plan for us and He will make all things work together for the fulfillment of that plan. Then we go on into Romans 8:29 and realize that God is using problems and suffering to work out His purpose in us. He is conforming us to the image of His Son, getting us ready for glory!

QUESTION 45

Compare Romans 8:29, Genesis 1:26-27 and 2 Corinthians 3:18. What do these Scriptures say about God's image? *(Select all that apply.)*

    A. It is only found in the Trinity.

    B. The whole creation bears it.

    C. Humans are created in it.

    D. Christians are being transformed back into it.

Romans 8:29-30 contains five important theological terms. This diagram demonstrates the relationship that exists between these terms.

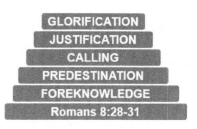

The word *foreknowledge* reminds us that God knows us and knows how to perfect or complete our salvation. He knew us before we were born. He knew which persons would respond to His offer of salvation and which ones would reject it. Then He planned what He would do for those who would become His sons. He predestined or foreordained us to be conformed to the image of His Son. Now He is carrying out the plan that He made before He created the world. He calls, justifies, glorifies. Nothing can stop Him! His plan will succeed! The God who has planned the universe and guides the planets in their orbits has foreordained our course and will lead us safely home.

QUESTION 46

Romans 8:29-30 gives us better insight into the relationship of these five important theological terms: foreknowledge, predestination, calling, justification, and glorification. We can see how each one grows out of, and depends upon, the preceding one. In your Life Notebook list these terms in a chart under three columns, Past, Present, and Future as you might present them on a chalkboard or poster. Under Present, list those that people experience now. Under Future, list what is completed in the future, even if it has already begun. (See example on next page.)

Perfection of Our Salvation

PAST	PRESENT	FUTURE

Are you surprised that Paul did not mention sanctification in tracing the development of our salvation? Do you suppose it is because sanctification is really a part of our glorification? The difference between them is one of degree, not of kind. Sanctification is progressively becoming like Christ here and now. Glorification is perfect sharing in Christ's nature and inheritance there and then. Sanctification is glory begun; glory is sanctification completed.

God's call is an important part of our salvation. He calls us through the gospel message and through the work of the Holy Spirit urging us to accept Christ as our Savior. Jesus said, "No one can come unto me unless the Father who has sent me draws him" (Jn 6:44). Christ commands us to take the gospel to the whole world so that all can hear the invitation. The Holy Spirit works with us calling people to Christ. Thank God that we have heard and responded to His call!

Security in the Father's Love (Rom 8:31-39)

Objective 10 – At the end of this topic, you will be able to enjoy a deep assurance of your safety in the love of God. You will be able to encourage yourself and others through frequent reference to this section of Romans 8.

"What then shall we say about these things?" asks Paul as he sums up his message of encouragement. Can we overcome our conflict with the flesh? Will our faith sustain us in the time of trial? Will Christ condemn us because of our weakness? Paul answers his question with the triumphant exclamation, "If

God is for us, who can be against us?" Could anything be more encouraging to our faith than the knowledge that God is for us? Paul recognizes that we will have opposition, but who can stand against the One who is for us? Romans 8:35-36 refers to the most violent kind of opposition, but God is able to make even these things work together for our good.

QUESTION 47

Which of the following are statements Paul makes statements about God in Romans 8:31-33. *(Select all that apply.)*

    A. God is for us.

    B. God did not spare His Son.

    C. Christ will come again.

    D. God delivered up His Son for us all.

    E. With Christ, God will freely give us all things.

    F. God justifies.

QUESTION 48

Compare Romans 8:1 with Romans 8:33-34. Match the questions with the actions which best fit.

Questions	*Actions*
What does God do?	He is interceding for us.
What has Christ done?	He died and rose again.
What is Christ doing now?	He justifies.

QUESTION 49

Romans 8:35-39 is among the most majestic passages in all of Scripture. In your Life Notebook, state in your own words and in one sentence the main message of this passage.

Three times in this passage Paul mentions Christ's love or God's love (Rom 8:35; Rom 8:37; Rom 8:39). This divine love is so powerful that it will not permit any power or force in the entire universe to separate the believer from God. This, of course, does not relieve the Christian of the responsibility of faithfulness to his Lord. But it does emphasize the glorious truth that when opposition is overwhelming, God's love for him will enable him to emerge as more than conqueror!

Lesson 5 Self Check

QUESTION 1

Which member of the Trinity is prominent in Romans 1:18–3:20?

    A. God the Father

    B. Jesus Christ the Son

    C. The Holy Spirit

    D. None of the above

QUESTION 2

Through whom do we receive deliverance from sin and death?

    A. Other people

    B. Jesus Christ

    C. Moses

    D. Paul

QUESTION 3

According to Romans 6:13, we can make our bodies instruments for either righteousness or _____?

    A. Peace

    B. Anger

    C. Unrighteousness

    D. Selfishness

QUESTION 4

Paul describes life in the spirit in Romans 6:8-12. According to verse 12, how should this affect our mortal bodies?

    A. We should fight the good fight.

    B. We should not let sin reign in our bodies.

    C. We should ask for forgiveness when we sin.

    D. We should seek that which is above.

QUESTION 5

In Romans 8:15, what title of the Spirit does Paul use in contrast with the spirit of fear?

    A. Spirit of adoption

    B. Spirit of peace

    C. Spirit of birth

    D. Spirit of God

QUESTION 6

What should our attitude be if we are slandered, criticized, threatened, or persecuted for following Christ? Why?

- A. We should rejoice since God will reward us with heaven because of our faithfulness.
- B. We should rejoice because it is an honor that God gives us to suffer with His Son and share in His reward.
- C. We should be angry because anger toward sin is the best response toward persecutors.
- D. We should be indifferent since it helps to shield us emotionally.

QUESTION 7

According to Romans 8:23-25, we have hope to walk faithfully with God because of the future liberation of the earth and manifestation of the sons of God. *True or False?*

QUESTION 8

Even though the Holy Spirit's intercession does not take the form of words, God the Father hears and understands because the Spirit is able to pray for us before we think of what we need so our prayers are not that essential. *True or False?*

QUESTION 9

The redemption of God's image in us _____.

- A. Is instantaneous
- B. Is gradual
- C. Will never be completed
- D. Is only for select believers

QUESTION 10

According to Romans 8:31-33, God is with us, Christ will come again, and God created the heavens and the earth. *True or False?*

Unit One Exam: Romans

QUESTION 1

In what year and from what city did Paul write his letter to the Romans?

- A. AD 57 from Philippi
- B. AD 58 from Philippi
- C. AD 57 from Corinth
- D. AD 58 from Corinth

QUESTION 2

Which is NOT one of the doctrinal topics that Paul develops in Romans?

- A. The Law
- B. The value of circumcision
- C. The promise of Abraham
- D. Abraham justified by faith
- E. The crucified Messiah
- F. The Second Coming

QUESTION 3

According to Romans 1:16, why is Paul not ashamed of the Gospel?

- A. He was a Jew.
- B. He was chosen to preach to the Gentiles.
- C. He believed.
- D. It is the power of God unto salvation.

QUESTION 4

In Romans 1:20 and 32, what does God say about the guilt of those who have rejected His truth and the sentence that they deserve?

- A. They are guilty, but God is merciful.
- B. They acted on what they knew and will not be condemned.
- C. They are without excuse and deserve to die.
- D. Some are guiltier than others and they will be judged individually.

QUESTION 5

How is the word "justification" used in the New Testament?

- A. It is only used to refer to the legal imputation of Christ's righteousness to the believer at the moment he believes
- B. It is only used to refer to a person being vindicated or proven to be right before men
- C. It usually refers to the legal imputation of Christ's righteousness to the believer, but sometimes refers to believers being vindicated before men by good works
- D. It is only used to refer to our becoming righteous as a result of both faith and works.

QUESTION 6

How did breaking the Law affect their rights and privileges as Jews according to Romans 2:25-29?

    A. They were now subject to the laws of chance.

    B. They were no longer Jews.

    C. They now needed to get their privileges reinstated in their local synagogue.

    D. They were no longer saved.

QUESTION 7

According to Romans 3:21, what is disclosed apart from the works of the Law?

    A. The righteousness of God

    B. The salvation for all who believe

    C. The love of God toward all men

    D. The hope for heavenly rewards

QUESTION 8

Who may receive the righteousness of God?

    A. The Jews

    B. The Gentiles

    C. The Greeks

    D. All who believe

QUESTION 9

According to Romans 4:12, who can claim Abraham as their spiritual father?

    A. Only Jews

    B. Only Jewish believers

    C. Only Gentiles

    D. All who follow his example of faith, Jews and Gentiles

QUESTION 10

Which form of baptism most clearly symbolizes the spiritual experience of a Christian according to Romans 6:3-5 and why?

    A. Pouring, because it pictures the outpouring of the Holy Spirit

    B. Immersion, because it pictures our union with Christ in death and resurrection

    C. Sprinkling, because it pictures God's sprinkling upon us

    D. No form of water baptism clearly symbolizes the spiritual experience of a Christian.

QUESTION 11

When Paul uses the term "law" what does he typically mean?

    A. The Old Testament

    B. The inner law of conscience

    C. The Mosaic law

    D. The rules made and enforced by government

QUESTION 12

Explain the role of the Law in Paul being incited to sin, according to Romans 7:7-8.

 A. The Law caused Paul to sin.

 B. The Law made it clear how to sin.

 C. The Law produced all kinds of wrong desires.

 D. The Law made Paul want to sin..

QUESTION 13

Which member of the Trinity is prominent in Romans 1:18–3:20?

 A. God the Father

 B. Jesus Christ the Son

 C. The Holy Spirit

 D. None of the above

QUESTION 14

Compare Romans 8:8 with 8:9. How do we know that "in the flesh" is referring to sinful human nature and not just to those who are alive in human bodies?

 A. For the Romans "the flesh" was commonly understood as referring to sinful human nature.

 B. The Romans were only concerned about physical concepts, but Paul wanted to expand their understanding.

 C. The Romans were alive and in their bodies, but Paul tells them that they are not in the flesh.

 D. The Romans had prohibitions against speaking of the flesh figuratively, so Paul was vague.

QUESTION 15

According to Romans 1:18, the basic reason the wrath of God is revealed against men is because they have rejected His truth. In Romans 1:21-32, what is the consequence of this rejection?

 A. God chose to forgive them.

 B. God gave them up to their sin.

 C. God gave them a second chance.

 D. God decided to ignore their sins.

QUESTION 16

The book of Romans is chiefly a book about the defense of the Pharisees. *True or False?*

QUESTION 17

God judges Gentiles by a different law than the Jews. *True or False?*

QUESTION 18

One facet of Abraham's faith that we see in Romans 4:20 is that he believed God even though there was no evidence to do so. *True or False?*

QUESTION 19

Paul's gloomy statements come to a climax in Romans 7:24 with the exclamation "who will rescue me...?" The significance of this exclamation is that God's rescue comes from outside ourselves. *True or False?*

QUESTION 20

According to Romans 8:23-25, because we know of the coming liberation of the earth and the manifestation of the sons of God it should give us hope to faithfully endure in our walk with him. *True or False?*

QUESTION 21

Even though the Holy Spirit's intercession does not take the form of words, God the Father hears and understands because the Spirit is able to pray for us before we think of what we need so our prayers are not that essential. *True or False?*

QUESTION 22

What is the condition we must meet in order to receive the benefits of the gospel?

- A. Obedience to the Mosaic Law
- B. Being baptized
- C. Obedience to my church's rules
- D. Justification by faith

QUESTION 23

God has revealed Himself to all mankind in two ways. According to Romans 2:14-15, one way is through conscience. According to Romans 1:19-20, what is the other way?

- A. Through Jesus
- B. Through nature
- C. Through the Mosaic Law
- D. Through the Temple

QUESTION 24

With what object in the Old Testament is the word "propitiation" related?

- A. Moses' staff
- B. The tabernacle
- C. The mercy seat
- D. The ten commandments

QUESTION 25

Paul said that a principle was at work in him keeping him from doing what he wanted to do. That principle was the Law of _____.

- A. Sin
- B. Selfishness
- C. Pride
- D. Anger

Lesson 5 Answers to Questions

QUESTION 1

Member of the Trinity	Scripture Division
God the Father	Romans 1:18–3:20
Jesus Christ the Son	Romans 3:21–5:21
The Holy Spirit	Romans 6–8

QUESTION 2: *Your answer*

QUESTION 3

   A. Father

   B. Son

   C. Holy Spirit

QUESTION 4: True

QUESTION 5

   B. The law of the Spirit of life

QUESTION 6: True

QUESTION 7

   C. The Spirit's

QUESTION 8

   C. In the likeness of sinful flesh

QUESTION 9: *Your answer*

QUESTION 10: Spirit

QUESTION 11

   B. Base nature

QUESTION 12: Unrighteousness

QUESTION 13: *Your answer should be one of the following:*

The Holy Spirit, Holy Spirit, Spirit

QUESTION 14

Partial Statements	Needed Word(s)
The spiritual mind obeys the things of the _____.	Spirit
The carnal mind obeys the things of the _____.	Flesh
The spiritual mind results in _____.	Life
The carnal mind results in _____.	Death
The spiritual mind will walk _____.	After the spirit
The spiritual mind receives no _____.	Condemnation

QUESTION 15

   C. The Romans were alive and in their bodies, but Paul tells them that they are not in the flesh.

QUESTION 16

   D. This person does not belong to Him.

QUESTION 17

   A. It is sown a perishable body and raised an imperishable body.

   C. It is sown in weakness and raised in power.

   D. It is sown a natural body and raised a spiritual body.

   E. It is sown in dishonor.

QUESTION 18: False

QUESTION 19: Flesh

QUESTION 20: *Your answer should be one of the following:*

The Holy Spirit, Spirit

QUESTION 21: *Your answer*

QUESTION 22

    A. They refer to the same thing.

QUESTION 23: *Your answer should be one of the following:*

Put to death, Kill

QUESTION 24

    D. It tells us that we need to follow the inner promptings of the Spirit rather than give in to the desires of the flesh.

QUESTION 25: *Your answer*

QUESTION 26: *Your answer should be one of the following:*

Slavery, Bondage

QUESTION 27

    A. This was the condition of the Roman Christians before they knew Christ.

    C. Some were in bondage to idols and afraid of them.

    D. Others were in bondage and fear under the Mosaic Law.

QUESTION 28

    A. Spirit of adoption

QUESTION 29

    B. A personal disposition or attitude

QUESTION 30: *Your answer*

QUESTION 31

    B. We will be glorified with Him.

    C. We will suffer with Him.

QUESTION 32

    B. We should rejoice because it is an honor that God gives us to suffer with His Son and share in His reward.

QUESTION 33: True

QUESTION 34: Sons

QUESTION 35

    A. It will be delivered from the bondage of decay into the glorious liberty of the children of God.

QUESTION 36

    B. The redemption of our bodies

    D. Our adoption

QUESTION 37: *Your answer should be one of the following:*

Endurance, Patience

QUESTION 38: *Your answer*

QUESTION 39: *Your answer*

QUESTION 40: Weak

QUESTION 41

    B. He intercedes for us with groanings too deep for words.

QUESTION 42

    C. God knows the mind of the Spirit, the Spirit always intercedes according to the will of God.

QUESTION 43: *Your answer*

QUESTION 44: *Your answer*

QUESTION 45

    C. Humans are created in it.

    D. Christians are being transformed back into it.

QUESTION 46: *Your answer*

QUESTION 47

    A. God is for us.

    B. God did not spare His Son.

D. God delivered up His Son for us all.

E. With Christ, God will freely give us all things.

F. God justifies.

QUESTION 48

Questions	Actions
What does God do?	He justifies.
What has Christ done?	He died and rose again.
What is Christ doing now?	He is interceding for us.

QUESTION 49: *Your answer*

Lesson 5 Self Check Answers

QUESTION 1

    A. God the Father

QUESTION 2

    B. Jesus Christ

QUESTION 3

    C. Unrighteousness

QUESTION 4

    B. We should not let sin reign in our bodies.

QUESTION 5

    A. Spirit of adoption

QUESTION 6

    B. We should rejoice because it is an honor that God gives us to suffer with His Son and share in His reward.

QUESTION 7: True

QUESTION 8: False

QUESTION 9

    B. Is gradual

QUESTION 10: False

Unit 1 Exam Answers

QUESTION 1
    C. AD 57 from Corinth

QUESTION 2
    F. The Second Coming

QUESTION 3
    D. It is the power of God unto salvation.

QUESTION 4
    C. They are without excuse and deserve to die.

QUESTION 5
    C. When God judges, He also takes into account opportunities that people have not had.

QUESTION 6
    B. They were no longer Jews.

QUESTION 7
    A. The righteousness of God

QUESTION 8
    D. All who believe

QUESTION 9
    D. All who follow his example of faith, Jews and Gentiles

QUESTION 10
    B. Immersion, because it pictures our union with Christ in death and resurrection

QUESTION 11
    C. The Mosaic law

QUESTION 12
    C. The Law produced all kinds of wrong desires.

QUESTION 13
    A. God the Father

QUESTION 14
    C. The Romans were alive and in their bodies, but Paul tells them that they are not in the flesh.

QUESTION 15
    B. God gave them up to their sin.

QUESTION 16: False

QUESTION 17: True

QUESTION 18: False

QUESTION 19: True

QUESTION 20: True

QUESTION 21: False

QUESTION 22
    D. Justification by faith

QUESTION 23
    B. Through nature

QUESTION 24
    C. The mercy seat

QUESTION 25
    A. Sin

Unit Two: Paul Applies His Gospel

Many outlines of Romans have Chapters 1–11 as theological, then Chapters 12–16 as practical. In our outline, however, we have preferred to treat Chapters 9–11 as part of Paul's practical application of the doctrine of justification by faith.

In Lessons 1–5, you saw Paul's development of the theology or doctrine of his gospel:

> Romans 1–3 **Condemnation**
>
> Romans 4–5 **Justification**
>
> Romans 6–8 **Sanctification**

In the final lessons of this course, you will see Paul's application of his gospel to:

> Romans 9–11 **Jews and Gentiles**
>
> Romans 12–13 **The Christian**
>
> Romans 14–16 **The Church**

If what Paul has written in Chapters 1–8 is true, how does it apply to your life and to the lives of people around you?

Lesson 6: The Gospel for Jews and Gentiles (Rom 9–11)

Introduction

As we look at Chapters 9–11, we can discover four reasons why Paul wrote what he did.

First, every Jew among his readers would want to know about the spiritual destiny of Israel. How could God's choice of Israel and His declared purpose of blessing the world through Israel be explained, considering that Israel as a nation had rejected the gospel? This subject of the spiritual destiny of the Jewish people was of intense personal concern to Paul. Even though he gloried in his ministry to the Gentiles, he was extremely burdened for his own people Israel. He wanted them to enjoy the benefits of the gospel, too.

Second, the question of God's promises to Israel and her spiritual destiny brings up the question of God's justice. Does Israel's rejection of the gospel mean that God must reject Israel? What about His covenant?

Third, if salvation is only by faith in Jesus Christ, how can people obtain this faith? If salvation is for Jews and Gentiles, what must be done so they can believe in the Lord Jesus Christ and be saved? An application of the gospel truth leads inevitably to the missionary responsibility of those who have the gospel.

Fourth, if salvation is only by faith in Jesus Christ, how does this affect the relationship between Jews and Gentiles? You have already seen how Paul deals with this practical problem in Galatians. But racial discrimination is not all one-sided. It seems possible the Gentiles in the church at Rome may have looked down on the Jewish Christians. And so Paul applies his gospel to racial problems.

Lesson Objectives

Topic 1 presents an Overview of Romans 9–11.

In Topic 1, you will review…

- The relationship between Romans 1–8 and Romans 9–-11
- Four reasons why Paul wrote Romans 9–11

Topic 2 focuses on Paul's first two reasons for writing these chapters. If the Jews are God's chosen people, why are they rejecting the gospel?

In Topic 2, you will discover…

- Why Paul is concerned for the Jews and why we should be concerned also
- How God's salvation plan is based on His justice and mercy
- Two Old Testament prophecies that predicted the partial salvation of Jews and the salvation of many Gentiles

Topic 3 focuses on Paul's third reason for writing these chapters. If Salvation is 'Only by Faith,' how can people obtain that faith?

In Topic 3, you will learn…

- What has caused Israel's tragic unbelief
- What a man or woman must do to gain salvation
- Why every Christian should be involved in world evangelism

Topic 4 focuses on Paul's fourth reason for writing these chapters. If God's plan is for both Jews and Gentiles, how should the two groups relate to each other?

In Topic 4, you will discover...

- Two ways in which the rejection of Israel is not total
- Three important lessons for Gentiles, who have been "grafted into" Israel
- God's future plan to revive and restore Israel
- How the riches of God's wisdom should cause Jews and Gentiles alike to humbly worship Him

Lesson Outline

Topic 1: Overview of Romans 9–11

Topic 2: God's Chosen People (9:1-29)

Paul's Concern for Israel (9:1-5)

Chosen in God's Justice and Mercy (9:6-22)

Chosen From Jews and Gentiles (9:23-29)

Topic 3: Salvation Only by Faith (9:30–10:21)

Israel's Tragic Unbelief (9:30–10:3)

Man's Part in Salvation (10:5-13)

World Evangelism (10:14-21)

Topic 4: God's Plan for Jews and Gentiles (11:1-36)

Not Total Rejection of Israel (11:1-16)

Gentiles Grafted In (11:17-25)

Israel Revived and Restored (11:25-31)

Riches of God's Wisdom (11:32-36)

Word List

We hope you will enjoy using the word study at the beginning of each lesson. Some of the words you already know, but they are used in a special sense in the lesson. Others are theological terms, and some are new words for many students. Please read the word study each time before starting the lesson. Refer back to it as necessary.

Baal (Rom 11:4) - Ancient Canaanite sun god, or the god of fertility and the flocks.

Election (Rom 9:11) - God's sovereign choice and the people so chosen by Him.

Lord of armies (Rom 9:29) - Lord of hosts and the One who executes judgment.

Mercy, etc. (Rom 9:15) - kindness shown to a person who deserves or expects severe treatment or punishment. *Compassion* - pity for those who suffer, with the desire to help. Mercy comes from compassion.

Topic 1: Overview of Romans 9-11

How do Chapters 9–11 of Romans fit into Paul's presentation of justification by faith? Some people say that these chapters are a parenthesis, a side issue apart from his main argument. Others think that they are an important part of Paul's theme and argument for justification by faith. There is substantial evidence confirming the latter interpretation.

> Objective 1 – At the end of this topic, you will be able to state the relationship between Romans 1–8 and Romans 9–11. You will be able to give four reasons that Paul probably had for writing what he did in Chapters 9–11 to the church at Rome.

What evidence is there that Romans 9–11 are an integral part of Paul's main argument? First, we find that in the latter part of Chapter 8 Paul mentions the doctrines of God's foreknowledge and foreordination. Then in Chapters 9–11 he applies these truths to Jews and Gentiles. Second, Paul talks in Chapter 8 about the final redemption of the believers and the deliverance of creation from the bondage it experiences because of man's sin. Then in Chapters 9–11 he goes into further detail about end-time events, especially as they relate to his people Israel. He also ends this section with an unfolding of the divine purpose in history.

As presented in the Introduction to this lesson, Paul had at least four reasons for writing Chapters 9–11 to the church at Rome:

1. Personal - concern for Israel's spiritual destiny
2. Doctrinal - need to show God's justice in dealing with Israel
3. Practical - racial problems between Jews and Gentiles
4. Practical - missionary responsibility

QUESTION 1

In order to get the impact of this important section of Romans, please read over your outline of Romans 1–8. Fortunately, you have just reviewed this material in your unit test. Now, with your lesson outline before you, read Romans 9–11. Use a modern speech version if you have one. Look for evidence of Paul's reasons for writing these chapters. Afterward, open your Life Notebook and write any impressions you may have received from this reading.

Topic 2: God's Chosen People (Rom 9:1-29)

Paul concluded Chapter 8 by describing the totality of God's love for those who have trusted in Christ as their Savior. What an encouragement it is to know that "nothing can separate us from the love of God in Christ Jesus"! But what about the many Jews who have not yet accepted God's salvation? Here in Romans 9 Paul turns his attention to his fellow Israelites, who for the most part are separated from God's love. He begins the chapter by expressing his deep concern for them. Then he addresses two very important questions: Has God's promise to His chosen people failed? How can God treat the Israelites with justice and yet be merciful at the same time?

Paul's Concern for Israel (Rom 9:1-5)

> Objective 2 – At the end of this topic, you will be able to explain and appreciate more deeply the debt that Christianity owes to first century Israel. You will be able to pray more earnestly for the spiritual restoration of Israel.

In the following discussion of Romans 9–11, care must be taken not to confuse the references to "Israel" with modern-day political Israel. In these chapters, Paul's primary objective is to explain why the Jewish people of the first century had rejected Jesus as their Messiah. Most Israeli Jews today also reject Jesus as Messiah and consequently are not part of the family of God. God is not obligated to fulfill His covenant promises with *unbelieving Israel*. Yet God does love the Jewish descendants of Abraham, and will ultimately fulfill His covenant promises with a future generation that turns to Him in faith. In the meantime, a Jewish person *as an individual* may turn to Jesus in faith and be saved. Such an individual is what the Bible calls a member of the "believing remnant."

The first problem that Paul deals with is Israel's resistance to the gospel. In Romans 9:1-3, Paul uses words that reveal a deep sadness toward his fellow Jews. Why was Paul so sad? He realized that most of the Israelites had rejected God's offer of salvation through Christ and that there was no other way for them to be saved. As a result, they faced a terrible national catastrophe, predicted by Jesus (Mt 23:37-39), and ultimately fulfilled by the Roman invasion and destruction of Jerusalem in AD 70.

Before answering Question 2, please lookup the following verses where the Greek OT uses the same Greek word that is translated "accursed" in Romans 9:3 are used. (Lev 27:28; Num 21:3; Josh 6:17; 7:12; Judg 1:17; 1 Chron 2:7; Zech 14:11).

QUESTION 2

Based upon the usage of accursed in the Bible Paul used (the Greek OT), what did Paul mean in Romans 9:3 when he said, "I could wish that I myself were accursed"?

  A. He was willing to give up his eternal salvation.

  B. He was willing to endure divine discipline.

  C. He was willing to give up his life in order that they might be saved.

  D. He was willing to endure the judgment of God in time if that would save his people.

QUESTION 3

Compare Paul's willingness to sacrifice his own soul to save his people (Rom 9:3) with Moses' prayer in Exodus 32:32. There are six references to the "book of life" in the Old Testament (Ex 32:32, 33; Ps 69:28; Isa 4:3; Ezek 13:9; Dan 12:1). Please read these verses. Do you think that when Moses spoke of having his name wiped from the book of life that he was referring to loss of salvation or loss of physical life? Was he offering to face condemnation of hell in order to save his people or was he speaking of being willing to die for them? Whatever it means for Moses, this is what Paul meant as well. Summarize your conclusions in your Life Notebook.

Of course, we know that neither Moses nor Paul could save Israel from the coming national catastrophe by dying for them or with them. Nevertheless, they serve as a powerful example for us to follow. A comparison of their attitudes in Galatians 3:13; 2 Corinthians 5:21; and John 3:16 reveals that they both had a sacrificial love, like God's love and Christ's love.

QUESTION 4

Do you have a burden for your own people who do not know Jesus Christ? What about your relatives? Are you concerned for them and for your friends? For people that you do not even know? Open your Life Notebook and make a list of the people for whom you have the greatest concern and begin to pray for them.

Take a moment to read about Paul's motivation for ministry as described in 2 Corinthians 5:14-16. Notice that the love of Christ gives Paul a different view of himself and others (2 Cor 5:16). We can have the same love of Christ that Paul had as a motivating force in our lives. Perhaps you remember that in Romans 5:5 Paul tells us that the love of God has been poured out in our hearts by the Holy Spirit. Pray that God will so pour His love into your heart that you will have a burden for the unsaved and will use every opportunity to tell them the good news of Jesus Christ.

QUESTION 5

God gives us a love for people and a desire for their salvation. There are good ways and mistaken ways of expressing this love. Which of the options below would you say are the best ways of showing love? *(Select all that apply.)*

    A. Pray earnestly for people to accept Christ.

    B. Tell God that if your loved ones cannot go to heaven, you do not want to go there either.

    C. Give up some of your own comforts and desires in order to give others the gospel.

    D. Do good works or make yourself suffer and ask God to put it to the credit of those who are not following Christ.

In Romans 9:4-5, Paul lists eight blessings which his people, Israel, have enjoyed. The last is the greatest: Christ as one of them! These blessings make Israel's unbelief all the more serious and at the same time perplexing. Why did they fail? What went wrong? Paul will deal with that problem later. In the meantime, let's consider our own debt toward Israel and see what our attitude should be.

QUESTION 6

As you read the list of blessings that Israel received from God, think of each one in relationship to you. What if Israel had not received that blessing and passed it on? Of the items below, which ones would make a difference in your life, if they had not been passed on to you, and why? Open your Life Notebook and record your thoughts.

- Adoption (chosen to be God's children)
- Covenants
- Law (includes the Old Testament)
- Service of God (worship and work)
- The promises (in the Old Testament)
- Jesus Christ the Messiah

QUESTION 7

The more you meditate on this list, the more you will want to thank God for the role Israel played in history and the heritage we have received from her. Stop now and pray for God to send a real spiritual awakening among Jews worldwide. Make an entry in your Life Notebook.

Chosen in God's Justice and Mercy (Rom 9:6-22)

> Objective 3 – At the end of this topic, you will be able to point out and appreciate the justice and mercy of God in His sovereign choice and dealings with individuals and nations.

You have probably noticed by now that to understand Paul's application of a doctrine we must go back and review the doctrine. And so, in Lessons 6-7 you will be doing quite a bit of review. This comes at a good time, too, because it will help get you ready for the final exam.

Now that we are to study about God's choice of Israel, it is very important that you go back and review the material presented on Romans 8:28-30. Notice the relationship between foreknowledge and election. If you have studied the Galatians course, remember the fact that predestination or election has to do with the accomplishment of God's will and purpose. God chooses whom He pleases in order to bring to pass His will for this world.

God Keeps His Word

Paul has a deep, deep concern for the many people of Israel who have refused to accept Jesus as their Savior and Messiah. He begins this section with an implied question: "Does Israel's rejection of Christ mean that the Word of God has failed?"

The answer to this question appears in Romans 9:6-12. To show that God's purpose has not failed and that God keeps His covenant, Paul refers back to Abraham.

QUESTION 8

Compare Genesis 12:1-3 and Genesis 18:17-19 with Romans 9:4-6. For what purpose did God choose Abraham and his descendants? *(Select all that apply.)*

    A. To multiply and fill the earth

    B. To be His people

    C. To be a blessing to all nations

    D. To be an example of righteousness

Part of God's plan in choosing Israel was to have a people of His own and to bless all the nations. Did His plan fail in either of these respects? In Romans 9:4-6, Paul says, "No." The key to understanding this is that throughout Old Testament history God's will and purpose were handed down and accomplished through an inner group, an elect minority, and not through the nation of Israel as a whole. The word *remnant* is often used in the Bible for those Jews who faithfully served the Lord.

QUESTION 9

In Romans 9:8, the remnant is called children of the _____.

QUESTION 10

Compare Romans 2:28-3:4 with Romans 9:4-8. Note Romans 3:3 and Romans 9:6. How can Paul say that God's promise has not failed?

    A. We know that God never fails.

    B. The promise was suspended for a time.

    C. The time to determine success or failure had not yet come.

    D. The promise is actually fulfilled to all those who believe.

QUESTION 11

In Romans 9:10-13, we have an illustration of God's sovereign election or choice. How do Romans 9:11-13 illustrate the principle given in Romans 8:29? *(Select all that apply.)*

    A. God caused Jacob to turn to Him and Esau to be a rebel.

    B. God chose the brother best suited for His purposes.

    C. Before they were born, God knew who Jacob and Esau would become.

    D. God's purpose was to show His people that He was in control.

    E. This is an example of predestination based on God's foreknowledge.

God is Both Merciful and Just

The illustration of the doctrine of divine election, or predestination, in Romans 9:10-13 brings up the question of God's justice or His fairness in choosing some and rejecting others. So in Romans 9:14 Paul says, "There is no injustice with God, is there?" He answers, "May it never be!" All through Romans you have seen Paul's pattern of anticipating the questions of his readers and then answering them. Paul's question in Romans 9:6 was implied. Here his question is clearly stated.

Paul presents an answer in Romans 9:15-18 that should be obvious to everyone--God is free to choose anyone He wants to. He is God, our Creator, and the sovereign Ruler of the universe. He has a right to do as He pleases with His creation. Paul illustrates this by pointing out that God accomplished His purposes in the Old Testament not only through the faithful remnant in Israel but also through pagan rulers like Pharaoh.

Based on Romans 9:17-18, some people have thought that God predestined Pharaoh to be lost and hardened his heart. These verses are not referring to Pharaoh's salvation, but to his refusal to let Israel go free (see Ex 11:9-10). The statement that God hardened his heart must be interpreted in the light of other Scriptures which clearly say that Pharaoh hardened his own heart (Ex 8:15; Ex 8:32; Ex 9:34). God is not the author of evil. He does not inspire men to do evil and then punish them for it. But He does use even the actions of wicked men to fulfill His purpose. Pharaoh hardened his heart and was determined not to let the Israelites go, so God hardened it even more. In the conflict that resulted, the Israelites saw the power of God and His love for them manifested in a way that strengthened their faith in God. Even the neighboring nations were convinced of God's power (Josh 2:10).

Compare Romans 9:17 with Exodus 9:13-26. Notice especially Exodus 9:16 and Exodus 9:20. Now compare these with Exodus 12:36-38.

QUESTION 12

In what way can you see the goodness of God and His mercy even in hardening Pharaoh's heart? *(Select all that apply.)*

    A. The world learned that the God of the Israelites fought for His people.

    B. God sent the plagues to punish Pharaoh for his lack of faith.

    C. Many Egyptians saw and were convinced of His power.

    D. Through faith in God's Word, some Egyptians escaped some of the plagues.

    E. God helped the Israelites gather much wealth as they left Egypt.

    F. Many Egyptians joined Israel to follow God's leading.

QUESTION 13

Now let's apply a rule that we have used for discovering the emphasis of a passage; find the key words. What word does Paul repeat most often in Romans 9:14-24?

It should now be clear that the main topic of this passage is mercy, not condemnation. Make a note of each time the word *mercy* occurs in these verses. Paul discusses divine election in connection with God's desire to show His mercy to man in the fullest possible way. He uses His freedom of action in offering mercy to all, not in condemning anyone He wanted to condemn. Going back to the question in Romans 9:14, anyone who knows God and understands that He is perfect should not worry over whether or not He will do the right thing. He is just and merciful and all that He does is right.

No One Deserves God's Mercy

Paul anticipates another question in Romans 9:19. Some of his readers might say, "God has no right to find fault, because who can resist His will?" Paul is emphasizing here the sovereign right of God our Creator to do with us whatever He wants to. He points out the foolishness of blaming God for what we are (Rom 9:20). Someone has said, "To know God is to serve Him: there is no other response that is intelligent." If God is God, perfect in justice, love, and mercy, we should trust Him even if we cannot understand why some people are saved and others are lost.

In Romans 9:21, Paul speaks of vessels for special or ordinary use. The word *vessel* speaks of service, of a purpose that it is to be used for. Paul uses this same figure of speech in 2 Timothy 2:20-21 where he speaks of responsibility in deciding which type of vessel we want to be.

QUESTION 14

Suppose you are trying to lead a friend into a life of complete commitment to Christ. He prays, but somehow does not seem to find the deliverance from sin that you tell him about. He points out Romans 9:18-21 and tells you God has made him for dishonor and destruction. He says he is like Pharaoh, predestined to be lost. How would you answer him? *(Select all that apply.)*

   A. Pharaoh hardened his own heart first.

   B. The passage is not actually addressing salvation.

   C. 2 Peter 3:9 shows that God does not want anyone to be lost.

   D. The friend needs to work harder on his commitment to Christ.

A comparison of Romans 9:22-23 reveals that we should not be surprised by God's judgment of mankind. Every person is a sinner and deserves His wrath. What should surprise us is that God has decided to hold back His wrath for a period of time in order to pour out His mercy on certain ones whom He has chosen!

QUESTION 15

Suppose you and a friend are talking about world conditions. Referring to terrible injustice in a certain area, he says. "If there is a God of justice, why doesn't He wipe those people off the face of the earth?" How would you answer him? (See Rom 9:22-24.) *(Select all that apply.)*

   A. If God treated us as we deserved, the human race would have been wiped out long ago.

   B. God needs mankind for companionship and worship.

   C. He has promised never again to purge the earth of mankind.

   D. As long as there are any righteous people remaining on the earth, God will not bring His judgment.

   E. His mercy causes Him to patiently endure many things which will eventually be judged and punished.

   F. While God, in His mercy, is withholding His judgment, many additional people are being saved.

This section of Romans should remind us of our key passage for this epistle, Romans 1:16-18. Take a moment to go back and reread it. Righteousness includes God's wrath against those who reject His truth, but God chooses to deal patiently with us in mercy and give us all an opportunity to be saved.

Chosen from Jews and Gentiles (Rom 9:23-29)

Objective 4 – At the end of this topic, you will be able to point out two prophecies about the remnant and God's acceptance of Gentiles. You will be able to explain how they have been fulfilled.

Perhaps you have wondered why we ended the last section of our outline at Romans 9:22 instead of including Romans 9:23-24. They belong to one section just as much as they do to the other. In fact, the theme of God's mercy runs right through Romans 9:29. We have chosen to include Romans 9:23-24 in this section to show that the vessels of mercy prepared for glory include both Jews and Gentiles.

QUESTION 16

Think back on Paul's mention of the term "for glory" in Romans. Review Romans 3:23; 8:17; 8:30; 9:3; 9:23. Based on these verses, we can conclude that we are vessels made to be filled with His glory both in the present and in the future. *True or False?*

In Romans 9:25-26, Paul uses the life and message of the prophet Hosea to show God's mercy to both Jews and Gentiles. God's message through Hosea is an outstanding revelation of God's love, patience, and mercy to disobedient Israel. In Hosea 1–3, we see that God compared Hosea's unfaithful wife to His own people, Israel, in their idolatry. Hosea's wife gave birth to two children of whom Hosea may not have been the father. God told Hosea to give them names that meant "not favored" and "not my people." God applied these names to the disobedient children of Israel, showing His attitude toward them in their sins. And yet, He pointed to a day when the word *not* would be removed from their names.

Paul takes this promise of God's mercy and applies its principle to the Gentiles. They were not the people of God. They were not favored. But God in His mercy has given them the gospel. His choice goes beyond Israel.

QUESTION 17

To whom is Paul referring primarily in Romans 9:26 as children of the living God?

    A. Spiritually restored Israel

    B. Gentiles who believe in Christ

    C. The whole nation of Israel

    D. The Jewish remnant

In Romans 9:27-29 Paul shifts his focus away from the Gentiles and quotes two prophecies from Isaiah that refer to the Jewish remnant.

QUESTION 18

In Romans 9:27-28, he quotes Isaiah 10:22-23. What is the main message in these verses?

    A. God executes judgment on the earth but saves all of Israel, His people.

    B. God's judgment falls chiefly on His people and only a few are saved.

    C. God's judgment comes on all the earth and relatively few of Israel are saved.

    D. God's judgment comes on all the earth, but those who accept Jesus are saved.

QUESTION 19

In Romans 9:29, Paul quotes Isaiah 1:9, referring to Genesis 18-19. What is he emphasizing?

    A. The sins of Israel were like those of Sodom and Gomorrah.

    B. God's wrath, as a reaction of His holiness against sin, will destroy unbelievers as completely as He destroyed Sodom and Gomorrah.

    C. Sinful Israel, like Sodom and Gomorrah, deserved total destruction, but God in His mercy saved a remnant.

    D. As Lot was saved from Sodom by God's mercy in answer to Abraham's prayer, we should pray for the salvation of Israel.

Notice that the salvation of a remnant is proof of God's mercy and also of His faithfulness to His covenant with Israel. And the very existence of the remnant assures us that God will keep His promise to restore Israel as a nation.

Of Paul's various reasons for writing Chapters 9–11, his main topic in these verses has been proof of the justice of God. Paul's approach has been to answer questions that he anticipates will be raised against his doctrine, questions that seem to be directed against God Himself. Woven throughout his answers we find one main thought: God is a God of mercy. The topic of mercy is woven throughout the argument from Romans 9:14-29. It is good for us to note it here and always remember that if it weren't for God's mercy, no one would be saved!

Topic 3: Salvation Only by Faith (Rom 9:30-10:21)

In discussing the plight of the Israelites, Paul has focused thus far on God--His sovereignty, justice, and mercy. Now he turns his attention to man and the personal responsibility that each one has to respond to the message of the gospel. In this section of Romans, Paul challenges those who are already saved to consider their responsibility to proclaim the gospel to those who have not heard.

Israel's Tragic Unbelief (Rom 9:30-10:4)

> Objective 5 – At the end of the topic, you will be able to show how Paul applies his doctrine of justification by faith to Israel. You will be able to explain his reference to the stumbling stone and the tragedy of Israel's attitude.

It sometimes seems that God, in His sovereignty, completely brushes aside the will of man. Did you get that feeling in most of Romans 9? Now Paul goes on to emphasize the *responsibility of man* in all his relationships with God. Once more we see Paul's great concern for the salvation of his people Israel.

QUESTION 20

In Romans 9:32-34, we see Israel's basic problem, the same one that we saw in Galatians. They wanted to save themselves by keeping the Law and would not trust Jesus Christ for their salvation. *True or False?*

Israel's failure to receive God's promise, then, is not God's fault but Israel's. Because of their unbelief and refusal to accept God's plan revealed in the gospel (Rom 9:32-33; 10:3), they are lost. They rejected God's way of righteousness and therefore prevented God from helping them. Their lost condition was not because God was unwilling to see them, but because Israel was unwilling to accept salvation on God's terms--only by faith in Jesus Christ.

QUESTION 21

Compare Romans 9:32-33 with Isaiah 8:13-15. Isaiah says the stumbling stone is _____.

    A. The Lord of armies

    B. Idols

    C. The Law

    D. Assyria

The fulfillment of Isaiah 8:14 is Jesus Christ. In the course of history, He became the "stumbling stone" for those in Israel who refused to believe (1 Pet 2:7-8)

QUESTION 22

Compare Psalm 118:22-23; Isaiah 28:16; Matthew 21:33-46 with 1 Corinthians 1:23 and Ephesians 2:20-22. What do the prophetic passages teach? *(Select all that apply.)*

    A. The religious leaders of Israel ("the builders") would not recognize the Messiah.

    B. Israel's leaders would "stumble over" the Messiah, reject Him, and kill Him.

    C. The efforts of the religious leaders would fail because they had chosen the wrong "cornerstone."

    D. Because the religious leaders rejected the Messiah, God would reject them and give His salvation to others.

The Gentiles were finding salvation and God's righteousness simply by believing in Christ. And so were some Jews. But the nation as a whole would not recognize that faith in Christ was God's way of righteousness for them.

As Paul applies the gospel of salvation by faith to Israel, we see clearly that those who reject Christ are not saved. Paul is not the only one who taught this. Read 1 Peter 2:3-8. We either recognize Christ as the main cornerstone or we have no part in God's spiritual temple. If we believe in Him, we will not be put to shame or disappointed. If we reject His claims and stumble over Him, we fall and destroy ourselves. The preaching of the gospel has one of these two effects on people: either they find in it a refuge or stumble over it and fall into judgment.

The word salvation basically means deliverance. In some cases, this refers to salvation from the eternal consequences of sin, that is, from hell (by believing the gospel), but in other cases salvation speaks of deliverance from some earthly threat or catastrophe. Therefore, the context must carefully be considered to discern what kind of salvation is in view. For example, when Paul says that a woman will be saved through childbearing (1 Tim 2:15), it is certain that it does not mean that having a child will save her from damnation! When he tells Timothy, "Watch your life and doctrine closely. Persevere in them, because if you do, you will save both yourself and your hearers" (1 Tim 4:16, NIV), he does not mean that Timothy, who is already regenerate and justified, will be saved from damnation if he perseveres in good works. When the disciples cried out during the storm at sea, "Lord save us! We are about to die!" (Matt 8:25), what they wanted was to be delivered (rescued from drowning). In each of these passages, salvation from temporal threats or dangers, not the eternal consequences of sin, is in view. Recognizing this flexibility about the word "salvation" will help us better understand Paul's use of the term in Romans 10.

QUESTION 23

After reading Romans 10:1, read the following passages that Paul draws upon in this context: Romans 9:27-28; Isaiah 10:22-23; Romans 9:29; Isaiah 1:9; Romans 10:13; and Joel 2:32. In these verses, Paul speaks of "salvation" in regards to Israel as a nation. Be careful to consider the OT context in which these passages are found. What kind of salvation is in view in each instance? Temporal, eternal, or a combination of both? Record your conclusions in your Life Notebook.

In Romans 10:1-4, Paul explains why the nation of Israel faced a national catastrophe --being under God's discipline and missing out on His blessings (cf. Matt 23:37-39 and Acts 3:19-20). They had rejected Jesus as their Messiah, and so were rejecting the free gift of righteousness granted to those who believe on Christ. Instead they were trying to establish their own righteousness through their self-efforts at keeping the Mosaic Law. Yet they would never gain God's favor in that way. Paul longed for their national salvation/deliverance (being restored to God as a nation; see Romans 11:26), but this also required their salvation at the individual level from the eternal consequences of sin.

Romans 10:2 shows us that in order to be effective, faith must be founded on true knowledge. Neither sincerity nor zeal are proof that our faith is all right. Zeal, in itself, is neither good nor bad; it depends on its object--what we are zealous for.

After focusing on unbelief at the end of Romans 9, Paul gives clear teaching about what faith is. He begins the chapter by complimenting the Jews for their zeal, but also points out how that zeal contributes to their problem of unbelief. Have you ever heard someone say, "It does not matter what you believe--just as long as you are sincere"? Do you think Paul would agree to that? To the contrary, he shows us that people can be sincerely wrong!

Sincere faith can be deadly if it is not based on truth. A believer may have perfect faith that the water in a certain stream is pure and so he drinks from it. But upstream someone has been dumping garbage into the water. Will the fact that he believes the water is pure keep him from getting sick? No! His sincerity will not save him. His faith was based on error, not on knowledge of the truth.

Paul is an important example of the danger of misplaced faith. Before he became a Christian, he helped stone Stephen and persecuted many other Christians. He describes his wrong behavior in 1 Timothy 1:12-16. Romans 10:3 shows what happens when people have religious zeal that is not based on God's truth.

They try to establish their own righteousness and do not submit to or accept the righteousness of God. Israel's tragedy was that their faith was based on their own concept of how to find right standing with God by keeping the Law and they rejected the knowledge that the gospel brought them.

In Romans 10:4, Paul concluded this paragraph on Israel's tragic unbelief by pointing out that righteousness was never meant to be a result of man's effort to keep the Law. The Law was a temporary arrangement revealing that God was holy and man could not live up to His righteousness. To the extent the Jews obeyed the Law, they were blessed. But salvation (having a righteous standing with God) was never based on keeping the Law (for no one could do that). Rather, it served to prepare the people for the coming of Christ and His death on the cross. Once Christ died on the cross, the Law's purpose was completed and so came to an end. Faith in Christ is what results in righteousness. Paul now turns to explain this in verses 5-13.

Salvation Based on Faith in Christ (Rom 10:5-13)

Objective 6 – At the end of this section, you will be able to explain to another person who desires to be spiritually "saved" what he must do. The gospel message is that simple faith alone in Christ alone is what saves, not our human efforts. This is a truth that is consistent with what God had previously revealed in the Old Testament.

While studying about Israel's tragic unbelief, you have already seen that the righteousness of God is revealed through the gospel and that man's part in salvation is to place his faith in the Lord Jesus Christ.

Have you ever seen anyone who thought it must be very hard to become a Christian? Throughout the centuries, Christians have often added many things to the gospel. Some have said that one must be baptized to be saved. Others have stressed that one must confess Jesus publicly. While important, do these additions to simple faith in Christ have anything to do with how one becomes a Christian? In Romans 10:6-8, Paul assures us that the way to be saved is very simple. Christ has already come down from heaven to save us. He has already been raised from the dead. He has finished the work of redemption and one only needs to believe from the heart to be justified. This is the message of the gospel. In this section, Paul draws upon several verses from Deuteronomy 30:12-14 to support his contention that salvation is by faith alone. These verses originally appeared in a context of Israel's failure to keep the

Law and God's plan to one day "circumcise their hearts" (Deut 30:6). This anticipated the new covenant, looking forward to what God would do in their hearts by the Holy Spirit (Rom 2:29).

Paul saw in the words of Deuteronomy 30:14 ("the word is near you, in your mouth and in your heart") a person's relationship to God based on faith, not one's self-efforts to keep the Law. Hence, he refers in Romans 10:8 to the gospel as "the word of faith that we preach." Paul's point is that the gospel message is consistent with the truth found in Deuteronomy 30:12-14.

In Romans 10:9-10, Paul highlights the words "mouth" and "heart" that were mentioned in Deuteronomy 30:14 and reveals their correspondence to faith in Christ. This involves confessing that Jesus is the Lord, and believing that God the Father resurrected Him from the grave. This is the heart of the Christian faith. Paul did not mean to suggest that these were two separate steps (as though "confession" was an additional step to "believing"). By "confession," then, Paul does not have in mind a separate action to be saved, but is thinking of the normal outward expression of faith of who one believes Jesus to be. Notice in Romans 10:9 that they are a "package deal" by which one is saved. This is further confirmed in Romans 10:11, the next verse: "Everyone who believes in him will not be put to shame." The crucial issue is that one "believes." That is also why Paul introduced this discussion as "the word (or message) of faith that we preach" (Rom 10:8).

QUESTION 24

What Paul has said in Romans 10:8-10 is consistent with what is revealed elsewhere in the New Testament. Look up the following verses that speak about "salvation": John 3:16; 3:18; Ephesians 2:8-9; Titus 3:5; Revelation 21:6, According to these verses, what is consistently emphasized about how one is saved? Please open your Life Notebook and summarize your thoughts.

QUESTION 25

According to Paul, what is required to obtain justification and the forgiveness of sins which saves us eternally?

    A. Believing in the heart

    B. Believing and confessing Christ as one's Lord

    C. Confessing Christ publicly

    D. Confessing Christ publicly and believing that God raised him from the dead.

Paul found support for the idea that the key to salvation is in "believing" (that is, through faith) in the words "Everyone who believes in him will not be put to shame," a quotation from Isaiah 28:16. Furthermore, the word "everyone" suggests that "believing" is something all can do... whether they are Jew or Gentile. That Paul is thinking of the universality of the gospel message is clear by what he says in the next verse: "For there is no distinction between the Jew and the Greek, for the same Lord is Lord of all, who richly blesses all who call on him."

Paul deliberately chose to use the words "who call on him," because they were used in the Old Testament regarding Israel's salvation. Paul quoted Joel 2:32 to this effect: "everyone who calls on the name of the Lord will be saved." Peter also had quoted these same words of Joel in his sermon on the day of Pentecost (see Acts 2:21). In its original context, Joel 2:32 was part of a longer passage describing events that would come about in "the day of the Lord." [The "day of the Lord" refers here to a time of God's judgment in the future]. In "that day," Jerusalem will be under heavy assault, but some will escape (or be delivered) at that time by "calling upon the Lord." To use the words of Joel, they "will be saved." In one sense, the salvation in view is physical, that is, deliverance from the terrible things that are happening at that time. Yet on the other hand, spiritual salvation is also involved, because those who turn to the Lord and call upon Him at that time are those who have come to believe in Jesus (compare Zech 12:10). So, even though the Joel 2 passage is looking at a unique time in history (Israel's prophetic future), Paul can draw from this a valid principle that he saw as applicable for all people and at all times.

The idea of "calling upon the name of the Lord" is not synonymous with exercising saving faith. This phrase is used many times in the Old Testament, yet with other things than salvation from sin in view.

QUESTION 26

Look up the following references where the idea of "calling upon the name of the Lord" is used; Genesis 12:8; Psalm 99:6; 116:4; and 1 Kings 18:24-26. Which of the following might be included in the activity of calling upon the name of the Lord? *(Select all that apply.)*

    A. To worship Him

    B. To be delivered from a dangerous or threatening situation

    C. To seek a favorable answer from the Lord in response to prayer or inquiry

    D. To visit the temple site

The idea of calling upon the name of the Lord in some cases has "worshiping" Him in view (e.g., Ps 116:17). More often, however, one calls upon the name of the Lord to seek His help or deliverance. In surveying the various places where the phrase "to call upon the name of the Lord" is used, a possible definition might be:

"to beseech the Lord in prayer, especially in moments of need or desperation, that He would respond favorably to one's request and be moved to act."

In the context of Romans 10, Paul's over-riding concern is the plight of the Jewish people. As a nation, they had failed to recognize Jesus as Messiah and believe in Him. Ultimately, he hopes for their national salvation, when the nation will be restored to God (Rom 11:12, 15, 26). This will happen when they finally call upon the name of the Lord to rescue them in "the day of the Lord." Yet for that to happen, they must believe in Him...putting their faith in the Lord Jesus Christ (Zech 12:10; Matt 23:37-39).

People everywhere—whether Jew or Gentile--need the Lord. They need the Lord to rescue them. While Joel 2:32 looks to a future time when Israel as a nation calls on Him (and are "saved"), so a principle extends to all people who need God's help and for Him to rescue them out of their spiritual darkness. The key is to believe in Him and call on His name in response to the gospel message.

Proclaiming the Gospel of Salvation (Rom 10:14-21)

> Objective 7 – At the end of the topic, you will be able to show how the conditions for salvation relate to our responsibility for world evangelism. You will be able to apply the knowledge in your own life and ministry.

In Romans 10:14-15, Paul traces the steps in reverse that lead to Israel calling on the name of the Lord. They cannot do so if they have not first believed, and this implies that they first need to hear and to have someone who preaches the good news to them. What is true of Israel, however, is true of all men everywhere. There is a need for getting the gospel message ("the righteousness based on faith") to them. Paul cites Isaiah 52:7 in appreciation of those who are involved in doing so: "How beautiful are the feet of those who preach the good news!" (Rom 10:15; ESV). These words were first spoken about men who carried the good news from Babylon to Jerusalem that the years of Israel's captivity were over and that the Jewish people would soon be returning to their own land. What a welcome those messengers must have received! But in proclaiming the gospel message, we are bringing news of deliverance from a far more significant type of captivity. For all who believe, Christ breaks the fetters of sin and restores them to fellowship with God.

All through Romans we have seen that believing in the Lord Jesus Christ is the only way to enter into a right standing before God and live a life of victory over sin. This leads us to an inevitable responsibility. We must share the good news that Christ has brought salvation for all who will accept it.

Of the many reasons behind what Paul wrote in Romans 9–11, Romans 10:11-15 make it clear that his main emphasis here is missionary responsibility. We need to proclaim the gospel, so that all people will have the opportunity to believe and call on the name of the Lord.

QUESTION 27

What words in Romans 10:11-13 remind you that Christ died for all and that the gospel is for all peoples everywhere? *(Select all that apply.)*

 A. "Everyone"

 B. "No distinction"

 C. "Lord of all"

 D. "Blesses all who call on Him"

QUESTION 28

Who takes the gospel message to those who have not heard it (Rom 10:14-15)?

 A. Those who preach or proclaim to others

 B. The Jews

 C. Paul

 D. The apostles

The world needs preachers who are sent by God. God's plan for men to answer His call to salvation demands that we answer His call to service. Angels are not commissioned to preach the gospel; we are.

QUESTION 29

In your Life Notebook, write out how you have been involved in helping to get the gospel message of salvation in Christ out to others. Have you had the joy of seeing firsthand another person come to faith in Christ? Try to describe what happened and what the outcome was. Be prepared to share with others in your group.

In Galatians 1-2, Paul defends his call and commission, showing that they were not from men. Instead he was sent by the Lord. And if we want souls to find Christ today, those who preach the gospel to them must be called and sent by God. The book of Galatians shows that the church recognizes that call and has the responsibility to send out missionaries. Paul's challenge causes us to recognize our responsibility to go and to send missionaries through our offerings. And it calls us to pray as we remember also the Lord's words, "The harvest is abundant, but the workers are few. Therefore ask the Lord of the harvest to send out workers into His harvest" (Lk 10:2). "And how are they to preach unless they are sent?" (Rom 10:15)

QUESTION 30

Compare Romans 8:30 with Romans 10:12-14. Open your Life Notebook and answer the following questions. What do you learn about your salvation through these two passages? Are there any questions that come to your mind that you would like to discuss further?

QUESTION 31

It is by hearing the preached _____ of Christ that faith comes to people so that they can believe in Christ and be saved (Rom 10:17).

Since this is so, let your preaching and teaching be centered on the Word of God. Hearing the Word of God will produce faith in the people you minister to. If you want people to have faith for salvation, preach what the Bible says about salvation. God will use the clear teaching of His Word to move men and women to trust in Christ as their Savior.

QUESTION 32

Read Romans 10:13. The act of a believer seeking help in the difficulties of life are described as calling on _____.

Receptivity to the Gospel

QUESTION 33

Now let's look at Romans 10:18-21. What two Old Testament prophetic passages does Paul quote to show that thus far the Jews have not been very receptive to the gospel message? *(Select all that apply.)*

    A. Isaiah 65:2

    B. Leviticus 26:21

    C. Isaiah 51:1

    D. Deuteronomy 32:21

We see evidence in these verses that God intends to use the Gentiles to provoke Israel to jealousy. This concept is developed further in Romans 11. Historically, we might say that Moses' prophecy was fulfilled as God used the Gentile nations as His instrument of judgment to punish Israel for her sins. But Paul refers here to the Gentiles' acceptance of the gospel, which was foreseen by Isaiah.

In summary, we see here that God freely offers His salvation to both Jews and Gentiles. Notice His patience with Israel and sorrow over her unbelief in Romans 10:21.

QUESTION 34

In light of Romans 10:18-21, where do you believe that God wants us to give people the Word of God and invite them to Christ?

    A. Especially where people are responsive to the message

    B. Especially to the unevangelized Gentiles

    C. Especially to the Jews

    D. To everybody, everywhere, whether they want to hear the message or not

Topic 4: God's Plan for Jews and Gentiles (Rom 11:1-36)

As presented in the Introduction to this lesson, Paul had at least four reasons for writing chapters 9–11 to the church at Rome. Thus far, he has expressed his deep concern for Israel's spiritual destiny, discussed God's justice in dealing with Israel, and challenged Christians to bear responsibility for spreading the gospel throughout the whole world. In this final section, Paul discusses racial problems between Jews and Gentiles. He does so in the context of God's future plans for Israel.

Not Total Rejection of Israel (Rom 11:1-16)

> Objective 8 – At the end of the topic, you will be able to point out two ways in which the rejection of Israel is not total.

Please read "God's Temporary Rejection of Israel."

God's Temporary Rejection of Israel (Rom 11:22)

> Behold then the kindness and severity of God; to those who fell, severity, but to you, God's kindness, if you continue in His kindness; otherwise you also will be cut off. (Rom 11:22, NASB95)

Cut off! Does this mean that it is possible for a true believer who once partook of the Abrahamic promise to be cut off from it and lose his salvation? This passage has understandably troubled many.

What goes on here? Before looking at this verse in Romans, let's back up and get an overall view of the context. For two chapters Paul has been focusing on God's purpose for national Israel. Now he explains that even though the kingdom has temporarily been taken from Israel (Mt 21:43) and the nation is temporarily no longer at the center of God's purposes, one day His plans for His chosen people will finally be realized. One day they will no longer be an object of His divine displeasure and they will experience "salvation" when the "Deliverer will come from Zion" and removes the ungodliness (Rom 11:26).

In the first ten verses (Rom 11:1-10), Paul makes it clear that God has not rejected His people. This, he says, is proven by the fact that there is a remnant of which Paul and other Jewish believers are a part. But was Israel's fall, a final fall? Does national Israel still have a future? It seems evident that there were those among his readers in the Roman church who thought Israel did not have a future. Paul viewed this Gentile viewpoint as "arrogant" (see Rom 11:19-20).

In Romans 11:11 Paul makes this explicit. Israel's fall is temporary.

> Again I ask: Did they stumble so as to fall beyond recovery? Not at all! Rather, because of their transgression, salvation has come to the Gentiles to make Israel envious.

Since Israel has been set aside in the purposes of God, salvation has come to the Gentiles. Does this mean that Gentiles can now experience personal salvation from hell but formerly they could not? Of course not! Because of Israel's rejection of Jesus as her Messiah, the gospel message of salvation is now going out to all the nations of the world (compare Acts 1:8). Yet there is still a place for national Israel in the plan of God (at least for those who turn to Jesus in faith).

> But if their transgression means riches for the world, and their loss means riches for the Gentiles, how much greater riches will their fullness bring! (Rom 11:12)

What are these riches for the world that have now come to the Gentiles? First and foremost is the blessing of salvation in Christ and the gift of eternal life. In addition are the numerous "riches" that have come to both individuals and nations by the advance of Christianity. The blessings to the Gentile world through the influence of Gentile biblical Christianity is well documented. Slaves have been freed, nursing and public schools came into existence, child labor laws were abolished, and the status of women elevated. Because of the gospel, millions of Gentiles have experienced salvation and transformed lives

Furthermore, because they have been grafted into the olive tree (Rom 11:17), Gentiles have been exposed to and have embraced the Jewish Scriptures. Riches indeed!

This came about because of Israel's loss. What did they lose? Paul is not speaking of the loss of individual salvation; he is speaking in national terms. *What the nation of Israel as a group lost was their role as the centerpiece of God's purposes in history.* It was God's intent as expressed in the promises to Abraham, that through Israel, blessing would come to the nations. This loss, however, is temporary. Paul continues:

> But if some of the branches were broken off, and you, being a wild olive, were grafted in among them and became partaker with them of the rich root of the olive tree, do not be arrogant toward the branches; but if you are arrogant, remember that it is not you who supports the root, but the root supports you. (Rom 11:17–18, NASB95)

Why does Paul use the metaphor of an olive tree? Commonly in the OT, olive oil was associated with blessing. An abundant oil harvest signified divine blessing (Joel 2:24; 3:13). The loss of the olive oil was a loss of blessing and Israel was to endure in faith in the face of the loss of this valuable agricultural produce (Hab 3:17). The metaphor is very appropriate. Israel was to be a channel of blessing to the entire world.(Isa 60:1-3; 62:1-3; Mic 4:1-4; Zech 8:11-13; 20-23). This was God's promise to Abraham (Gen 12:1-3). The fruit of the olive was used in almost every aspect of Jewish life. Olive wood was used for fuel and for carpenters; olive oil was used for food and medicine; olives were picked and eaten. A fruitful person enjoying God's favor is "like a green olive tree in the house of the Lord" (Ps 52:8). *The metaphor of the olive tree speaks of blessing and fruitfulness and not final entrance into heaven or deliverance from hell.*

In Romans 11:13-25, Paul begins to rebuke Gentile Christians because of their presumptuous boasting that they had replaced Israel as the channel of God's blessing to the world (Rom 11: 17-18). It appears that the Roman Gentile Christians not only misunderstood their place in the divine plan to bless the world but also God's dealings with His chosen people. Because the majority of Jews had failed to accept Paul's gospel, some Gentile Christians erroneously concluded that God's rejection of the nation was permanent. Furthermore, they saw themselves as displacing the broken-off branches and boasted in their new-found status.

God had said to Abraham and his seed, "in you all the families of the earth will be blessed" (Gen 12:3, NASB95). But they failed to fulfill that role and, as Jesus put it, *"Therefore I say to you, the kingdom of God will be taken away from you and given to a people, producing the fruit of it "* (Mt 21:43, NASB95).

But unnatural branches, the Gentiles, were grafted into the place of Abrahamic blessing. Israel has been set aside and now God is using the Gentiles to be the instruments of His purposes in history.

If, due to Jewish national rejection of Messiah, the Gentiles were grafted into the place of blessing, think what will happen when the Jews return to the Messiah. It will be like "life from the dead," magnificent universal righteousness in the coming thousand-year kingdom of God.

> You will say then, "Branches were broken off so that I might be grafted in." Quite right, they were broken off for their unbelief, but you stand by your faith. Do not be conceited, but fear; for if God did not spare the natural branches, He will not spare you, either (Romans 11:19–21, NASB95).

For centuries, Gentile conceit has concluded that they have permanently replaced Israel, and that the Gentile church is the "New Israel." However, we know from the book of Revelation, that it will be 144,000 believing Jews who will be sent out to evangelize the world. One day God will set the Gentiles aside as his channel of blessing. We can already see that Gentile Christendom is falling away from the teaching of Paul. Not only is the difference disappearing between the church and the surrounding culture (primarily in the West), but the message of Paul is no longer preached.

Paul warns the Gentiles that just as the Jewish nation was cut off nationally, so they too can be cut off. This suggests that there were Gentiles in the Roman church advocating this viewpoint.

> Behold then the kindness and severity of God; to those who fell, severity, but to you, God's kindness, if you continue in His kindness; otherwise you also will be cut off.

> And they also, if they do not continue in their unbelief, they will be grafted in, for God is able to graft them in again. (Rom. 11:22-23)

God will once again return his chosen people as his agency to bless the world as the OT Scriptures abundantly predict. The natural branches will one day be grafted into the place of centrality in the creation purposes of God.

Currently the Gentiles experience the "kindness" of God. They are currently the channel through whom he works. Israel has been set aside. But, like national Israel, they too can be "cut off," removed from the olive tree. The olive tree is not a metaphor for "being saved." As pointed out above, it is a metaphor for being the channel of blessing to the world. This passage has absolutely nothing to do with the idea that individuals can lose salvation.

The danger then to which Paul refers is that the believing gentiles as a group, like national Israel, can be cut off from the current position they enjoy. Harrison notes:

> This should not be understood on an individual basis as though Paul were questioning their personal salvation. The matter in hand is the current Gentile prominence in the church made possible by the rejection of the gospel on the part of the nation of Israel as a whole. Let Gentile Christians beware. Their predominance in the Christian community may not last" (Everett F. Harrison, "Romans," in *The Expositor's Bible Commentary*, ed. Frank E. Gabeline and Everett F. Harrison (Grand Rapids: Zondervan, 1976), 10:122)

What applies to the church in general can, of course, be applied to individuals within it. The Lord Jesus spoke of dead or useless branches being cut off from fruit bearing and communion in John 15:2, 6. The writer of Hebrews warns his readers that we are partners, sharers in the final destiny of man as co-heirs with Christ, only if we persevere in faith until the end (Heb 3:14). All Christians will be in the kingdom, but only those who persevere in faith will inherit the kingdom, that is, rule with Christ there.

You have seen how Paul deals with several questions about Israel in Chapters 9–11. In Romans 9:6, we considered whether or not God's promise to Israel had failed. In Romans 9:14, Paul took up the question of God's justice. Now, in the light of Israel's rejection of the Messiah, we might ask, "Does this mean that God has completely rejected Israel?" Paul's answer to this question is very clear in Romans 11:1.

QUESTION 35

The fact that Paul was an Israelite is positive evidence that God has not totally rejected Israel (Rom 11:1). *True or False?*

QUESTION 36

Which group comprised the remnant, according to the election of grace in Paul's time, that he refers to in Romans 11:5-7? *(Select all that apply.)*

   A. Paul himself

   B. Thousands of Jews who had accepted Christ and were saved by grace

   C. All the Jews scattered abroad

   D. Only those who were faithful to keep the Law

Paul usually speaks of the elect as those God has chosen from Jews and Gentiles, but here he is referring to the Jewish Christians to show that God has not totally rejected Israel. The existence of the remnant proved that God had not abandoned Israel or given up His purpose for her.

Notice, however, that according to Romans 11:7-10, blindness had come to those who refused to accept the light. We have already seen this principle of retribution at work in Romans 1.

Romans 11:11-16 shows us that God's apparent rejection of Israel is only temporary. God is using Israel's temporary rejection of the Messiah to give the Gentiles an opportunity to receive the gospel and share its benefits on an equal footing with the Jewish believers in Christ. Paul writes that in light of Israel's rejection of Jesus, "salvation has come to the Gentiles." Primarily this entails the obvious blessing for Gentiles of eternal life and the provision of the Holy Spirit. Yet the Apostle Paul also anticipated that God would eventually fulfill His plans with Israel as a nation. According to Romans 11:12, "Now if their transgression means riches for the world and their defeat means riches for the Gentiles, how much more will their full restoration bring?" Later in the chapter (see Rom 11:25-27), Paul will explain that this restoration of Israel will come about in conjunction with the second coming of Christ. Only those Jews who turn to Jesus Christ in faith will be included in this restoration.

QUESTION 37

What else do we know is true about Israel's failure and the gospel going out to Gentiles? *(Select all that apply.)*

   A. God will use the spread of the gospel to Gentiles to provoke the nation of Israel to jealousy.

   B. The Jews that continue to offer animal sacrifices will be "saved" because of God's mercy.

   C. Now that salvation has gone out to the Gentiles, there is no longer a need to preach the gospel to the Jews.

   D. Although the focus in this age is on Gentiles responding to the gospel and being saved, the Apostle Paul still anticipated a time in the future when God's promises to Israel would be fulfilled and the nation restored.

Do you remember what problems Christianity faced when the Judaizers tried to force all Gentile Christians to become Jews? Paul's conflict with Peter at Antioch, the Council at Jerusalem, and Paul's letter to the Galatians all helped turn the tide for Christian liberty. Imagine how it might have been if Israel as a nation had accepted Christianity and the early church had been dominated by the decisions of the Sanhedrin about the Gentile converts! The temporary rejection of Israel opened the way for the worldwide preaching of the gospel without racial prejudice or national complications.

QUESTION 38

In the article on God's Temporary Rejection of Israel (refer to this Article placed earlier in the lesson), the author lists at least three "riches to the world" which have come to the Gentile world as a result of Jewish rejection of the Gospel. What are they? Is there anything you would add?

God in His great wisdom has been using the conversion of the Gentiles to stir up the interest of the Jews in the gospel. After all, who received the revelation of the true God and handed it down from generation to generation in the Scriptures? To whom was the covenant given? What people had waited and prayed for the Messiah to come for centuries? And why should the Gentiles receive all the blessings to be found in Christ? Wasn't He a Jew? Why should the Jews shut themselves out from the spiritual riches that the Gentiles had found in Christ? We have seen that Paul preached to the Jews first and then to the Gentiles. As an apostle to the Gentiles, he was happy to have such a ministry (Rom 11:13), but he hoped and prayed that God would use even this to stir up the interest of his own people (Rom 11:14).

QUESTION 39

When Paul spoke of Israel's "loss" he meant:

    A. Israel had permanently lost its right to rule in the future kingdom

    B. Israel has lost its role as the centerpiece of God's purposes in history.

    C. The Jewish nation has lost the opportunity find salvation.

    D. Israel has been replaced by the church which is the "New Israel."

Gentiles Grafted In (Rom 11:17-25)

Objective 9 – At the end of the topic, you will be able to give three important lessons taught by the parable of the olive tree.

QUESTION 40

In Romans 11:17, who do the branches represent? *(Select all that apply.)*

    A. The branches broken off are unbelieving Jews.

    B. The branches broken off are those who have wandered away from the faith.

    C. The wild olive branches grafted in are those who once wandered away but have since returned to an active faith.

    D. The wild olive branches grafted in are Gentile Christians.

Have you ever watched a person graft a branch from one tree into another? You may have a tree that produces sour oranges. You can cut a branch close to the trunk and place in the incision a small branch cut from a tree that bears sweet oranges. Wrap it well to hold it there until it becomes a part of the tree. The original branch is cut off. The new branch receives its life from the tree but produces its own sweet oranges.

Paul says in Romans 11:24 that God reversed the ordinary process and in His mercy grafted the wild olive into the good tree. Because the wild olive is still an olive, there is not a problem with this process.

QUESTION 41

In "God's Temporary Rejection of Israel" the author explains what the metaphor of an olive tree would have meant to a first-century Jew. What is the meaning of that metaphor? What does it mean that natural branches were cut off? Does this mean that national Israel lost salvation?

It is only in Christ, who in His humanity was of the seed of Abraham, that we have any right to enjoy the blessings of spiritual life. And where would Christianity be today if it were not for the missionary work of such great Jewish evangelists as Peter, Paul, and Philip? And how would we know how to find God without the Bible that we have received from Jewish writers? Let's thank God for the olive tree!

QUESTION 42

In "God's Temporary Rejection of Israel" the author explains the meaning of being "cut off." Please open your life Notebook and summarize what this means. Do you agree or disagree with the author's conclusion? Why or why not?

Israel Revived and Restored (Rom 11:25-31)

Objective 10 – At the end of the topic, you will be able to state what God's plans are for Israel's future.

Romans 11:25 is the climax of the passage about the olive tree and leads us right into a clearer revelation of Israel's future. It is clear from Romans 11:23-25 that the rejection of Israel is only temporary. A future restoration is coming. If God shows mercy to the Gentiles, how much more will He show mercy to His people Israel!

QUESTION 43

Compare Romans 11:25-26. What conditions or events show us when Israel will be restored? *(Select all that apply.)*

A. When the Gentiles have had a reasonable amount of time to accept Christ

B. When signs of Christ's return are at their peak

C. When the Deliverer comes out of Zion

D. When the full number of the Gentiles has come in

The fullness of the Gentiles coming in reminds us of the worldwide proclamation of the gospel and the great company of Gentile believers that God is grafting into the olive tree. He alone knows when that number will be complete. This period may be compared with the "time of the Gentiles" that Daniel mentions in his prophecies. The Deliverer who comes out of Zion is the Lord Jesus Christ, the Messiah who will return to earth to establish His kingdom in glory.

QUESTION 44

According to Romans 11:26-27, the restoration will be spiritual in nature. *True or False?*

This restoration will take place when Jesus comes back to earth. Romans 11:26 is speaking of Israel as a whole but does not mean that every Israelite will be saved on the basis of his ethnicity.

For a fascinating study of prophecies about this time of national repentance, you may want to look at Zechariah 12–14. At this time, Israel will recognize Jesus as their Messiah and repent for having crucified Him (Zech 12:10; 13:6). When they struck the Shepherd, Jesus, His followers were scattered, but God protected a remnant. He will bring them through a time of great suffering and claim them as His people (Zech 13:7-9). Nations will come to fight against Jerusalem, but Christ will come to deliver His people and establish His reign (Zech 14).

Many other Old Testament prophecies tell of the coming of the Messiah in glory to establish His everlasting reign over Israel and the whole earth. Those prophecies will be fulfilled. God has not repented or changed His mind about His call and promise to Abraham and his seed. He has not forgotten His promise to David. He does not repent of His promises to Israel. His gifts and callings can be depended on (Rom 11:29).

Even now as we are getting closer to the time for Jesus to come again, God has begun a spiritual awakening among the Jews. Many are accepting Jesus as their Savior. We should pray for them, share the gospel with them, repay the debt we owe them (Rom 11:30-31), and rejoice in their restoration through the mercy of God!

Riches of God's Wisdom (Rom 11:32-36)

Objective 11 – At the end of the topic, you will be able to appreciate more deeply God's wisdom, ability to accomplish what He purposes, and faithfulness to His promises.

In Romans 11:32, Paul sums up his argument about the relationship of the Jews and Gentiles. There will be no boasting about racial superiority and special privileges in God's kingdom and no pride in our own goodness or looking down on others as vile sinners. God has shown that the whole world has sinned. Israel's pride in being God's chosen people has been humbled through her sin of unbelief. God has shown those of us who are Gentiles that we can come to Him for mercy.

Look back at Romans 11:30-32 and notice the emphasis on God's mercy. We see here the love and wisdom of God in bringing men and nations to repentance and faith so that He can save them in His abundant mercy.

In Romans 11:33-36, Paul is overwhelmed with the great plan of salvation that he has been discussing. He has anticipated questions or perhaps repeated questions with which others had challenged his presentation of God's plan in the gospel. He has dealt with the perceived injustice of God in relation to Israel's unbelief and rejection. He has shown us God's plan for the worldwide proclamation of the gospel and the salvation of Jews and Gentiles alike through faith in Christ. We have seen how God has used even Israel's unbelief to give an opportunity for the salvation of the Gentiles. And now we can look forward to the restoration of Israel and the joint sharing of Jews and Gentiles in Christ's eternal reign. No wonder Paul concludes this section with an outburst of praise to God! We join with Paul in saying, "O the depths of the riches both of the wisdom and knowledge of God! To whom be glory forever. Amen."

Lesson 6 Self Check: Romans

QUESTION 1

What did Paul mean in Romans 9:3 when he said, "I could wish that I myself were accursed"?

   A. He was willing to give up his eternal salvation.

   B. He was willing to endure divine discipline.

   C. He was willing to give up his life in order that they might be saved.

   D. He was willing to endure the judgment of God in time if that would save his people.

QUESTION 2

In Romans 9:8, the remnant is called children of _____.

   A. Israel

   B. Salvation

   C. God

   D. Promise

QUESTION 3

To whom is Paul referring primarily in Romans 9:26 as children of the living God?

   A. Jews

   B. Gentiles

   C. Jewish believers

   D. Pagans

QUESTION 4

In Romans 9:27-28, Paul quotes Isaiah 10:22-23. What is the main message in these verses?

   A. God executes judgment on the earth but saves all of Israel, His people.

   B. God's judgment falls chiefly on His people and only a few are saved.

   C. God's judgment comes on all the earth and relatively few of Israel are saved.

   D. God's judgment comes on all the earth, but those who accept Jesus are saved.

QUESTION 5

Compare Psalm 118:22-23; Isaiah 28:16; Matthew 21:33-46 with 1 Corinthians 1:23 and Ephesians 2:20-22. Which of the following prophecies does the Bible not teach?

   A. The religious leaders of Israel ("the builders") would not recognize the Messiah.

   B. Israel's leaders would "stumble over" the Messiah, reject Him, and kill Him.

   C. The efforts of the religious leaders would fail because they had chosen the wrong "cornerstone."

   D. Because the religious leaders rejected the Messiah, God would reject them and give His salvation to others.

QUESTION 6

What is the essential ingredient of salvation?

- A. Faith
- B. Obedience
- C. Baptism
- D. Repentance

QUESTION 7

According to Romans 10:17, it is by hearing the preached word of Christ that faith comes to people so that they can believe in Christ. *True or False?*

QUESTION 8

According to Romans 11:5-7, the remnant of the election of grace only included Gentiles. *True or False?*

QUESTION 9

In Romans 11:17, the broken off branches refer to unbelieving _____.

- A. Gentiles
- B. Christians
- C. Pagans
- D. Jews

QUESTION 10

According to Romans 11:25-26, Israel will one day be restored. *True or False?*

Lesson 6 Answers to Questions

QUESTION 1: *Your answer*

QUESTION 2

D. He was willing to endure the judgment of God in time if that would save his people.

QUESTION 3: *Your answer*

QUESTION 4: *Your answer*

QUESTION 5

A. Pray earnestly for people to accept Christ.

C. Give up some of your own comforts and desires in order to give others the gospel.

QUESTION 6: *Your answer*

QUESTION 7: *Your answer*

QUESTION 8

B. To be His people

C. To be a blessing to all nations

QUESTION 9: Promise

QUESTION 10

D. The promise is actually fulfilled to all those who believe.

QUESTION 11

B. God chose the brother best suited for His purposes.

C. Before they were born, God knew who Jacob and Esau would become.

E. This is an example of predestination based on God's foreknowledge.

QUESTION 12

A. The world learned that the God of the Israelites fought for His people.

C. Many Egyptians saw and were convinced of His power.

D. Through faith in God's Word, some Egyptians escaped some of the plagues.

E. God helped the Israelites gather much wealth as they left Egypt.

F. Many Egyptians joined Israel to follow God's leading.

QUESTION 13: Mercy

QUESTION 14

A. Pharaoh hardened his own heart first.

B. The passage is not actually addressing salvation.

C. 2 Peter 3:9 shows that God does not want anyone to be lost.

QUESTION 15

A. If God treated us as we deserved, the human race would have been wiped out long ago.

E. His mercy causes Him to patiently endure many things which will eventually be judged and punished.

F. While God, in His mercy, is withholding His judgment, many additional people are being saved.

QUESTION 16: True

QUESTION 17

B. Gentiles who believe in Christ

QUESTION 18

C. God's judgment comes on all the earth and relatively few of Israel are saved.

QUESTION 19

C. Sinful Israel, like Sodom and Gomorrah, deserved total destruction, but God in His mercy saved a remnant.

QUESTION 20: True

QUESTION 21

A. The Lord of armies

QUESTION 22

    A. The religious leaders of Israel ("the builders") would not recognize the Messiah.

    B. Israel's leaders would "stumble over" the Messiah, reject Him, and kill Him.

    D. Because the religious leaders rejected the Messiah, God would reject them and give His salvation to others.

QUESTION 23: *Your answer*

QUESTION 24: *Your answer*

QUESTION 25

    A. Believing in the heart

QUESTION 26

    A. To worship Him

    B. To be delivered from a dangerous or threatening situation

    C. To seek a favorable answer from the Lord in response to prayer or inquiry

QUESTION 27

    A. "Everyone"

    B. "No distinction"

    C. "Lord of all"

    D. "Blesses all who call on Him"

QUESTION 28

    A. Those who preach or proclaim to others

QUESTION 29: *Your answer*

QUESTION 30: *Your answer*

QUESTION 31: *Your answer should be one of the following:*

Word, gospel

QUESTION 32: *Your answer should be one of the following:*

The name of the Lord, The Lord, His name, The Lord's name

QUESTION 33

    A. Isaiah 65:2

    D. Deuteronomy 32:21

QUESTION 34

    D. To everybody, everywhere, whether they want to hear the message or not

QUESTION 35: True

QUESTION 36

    A. Paul himself

    B. Thousands of Jews who had accepted Christ and were saved by grace

QUESTION 37

    A. God will use the spread of the gospel to Gentiles to provoke the nation of Israel to jealousy.

    D. Although the focus in this age is on Gentiles responding to the gospel and being saved, the Apostle Paul still anticipated a time in the future when God's promises to Israel would be fulfilled and the nation restored.

QUESTION 38: *Your answer*

QUESTION 39

    B. Israel has lost its role as the centerpiece of God's purposes in history.

QUESTION 40

    A. The branches broken off are unbelieving Jews.

    D. The wild olive branches grafted in are Gentile Christians.

QUESTION 41: *Your answer*

QUESTION 42: *Your answer*

QUESTION 43

    C. When the Deliverer comes out of Zion

D. When the full number of the Gentiles has come in

QUESTION 44: True

Lesson 6 Self Check Answers

QUESTION 1

    D. He was willing to endure the judgment of God in time if that would save his people.

QUESTION 2

    D. Promise

QUESTION 3

    B. Gentiles

QUESTION 4

    C. God's judgment comes on all the earth and relatively few of Israel are saved.

QUESTION 5

    C. The efforts of the religious leaders would fail because they had chosen the wrong "cornerstone."

QUESTION 6

    A. Faith

QUESTION 7: True

QUESTION 8: False

QUESTION 9

    D. Jews

QUESTION 10: True

Lesson 7: The Gospel and the Christian (Rom 12–13)

Lesson Introduction

In Romans, Paul follows a pattern which is common in his other epistles. After dealing with a doctrinal issue, he emphasizes its practical implications. He has presented a particular doctrine and then immediately discussed its application to life. A well-known theologian, F. F. Bruce, said concerning this practice, "Doctrine is never taught in the Bible simply that it may be known; it is taught in order that it may be translated into practice."

The Roman epistle itself is arranged in this same way. Chapters 1–11 deal primarily with the doctrine of justification by faith and Chapters 12–16 deal with the practical implications of that doctrine in the Christian life. (Chapters 9–11 are, in a sense, parenthetical. We have included them in Lesson 6 in the unit on the application of the gospel, but they also could be considered part of the doctrinal part of the book.)

Jesus illustrated the relationship between doctrine and practice when He said, "If you know these things, happy are you if you do them" (Jn 13:17). True happiness does not come from knowing about Christianity. It comes from living it!

Lesson Objectives

Topic 1 shows how dedication leads to transformation and affects our relationships with other Christians.

In Topic 1, you will examine…

- Your attitude toward God, focusing on the need to cooperate with God's transformation process
- Your attitude toward yourself, focusing on the humble use of your spiritual gifts
- Your attitude toward other Christians, focusing on practical ways to replace selfishness with sacrificial love

Topic 2 applies the gospel to our relationships with the world.

In Topic 2, you will discover…

- The importance of being a good citizen
- A basic rule for all your actions toward others in the world
- The importance of wisely using your time

Lesson Outline

Topic 1: Dedication and Transformation (Rom 12:1-21)

Attitude toward God (12:1-2)

Attitude toward Self (12:3-8)

Attitude toward Others (12:9-21)

Topic 2: Relationships with the World (13:1-14)

Good Citizenship (13:1-7)

Actions Determined by Love (13:8-10)

Wise Use of Time (13:11-14)

Word List

We hope you will enjoy using the word study at the beginning of each lesson. Some of the words you already know, but they are used in a special sense in the lesson. Others are theological terms, and some are new words for many students. Please read the word study each time before starting the lesson. Refer back to it as necessary.

Be devoted (Rom 12:10) - have warm brotherly love, be friendly and kind.

Bless (Rom 12:14) - ask God to give His favor to.

Conformed (Rom 12:2) - shaped in the mold of a set of standards, living by its ideals and values. *Transformed* - completely changed.

Contribute (Rom 12:13) - giving or sharing to meet the needs of God's people.

Exhortation (Rom 12:8) - encouraging, urging earnestly.

In harmony (Rom 12:16) - with the same attitude for all.

Lag in zeal (Rom 12:11) - be lazy, sluggish like a sloth.

Prophecy (Rom 12:6) - gift of speaking messages from God.

Resists such authority (Rom 13:2) - rebels against the authority or government, opposes what God has ordered.

Subject to (Rom 13:1) - obedient to.

Governing authorities - Paul is speaking chiefly of government, but the principle applies to other areas too. When described as *instituted by God*, they are established as part of human government and, as such, part of God's plan for carrying out justice in the world.

Topic 1: Dedication and Transformation (Rom 12:1-21)

What must we do as Christians in order to experience transformation in our daily lives? Romans 12 shows us the path. First, we must take steps to change the way we relate to God and to the world. This will quickly lead to changes in the way we view ourselves and the way we treat other Christians.

Attitude toward God (Rom 12:1-2)

> Objective 1 – At the end of the topic, you will be able to see how the doctrinal development of Romans 1–11 is the foundation for our decision to submit to the Lordship of Christ in Romans 12:1-2 and learn the implications of this decision in daily life.

The word *therefore* again gives us the relationship between the doctrinal and the practical sections of this letter. It points back to chapters 1–11 and forward to the appeal to offer ourselves as a living sacrifice to God. This is the only logical and acceptable response to all that God has done in providing salvation for us. This is our reasonable service. Instead of questioning God (as reflected in the questions of men answered by Paul in chapters 9–11), real faith worships and serves God. Real faith causes us to bow down in the presence of such marvelous grace and worship. Real faith says, "Here am I, Lord, send me" (Isa 6:8).

QUESTION 1

Paul says, "By the mercies of God I plead with you, give yourselves to God." What mercies do you think he is referring to? *(Select all that apply.)*

   A. The grace mentioned in the preceding eleven chapters

   B. The love mentioned in the preceding eleven chapters

   C. The blessings mentioned in the preceding eleven chapters

   D. God's mercy in Christ's death to save us when we were still enemies of God

Paul speaks of presenting our bodies as a living sacrifice. Different translations say that this is "your spiritual service of worship," or "the true worship that you should offer." Paul is using the language of the Old Testament worship. We have a contrast here between service under the Old Covenant and service under the New.

QUESTION 2

What are the three things that Paul begs the readers of his epistles to do in Romans 12:1-2? *(Select all that apply.)*

   A. Please God.

   B. Present our bodies as living sacrifices.

   C. Know the will of God.

   D. Not be conformed to this world.

   E. Be transformed by the renewing of our minds.

Sacrifice and Service

OLD COVENANT – LAW	NEW COVENANT – GRACE
The one making the offering gives the sacrifice	The one making the offering is the sacrifice
A dead sacrifice	A living sacrifice
The sacrifice appeases God	The sacrifice pleases God
Service is outward, ceremonial in nature	Service is inward, spiritual in nature
Service is duty	Service is worship
Appeal for service as a command of God	Appeal for service by the mercies of God

QUESTION 3

Romans 12:2 says that as a result of these actions we will know and experience God's _____.

QUESTION 4

How can we keep from being conformed to the world, its standards, and values? In Romans 8, you have read of a power that can help you resist this tendency; it is the power of the _____.

QUESTION 5

What relationship does this power have to the second command in Romans 12:2: be transformed? (See 2 Cor 3:18.)

   A. The Holy Spirit encourages us to transform our minds.

   B. The Holy Spirit does the work of transforming us.

   C. The Holy Spirit gives glory to the obedient.

   D. The Holy Spirit helps us to try harder to change.

By allowing the Holy Spirit to minister to our lives, we can both resist conforming to the age in which we live and also know and do the will of God. This transformation is an ongoing and progressive experience. As we continually yield to the Holy Spirit, He is able to conform us not to the age but to the image of

Christ. These two verses cover both the spiritual service of the believer (Rom 12:1) and the inner spiritual experience of the believer (Rom 12:2).

Service cannot be separated from the servant. The quality of service is determined by the quality of the servant. In a book discussing the life of a servant of God, E. M. Bounds said, "It takes 20 years to make a sermon because it takes 20 years to make a man." His meaning was that the sermon is for the most part the reflection of who the man is. The combination of service and inner spiritual experience in these two verses is no accident. Effective service for God will be determined by how much you are yielded to the Holy Spirit's ministry in your life.

QUESTION 6

Part of our transformation is our attitude toward the will of God. Match Paul's concept of God's will with the world's concept.

Paul's Concept of God's Will	The World's Concept of God's Will
Good	Not the best for us
Acceptable	Not acceptable
Perfect	Too demanding

Compare Paul's description of the will of God with the concept that the world has of it. Then see if your own attitude toward God's will needs to be changed to better reflect Paul's concept.

Notice that the transformation comes through the renewing of our minds--new thoughts and attitudes. What we fill our minds with affects our attitudes and our actions. Are our thoughts full of self-- of our own interests and desires? Or are they full of God and His Word? Part of the renewal of our minds comes through accepting Romans 12–16 as the pattern for our lives.

QUESTION 7

Suppose you are the pastor of a church whose members are very much conformed to this world. Their outlook on life is materialistic and self-centered. They follow the permissive moral standards of the world. To them, Christian service is a matter of helping people with physical or material needs. You are planning a series of Bible studies. How might a systematic study of Romans be used by God to transform your church? *(Select all that apply.)*

    A. The Holy Spirit uses the Word of God (e.g., to convict of sin and help many people see their lost condition and need of God).

    B. The picture of God's wrath against the world helps people see the danger in being conformed to the world and see that they are condemned to die for their sins.

    C. Through these Scriptures, people see the impossibility of meeting God's standards by their own efforts.

    D. People can see God's love in His provision of salvation, the provision of victory in the Holy Spirit, and God's way of keeping and transforming them.

    E. Romans 12–16 shows the pattern for transformation.

We have spent a great deal of time on the first two verses of Romans 12, but these are the theme of this whole section of the epistle. You will see that all the relationships and actions that Paul recommends in the rest of the epistle are a description of the transformed life.

Attitude toward Self (Rom 12:3-8)

> Objective 2 – At the end of the topic, you will be able to list seven ministry gifts of the Holy Spirit. You will be able to find your identity in the body of Christ and use your gifts with modesty and faith.

"Who am I?" This is the constant cry for identity that we hear from this lost and bewildered generation. In Christ we have found the answer. What a change the gospel has brought us--from condemned sinner in Romans 1–3 to members of the body of Christ in Romans 12! Christ is our Head, and all those who believe in Him are members of His body. Paul uses this figure of speech in four of his epistles (Romans, 1 Corinthians, Ephesians, and Colossians) to show us our relationships, privileges, and responsibilities.

How well we do our part as members of the body of Christ depends to a great extent on our attitude toward ourselves. First, we must recognize that we are not wise enough or strong enough to do anything by ourselves. We must depend on Christ our Head, the ability that the Holy Spirit gives, and the cooperation of the other members of the body. Second, we must realize that in Christ, with the power of His Spirit and the cooperation of the other members of the body, we can do anything God tells us to do.

QUESTION 8

Compare Romans 12:3 with John 15:5 and Philippians 4:13. Modesty and faith are two qualities that you should have according to these verses. *True or False?*

Paul points out that we must be modest and not overestimate our own ability or importance. But this must be balanced with faith in God and the confidence that He will help us do whatever He calls us to do.

In Romans 12:3, "according... to... the measure of faith" means according to the spiritual power or amount of faith that God gives to each Christian to carry out his special responsibility. We have already seen that we walk by faith in holy living. We also walk by faith in Christian service. God gives us a job to do. First, we must recognize we cannot do it right by ourselves. We look to God in faith and accept the work, knowing He will help us.

What Is Your Gift?

Romans 12:4-8

- Prophecy
- Ministry
- Teaching
- Showing Mercy
- Exhortation
- Giving
- Ruling

In Romans 12:1-2, Paul has told us that a proper reaction to the mercies of God is service. Here we are faced with the important question, "What kind of service am I to give?" Paul speaks now of the special abilities that God gives the various members of the body. They are spiritual gifts--abilities given by the Holy Spirit. The body has many members. Each one has its own specific task and ministry. Your church needs the gift God has given you!

QUESTION 9

Open your Life Notebook and answer the following question. List the seven spiritual gifts in Romans 12:6-8 and briefly describe how each one contributes to the local church and its work. In addition, compare the list of spiritual gifts in Ephesians 4:8-12 and 1 Corinthians 12:6-10 with Romans 12:6-8. What additional gifts are found in these texts?

QUESTION 10

Had you realized that all of these were gifts or abilities that the Spirit gives to Christians? What do you feel is your gift or ministry in the church? Open your Life Notebook and record your thoughts.

Take time now to thank God for the great honor and privilege of being a member of the body of Christ. Pray about your ministry and ask His help to do it effectively. Make an entry in your Life Notebook.

Attitude toward Others (Rom 12:9-21)

> Objective 3 – At the end of the topic, you will be able to compare the attitudes in a transformed life with those in a life that is conformed to the world. You will be able to cultivate those that God recommends for you.

These verses are closely related to the Sermon on the Mount. When you use these verses for Bible studies or in preaching, we suggest that you look in Matthew 5-7 for additional teaching on the subject. Please read these chapters now so you can see how Paul based his instructions for Christian life on the teachings of Jesus.

The twenty-seven commands found in Romans 12:9-21 are self-explanatory. Any problem here is not with understanding them but in practicing them.

QUESTION 11

What lesson does Matthew 7:24-29 teach us about putting into practice what we know about God and His Word? *(Select all that apply.)*

    A. It is easy to be distracted and foolishly fail to apply what Jesus has taught us.

    B. It is dangerous to hear the Word of God and then fail to apply it to our lives.

    C. Our lives will have a strong foundation if we follow Jesus' teaching and apply what we know.

    D. If we fail to apply what we know, God will bring stormy trials into our lives.

QUESTION 12

In Romans 12:9-21, the last twenty-six commands are simply ways of carrying out the first one. The first one is that love must be without _____.

Romans 12:9 sets the theme for this whole section. Divine love is the controlling principle of the Christian's life. This is genuine love, or divine love. This is the law of Christ; it is the law of love. Human love is conditioned upon the goodness or lovability of its object. God's love is not like that. If it were, you and I would never have been saved! It is a love which is centered more in the will than the emotions. He does not love us because we are lovable and deserving. He loved us when we were sinners.

Divine love pours itself out spontaneously from the life that is filled with the Spirit of Christ (see Rom 5:5). It makes it possible for us to forgive and love our enemies. If we love only those who love us, are we showing divine love (see Mt 5:46-47)? Divine love will make us feel the needs of others and do what we can to help them (Rom 12:15-16). Romans 12:21 is actually a summary of the Sermon on the Mount. By doing good and by the love of God in us, we are to serve our fellowmen.

Take time to read carefully the chart below which contrast the life "transformed" by the Word of God with the life "conformed" to the world.

Conformed Versus Transformed

Romans	Conformed	Transformed
12:9	Hypocritical love Accepts evil Rejects good	Sincere love Hates evil Holds onto good
12:10	Unkind Hardhearted Wanting to be honored	Kind Brotherly love Honoring others above self
12:11	Lazy, careless Indifferent to spiritual things Serving self	Diligent worker Enthusiastic in spiritual things Serving the Lord
12:12	Depressed, sad Impatient Prayerless	Rejoicing in hope Patient in tribulation Persevering in prayer
12:13	Selfish Inhospitable	Generous, sharing Hospitable
12:14	Cursing enemies	Blessings persecutors
12:15	Indifferent to welfare of others	Concerned, sharing joys and sorrows of others
12:16	Prejudice, favoritism Conceited	Same to all Humble
12:17	Evil for evil Dishonest	Good for evil Honest
12:18	Quarrelling	Peaceable
12:19	Avenging oneself	Leaving vengeance to God
12:20	Destroying enemies	Kind to enemies
12:21	Overcome by evil	Overcoming evil with good

QUESTION 13

Do the commands of this section relate to our attitudes toward Christians, unbelievers, or both?

    A. Christians only--not unbelievers

    B. Unbelievers only--not Christians

    C. Both Christians and unbelievers

    D. Only those in heaven

QUESTION 14

Why should we not avenge ourselves? (Rom 12:19)

    A. Because most people do not know how to properly take revenge

    B. Because the Scriptures teach us to be tolerant rather than judgmental

    C. Because it is God's responsibility to judge and punish wrongdoing

    D. Because we might get hurt

In Romans 12:19, Paul quotes Proverbs 25:22. The figure of speech *heap coals of fire on his head* is generally understood to mean causing someone to be ashamed of himself. His conscience accuses him and he recognizes his wrong when his enemy treats him kindly.

QUESTION 15

Suppose that someone in the church has criticized you and treated you unkindly. In what ways could you apply the principle stated in Romans 12:19? *(Select all that apply.)*

    A. Be kind.

    B. Make a special effort to be friendly.

    C. Show the person how his action hurt you.

    D. Ask the person's pastor to gently explain the offense.

QUESTION 16

Go back over Romans 12:9-21 phrase by phrase. Evaluate your daily life in regard to each of these commands. Make note of the ones where you feel that you are weak. Pray about your need and accept God's help to carry out your transformation in these areas. Remember that faith is a matter of receiving from God what He has promised. As a reminder to yourself, enter in your Life Notebook what, with the Lord's help, you are asking God to do to change your heart.

Topic 2: Relationships with the World (Rom 13:1-14)

As we take steps to change the way we relate to God and to the world, we will not only change the way we view ourselves and the way we treat other Christians, but also begin to act differently toward those around us who are not Christians. Romans 13 focuses on our behavior toward the people who govern us and also toward our neighbors who live and work around us. It concludes with an exhortation to not fall back into the temptations of this world.

Good Citizenship (Rom 13:1-7)

Objective 4 – At the end of the topic, you will be able to discuss the importance of Paul's words about government to the Roman Christians and to us; appreciate your government more; and be more aware of your responsibilities and opportunities as a Christian and a good citizen.

Why do you suppose Paul discusses a Christian's duty to his government at this particular point in his letter to the Romans? Let's look at some possible reasons that have been suggested.

    1. Part of Christian doctrine and application: Paul is giving a systematic presentation of Christian doctrine and its practical application. He cannot leave out this area of

responsibility for a transformed life. Our attitudes toward the government need to be directed by the Lord in the renewing of our minds.

2. A practical issue for the Christians at Rome: The Christians at Rome were in the political center of the Roman Empire. The question of their relationship to the government was very important to them. They faced the problem daily.

3. Lingering suspicions about the nature and motives of Christianity: The Christians needed to make their position clear in the eyes of the authorities at Rome. The Founder of their religion had been executed by the sentence of a Roman governor on the charge of trying to make Himself a king. This would put His followers under suspicion. Paul states their Christian position and their reasons for respecting those who were in authority.

4. Concern for the church as a whole: The obedience of the Christians in the capital would help counteract the suspicion and false accusations about them. But disobedience to the government could provoke a persecution against the church that might reach to the farthest corners of the Roman world.

5. Questions about whether obedience to government represents conformity to the world: Another reason for Paul to bring up the subject of obeying the laws might be what he had written in Romans 12:2: "Do not be conformed to this present world." How far does this command go? Should they be disloyal to the institutions and authority of the government? Should they respect and be subject to the emperor?

6. Correction of overemphasis on Christian liberty: Have you thought about the anti-law party that Paul wrote about in Galatians? Do you suppose there were some of them in Rome? Or could Paul be concerned that his strong emphasis on freedom from the Law in his letter to the Romans might make some of them think they did not need to obey the laws of the land?

QUESTION 17

Which members of the church are free from any responsibilities toward the civil government according to Romans 13:1?

Paul makes it very clear that every person is responsible to submit to governing authorities. The words *every person* are a Hebrew expression suggesting the idea of individual duty. Remember Paul is writing to the church; he is addressing Christians. The idea is that no person is exempt from this duty. No one has the special privilege by which he may ignore or feel himself free to violate the laws set by governing authority.

QUESTION 18

Why should a Christian submit himself to the authority of the government according to Romans 13:1-2?

A. To help assure that governments will not make life difficult for believers

B. To keep from embarrassing the church

C. To honor God who has given governments the right to rule

D. To avoid resistance and anarchy in the community

Paul is talking about the existing governmental powers. He says that they are in existence by divine order. Paul does not mean that everything the authorities do is in agreement with God's will. There are good and bad authorities. There are authorities that use their powers in harmony with God's will, and there are authorities who misuse their powers. Paul is not talking about the use of authorities here. He is talking about its origin and the right to rule. He is saying that all authorities have one thing in common, they are instituted by God. They derive their origin, right, and power from God.

QUESTION 19

Open your Life Notebook and describe some of the benefits which you and fellow countrymen enjoy because of your government and its work. Take time to pray for your country's leaders and thank God for the benefits which you enjoy under their leadership.

Romans 13:2-3 shows us that God has given human governments the responsibility of maintaining order and punishing those who violate that order. Paul describes a government that is a terror to evildoers, one that encourages right living and justice. Christians should certainly thank God for their government and pray for all those who have any responsibility in it. Do we?

QUESTION 20

What name for government leaders does Paul use in Romans 13:4-6 to show that they are not really the highest authority?

QUESTION 21

Romans 13:5 gives reasons why a Christian should obey the laws. What are they? *(Select all that apply.)*

    A. Because of the authorities' wrath

    B. Because subjection is more spiritual

    C. Because of the Christian's conscience

    D. Because it is a necessity to keep out of trouble

Do you understand the meaning of the phrases "because of the wrath" and "because of your conscience" in Romans 13:5? Paul is telling us that it is important to be in subjection to the government for two reasons. First, we need to obey in order to avoid punishment from authorities over us for breaking the law. Second, we do not want to be guilty of disobeying God, and that is ultimately what we do if we break the laws of our country.

But what if the authorities are a terror to those who do good? Even though Paul is not referring to evil government here, the question should be answered. Jesus teaches us to give to Caesar what belongs to Caesar and give to God what belongs to God (Mt 22:21). He stated this principle about paying taxes, but it goes beyond taxes.

Romans 13:7 teaches we are to pay everyone what is owed: taxes, revenue, respect, and honor. Notice that the honor and respect are based on the position that the person holds as a "minister of God" in human government. We can respect a person for his position even if some of his actions are not what they should be.

But we must still consider the problem of how far a Christian is obliged to obey the government. Certainly the Christians in Rome would have asked this question. Should they obey the law that everyone had to worship the emperor? Or should they worship God alone as His Word commanded them? When there is a conflict, which takes priority, God's or humans' authority? When Peter and the other apostles had to face this question, they said, "We ought to obey God rather than men" (Acts 5:29).

Read the stirring account of the apostles' decision and its results in Acts 4:1-31 and Acts 5:12-42. When there is a conflict between the requirements of men and the commands of God, the words of Peter still take effect. We should remember, though, that Peter's refusal to obey the authorities was clearly because

---

their order directly opposed Jesus' command to preach the gospel to every person, beginning in Jerusalem.

QUESTION 22

The religious authorities ordered them to stop speaking to people about Jesus. *True or False?*

We should especially notice that the emphasis here in Romans 13:1-7 is on obedience and respect for existing authority. Situations do arise when it is very difficult for a Christian to know what to do. When the commands of men seem to conflict seriously with the commands of God, we should certainly look to the Holy Spirit for His leading and for wisdom. We should remember to pray for those who are in such circumstances and that God will work out His solution.

QUESTION 23

In some areas of the world, the teachings of Romans 13:1-7 seem especially important for the church today. Do you feel that this is true in your area? If so, why? Open your Life Notebook and answer this question.

A spirit of lawlessness in the world makes it important for us to recognize what our attitudes should be. Some sincere Christians have gone against biblical principles in their zeal for social or political reform.

QUESTION 24

Open your Life Notebook and list by position some of the people in your government that you plan to respect. Underline and note those whom you plan to pray for often, asking that the Lord will help them to carry out their duties well.

QUESTION 25

Suppose that you hold a government position or shepherd those who do. How can you perform your duties as a minister of God or encourage those in your care to do so? How can you serve both God and your country better? How can you help other Christians see their responsibilities and opportunities as good citizens? Open your Life Notebook and record your responses.

Actions Determined by Love (Rom 13:8-10)

> Objective 5 – At the end of the topic, you will be able to state the basic rule for a Christian's actions and apply it in your life.

In Romans 13:8, Paul passes from the subject of paying what we owe the government to the subject of all debts and the basic rule for all our relationships with others.

QUESTION 26

Read Matthew 5:43-48; John 13:34-35; Luke 10:25-37; and Romans 13:8. Give the one basic rule that should guide us in all our relationships with others. Think about whether you accept to do so as part of your reasonable service to God.

   A. Pray for our enemies.

   B. Love our neighbors as ourselves.

   C. Love the Lord our God with all our hearts, souls, strength, and minds.

   D. Do not owe anything to anyone.

Let's think about what "owe no one anything" means. This does not prohibit Christians from having financial obligations. We may borrow from others in case of need (see Mt 5:42 and Lk 6:35). But we must meet our obligations. Psalm 37:21 says, "Evil men borrow, but do not repay their debt." It is wicked to borrow objects or money from people and then not do our best to return what we have borrowed in good condition or pay what we owe at the expected time. Why? We must consider the rights of other people and respect their property. Remember that how you behave towards others, with your finances and other areas of stewardship, can be either a positive or negative witness for the Lord.

QUESTION 27

Suppose you go to a town to start a church in the home of a Christian who lives there. You invite several of the businessmen of the town to the services. They come and hear the Christian testify about how he has been following Christ for ten years. He owes all of them money and makes no attempt to pay his bills. What do you think their feelings would be toward his testimony, your church, and the gospel? *(Select all that apply.)*

    A. They may be intrigued by the apparent contradiction between faith and life.

    B. They may possibly wish to talk with him about what he owes them.

    C. They might not want to have anything to do with Christ, the church, or the gospel.

    D. They may be impressed with such long-term commitment.

Paul suggests that there is one debt that we will be making payments on as long as we live. That is our debt to love our neighbor. To whom do we owe this debt of love? Only to our fellow Christians? Is it a debt that we owe only to those who love us, a love that we must return?

We have already discussed the motivating power of love. We saw in Romans 5:5 that only the love of God that the Holy Spirit gives makes it possible for us to love our neighbor as ourselves. Romans 13:8-10 shows us very clearly how divine love fulfills the law. It will help us joyfully carry out our responsibilities to God and our fellow man.

Wise Use of Time (Rom 13:11-14)

Objective 6 – At the end of the topic, you will be able to appreciate the urgency of the hour for you as a Christian and ways in which you plan to make the best use of your time.

In Romans 13:11-14, we have a new motivation for living a transformed life. It is the fact that our time is limited. We cannot afford to waste it on things that do not contribute to our one great purpose in life. We have presented our bodies to God as a living sacrifice. He has work for us to do and now is the time to do it. Jesus, the Light of the world, has come into our lives, and we want to share His light with others.

What kind of attitude toward time would you expect to find in a transformed life? In Romans 13:11-14, we see again the contrast between a life that is conformed to the world and one that has been transformed in its surrender to God. Paul speaks of some people who are asleep to their opportunities and responsibilities. They think only of themselves and their own comfort and pleasure. Even some Christians are only half awake. Paul is saying to us, "Wake up and let's get on with the job God has given us to do." Why? Because we do not have much time left.

QUESTION 28

Compare Romans 13:11 with Hebrews 9:28 and 2 Peter 3:10-14. What do the words "our salvation is now nearer" refer to? Open your Life Notebook and record your answer.

If you are able, use some study tools available to you to do your own study on the multifaceted biblical concept of "salvation" as referred to in Romans 13:11. In your Life Notebook, explain how this would affect your use of time and lifestyle as a witness for Christ.

Many Christians have a motto in their homes that says: "Perhaps Today?" It refers to Jesus' return. Fulfilled prophecies point to the fact that it must be soon. What if He returned today? With that thought, many follow the advice: "Don't go anywhere today where you would not like to be found when Jesus comes. Don't do anything you would not want to be doing when He comes. Don't say anything you would not like to be saying when Jesus comes." This is a good rule. Maybe we could make it even better by stating it positively: "Do the things today that you would like to be doing when Jesus comes."

> "If I only knew, if I knew for sure
>
> That the Lord would return this year.
>
> Which clamoring tasks would I do today?
>
> What things would I buy?
>
> How much would I pray?
>
> As I mixed with my friends,
>
> Just what would I say
>
> If I knew the time so near?
>
> If I only knew, if I knew for sure
>
> That ere six months were sped
>
> The skies would part at the trumpet's peal,
>
> What change in my plans
>
> Would the days reveal?
>
> Would the things I love hold the same appeal
>
> If I knew what lay ahead?
>
> If I only knew, if I knew for sure . . .
>
> O God can I be so blind?
>
> So enthralled with Time that I cannot see
>
> The beckoning hand of Eternity?
>
> Body and soul I belong to Thee,
>
> May my hours be wholly Thine."
>
> - L.J. Walker

QUESTION 29

Compare Romans 13:12-14 with Titus 2:11-14. Also see Ephesians 5:1-17. If we are looking forward to the return of Christ, what kind of life should we be living? *(Select all that apply.)*

    A. Decent

    B. Self-controlled

    C. Upright

    D. Godly

    E. In love

    F. Wise

The words *the day* in Romans 13:12 refer to the day when Jesus Christ, the Sun of Righteousness, will appear and bring a new day for this world (Mal 4:2). Just as the sun drives away the darkness, Christ the Light of the World will put an end to the "deeds of darkness" when He comes and establishes His kingdom of light. But we are members of His kingdom now. So we put on the "armor of light" as a protection against the powers of darkness around us. All through the Scriptures, light is a symbol of good and darkness a symbol of evil. We are urged to walk in the light (1 Jn 1:5-7). Here Paul tells us how we can do it. We are to put on the Lord Jesus Christ. He is our armor of light.

Paul speaks of putting on Christ in Romans 13:14 and also in Galatians 3:27. In Galatians he refers to our position--our union with Christ in His death and resurrection as symbolized in water baptism. Here in Romans he reminds us that this must also be a reality in our daily experience. In Christ--through His power--we can live a resurrected, transformed life, one that is not conformed to the world but will take Him to the world.

QUESTION 30

Read Romans 13:14. What new steps do you need to take to "put on the Lord Jesus Christ, and make no provision for the flesh"? In your Life Notebook, answer this question.

QUESTION 31

Our time to display the righteousness of God and tell people about Jesus may be limited because of the nearness of His return. Can you think of two other reasons why it is "high time" for us to wake up and do now whatever we can for God and the people around us? (See Jn 9:4; Eph 2:10; 1 Cor 3:10-15.) *(Select all that apply.)*

    A. God has good deeds prepared for us to perform in the present.

    B. So that our deeds will not be burned up in the fire of testing

    C. Time is short.

    D. God will reward us in heaven for our good deeds.

Benjamin Franklin, an American philosopher, once said, "Do not waste time; it is the stuff that life is made of." We have given our lives to Christ. Our time belongs to Him. Let's invest it wisely.

QUESTION 32

Open your Life Notebook, and answer the following question. How do you plan to improve the use of your time in view of the urgency of the hour?

Lesson 7 Self Check

QUESTION 1

When Paul said, "By the mercies of God I plead with you, give yourselves to God," which of the following mercies do you think He was referring to?

    A. The grace mentioned in Romans 1–11

    B. The love mentioned in Romans 1–11

    C. The blessings mentioned in Romans 1–11

    D. All of the above

QUESTION 2

What does Romans 12:2 say that we will know and experience as a result of being transformed?

    A. Peace

    B. Our desires

    C. God's will

    D. Eternal life

QUESTION 3

Modesty and _____ are two qualities that you should have according to Romans 12:3, John 15:5, and Philippians 4:13.

    A. Hope

    B. Ambition

    C. Courage

    D. Faith

    E. Happiness

QUESTION 4

What lesson does Matthew 7:24-29 NOT teach us about putting into practice what we know about God and His Word?

    A. It is dangerous to hear the Word of God and then fail to apply it to our lives.

    B. Our lives will have a strong foundation if we follow Jesus' teaching and apply what we know.

    C. It is easy to be distracted and foolishly fail to apply what Jesus has taught us.

    D. Following and applying Jesus' teaching demonstrates true faith in Him.

QUESTION 5

The commands in Romans 12 relate to our attitudes towards whom?

    A. Other Christians and unbelievers

    B. Jewish believers

    C. Unbelievers

    D. Pagans and Gentile believers

QUESTION 6

Why should a Christian submit himself to the authority of the government according to Romans 13:1-2?

    A. To help assure that governments will not make life difficult for believers

    B. To keep from embarrassing the church

    C. To honor God who has given governments the right to rule

    D. To avoid resistance and anarchy in the community

QUESTION 7

According to Acts 4:1-31 and Acts 5:12-42, the apostles disobeyed an order not to speak against the government. *True or False?*

QUESTION 8

According to Matthew 5:43-48 and Romans 13:8, the one basic principle that should guide our relationship with others is to "love your neighbor as yourself." *True or False?*

QUESTION 9

According to Romans 13:12-14, Titus 2:11-14, and Ephesians 5:1-17, what words might describe the type of life we are living if we are looking forward to the return of Christ? *(Select all that apply.)*

    A. Selfish

    B. Decent

    C. Self-controlled

    D. Worldly

    E. Godly

QUESTION 10

According to John 9:4, Ephesians 2:10, and 1 Corinthians 3:10-15, two reasons for us to live godly lives are: God has good deeds prepared for us to perform and God will reward us for our good deeds in heaven. *True or False?*

Lesson 7 Answers to Questions

QUESTION 1
- A. The grace mentioned in the preceding eleven chapters
- B. The love mentioned in the preceding eleven chapters
- C. The blessings mentioned in the preceding eleven chapters
- D. God's mercy in Christ's death to save us when we were still enemies of God

QUESTION 2
- B. Present our bodies as living sacrifices.
- D. Not be conformed to this world.
- E. Be transformed by the renewing of our minds.

QUESTION 3: *Your answer should be one of the following:*
Perfect will, Will

QUESTION 4: *Your answer should be one of the following:*
Holy Spirit, Spirit

QUESTION 5
- B. The Holy Spirit does the work of transforming us.

QUESTION 6

Paul's Concept of God's Will	*The World's Concept of God's Will*
Good	Not the best for us
Acceptable	Not acceptable
Perfect	Too demanding

QUESTION 7
- A. The Holy Spirit uses the Word of God (e.g., to convict of sin and help many people see their lost condition and need of God).
- B. The picture of God's wrath against the world helps people see the danger in being conformed to the world and see that they are condemned to die for their sins.
- C. Through these Scriptures, people see the impossibility of meeting God's standards by their own efforts.
- D. People can see God's love in His provision of salvation, the provision of victory in the Holy Spirit, and God's way of keeping and transforming them.
- E. Romans 12–16 shows the pattern for transformation.

QUESTION 8: True

QUESTION 9: *Your answer*

QUESTION 10: *Your answer*

QUESTION 11
- B. It is dangerous to hear the Word of God and then fail to apply it to our lives.
- C. Our lives will have a strong foundation if we follow Jesus' teaching and apply what we know.

QUESTION 12: Hypocrisy

QUESTION 13
- C. Both Christians and unbelievers

QUESTION 14
- C. Because it is God's responsibility to judge and punish wrongdoing

QUESTION 15
- A. Be kind.
- B. Make a special effort to be friendly.

QUESTION 16: *Your answer*

QUESTION 17: *Your answer should be one of the following:*
None, No one

QUESTION 18

    C. To honor God who has given governments the right to rule

QUESTION 19: *Your answer*

QUESTION 20: Servant

QUESTION 21

    A. Because of the authorities' wrath

    C. Because of the Christian's conscience

QUESTION 22: True

QUESTION 23: *Your answer*

QUESTION 24: *Your answer*

QUESTION 25: *Your answer*

QUESTION 26

    B. Love our neighbors as ourselves.

QUESTION 27

    B. They may possibly wish to talk with him about what he owes them.

    C. They might not want to have anything to do with Christ, the church, or the gospel.

QUESTION 28: *Your answer*

QUESTION 29

    A. Decent

    B. Self-controlled

    C. Upright

    D. Godly

    E. In love

    F. Wise

QUESTION 30: *Your answer*

QUESTION 31

    A. God has good deeds prepared for us to perform in the present.

    D. God will reward us in heaven for our good deeds.

QUESTION 32: *Your answer*

Lesson 7 Self Check Answers

QUESTION 1
    D. All of the above

QUESTION 2
    C. God's will

QUESTION 3
    D. Faith

QUESTION 4
    C. It is easy to be distracted and foolishly fail to apply what Jesus has taught us.

QUESTION 5
    A. Other Christians and unbelievers

QUESTION 6
    C. To honor God who has given governments the right to rule

QUESTION 7: False

QUESTION 8: True

QUESTION 9
    B. Decent
    C. Self-controlled
    E. Godly

QUESTION 10: True

Lesson 8: The Gospel and the Church (Rom 14–16)

Lesson Introduction

Paul continues to follow the pattern that is common in his other epistles. After dealing with a doctrinal issue, he emphasizes its practical implications.

His main focus here in Romans 14–16 is the church. The church is one of the principal means by which God desires to reveal His glory to a world that does not know Him. As you study this lesson, look for ways that Paul's teaching can be applied to your church.

Lesson Objectives

Topic 1 describes ways we should exercise brotherly love in the church.

In Topic 1, you will learn how God wants you to treat other Christians whose convictions and cultural backgrounds may be different from yours. Practical issues include…

- Not judging and quarreling
- Not causing others to stumble
- Helping and pleasing others
- Accepting others

Topic 2 examines practical responsibilities of the church.

In Topic 2, you will discover…

- Why teaching and spirituality are important responsibilities of the church
- Ten guidelines for success in world evangelism
- Three kinds of offerings that are a pattern for the church today
- The practical power of prayer in the church

Topic 3 describes methods for cultivating positive Christian fellowship.

In Topic 3, you will identify the activities that can strengthen a church, including…

- Recognition and commendation of those who serve well
- Quick correction of those who are divisive
- Cultivation of fellowship with other churches

Topic 4 focuses on Paul's concluding statements about the glory of God.

In Topic 4, you will consider God's glory as seen in the gospel and how it should motivate you to share it with others.

Lesson Outline

Topic 1: Brotherly Love in the Church (14:1–15:12)

Not Judging and Quarreling (14:1-13)

Not Causing Others to Stumble (14:13-23)

Helping and Pleasing Others (15:1-6)

Accepting Others (15:7-12)

Word List

We hope you will enjoy using the word study at the beginning of each lesson. Some of the words you already know, but they are used in a special sense in the lesson. Others are theological terms, and some are new words for many students. Please read the word study each time before starting the lesson. Refer back to it as necessary.

Confirm the promises (Rom 15:8) - fulfill and verify, show that the promises were true.

Disputes over differing opinions (Rom 14:1) - arguments about things that are not clear, discussions that will cause one to doubt or will perplex and trouble him.

Distressed by what you eat (Rom 14:15) - upset, troubled, or hurt because of what you eat.

Nothing unclean (Rom 14:14) - no food is ceremonially prohibited now for the Christian as many things were under the Law.

Root of Jesse (Rom 15:12) - a sprout from the root of Jesse the father of David, descendant of Jesse.

Topic 1: Brotherly Love in the Church (Rom 14:1-15:12)

Did you ever see Christians who had a hard time getting along with each other? Or a church that did not seem able to keep the people they led to the Lord? Or a church where visitors and prospective members did not feel welcome? Maybe we can find the root of some of the problems in Romans 14–15 as Paul applies his gospel to the church.

> Objective 1 – At the end of the topic, you will be able to describe and cultivate the right attitudes toward Christians whose convictions and cultural backgrounds may differ from yours.

Not Judging and Quarreling (Rom 14:1-13)

Paul introduces this whole passage on brotherly love in the church (Rom 14:1–15:13) with his statement in Romans 14:1. This is the theme for the rest of the passage. He discusses the relationship between Christian liberty and Christian love. We find similar passages in his first letter to the Corinthians.

QUESTION 1

In Romans 14:1-6, Paul mentions two problem areas in which the early Christians disagreed as to their Christian liberty. What were they? *(Select all that apply.)*

    A. What food they could eat

    B. Which person they should marry

    C. Which church they should attend

    D. Religious observance of certain days

QUESTION 2

Compare 1 Corinthians 8:1-13 and 1 Corinthians 10:23-33 with Romans 14:1-3. A weaker brother might be afraid to eat meat that had been sold in a market because he might think he is sinning by eating meat that had been offered to idols as a sacrifice. *True or False?*

Some did not believe that they could eat certain things because they were not permitted under the Jewish law. Others were afraid to eat any meat because much of it had been sacrificed to idols before it was sold in the public market. Their consciences would not let them eat it.

Others, like Paul, thanked God for whatever He provided for them to eat and ate it with faith knowing that it was sanctified by the Word of God and prayer (1 Tim 4:5). They enjoyed this liberty in Christ. However, some of them criticized those who did not have the same faith and ridiculed them.

On the other hand, those who did not have the faith to eat everything criticized those that did and thought they were sinning.

They had the same problem over keeping certain days as holy to the Lord. Some may have observed the Jewish Sabbath, some the first day of the week as the Lord's day, and others said that every day was for the Lord.

QUESTION 3

What attitude should a person who enjoys greater liberty in Christ have toward Christians whose conscience does not allow the same liberty about such things as food, observance of certain days, and similar matters? (Rom 14:1-9)

    A. Realize they are weak and hope someday they will hold the same convictions.

    B. Fellowship with them and do not quarrel over these issues.

    C. Realize that they are in sin and God will eventually bring conviction.

    D. Pray that God will allow them to become mature like them.

QUESTION 4

What should the attitude of a Christian whose conscience does not allow liberty about food, observance of certain days, and similar matters be toward other Christians who do not conform to their standards? (Rom 14:1-9)

    A. Should not judge or criticize

    B. Must not look down on them

    C. Realize that they are in sin and God will eventually bring conviction.

    D. Should take the persons aside privately and confront them on the issues

Paul points out that being offended because others do not agree with us in regard to these matters is a mark of being weak in the faith. In the same manner, the person who is stronger in faith in regard to these matters should not be offended if other Christians do not agree with their actions.

It is important to understand that Paul is not talking here about actions that are clearly sinful. There should be no disagreement among Christians when the Word of God clearly states that certain things are sin.

QUESTION 5

Think about the churches that you are acquainted with. What problems do you think Paul would mention if he were writing to them? In your Life Notebook, write out your thoughts on how Paul would address these problems. Keep in mind what we just studied on not taking offense or judging.

Christians still disagree over the same things that Paul wrote about. Similar areas of disagreement in church history that persist in modern times are questions of dress, ornaments, length of hair, and forms of entertainment. Different people have different convictions over these things. Judging one another's spirituality by such things and quarreling about them has greatly weakened many churches. Many people have been driven away from Christ by the harsh, critical spirit they have found in the church.

QUESTION 6

What reasons does Paul give for telling us why we are not to judge one another? (Rom 14:1-12) *(Select all that apply.)*

    A. God has accepted each one of us.

    B. It helps us to gain more favor with God.

    C. God will judge us all.

    D. Each of us must give an account to God.

Out of the problem about standards of conduct, Paul points out an important doctrinal truth: Christ is our Judge. Each one of us must give an account to Him. We have presented our bodies to God as a living sacrifice to serve Him. He is our Master and we must answer to Him.

In Romans 14:7, Paul says in effect, "None of us lives to himself. Each Christian lives out his life in Christ's sight and as His servant. He will help us and take care of us (Rom 14:4). He is able to make us stand! Does not that make you happy? But it is also true that what we do affects other members of the body of Christ. And so we must try to get along together and avoid attitudes and actions that hurt others."

In light of Romans 14:1-11, we can see that Romans 14:12 means that both the weak brother and the strong brother will have to answer personally to God for their conduct and for how they have treated one another. In matters of conscience and standards of conduct, we will all be judged by God for our attitude toward Christians who do not agree with us.

QUESTION 7

Suppose you are a pastor. Many young people are coming to Christ in your church. Some of the older members of your church are shocked at the way they dress, their loud enthusiastic singing, the kind of music they have in their youth services, and some of the expressions they use in their testimonies. A few leading members of the church threaten to leave unless you do something about it. They are deeply distressed at what they consider worldliness and lack of respect for the house of God. What would you do? In your Life Notebook, outline the specific approach you would take to address this problem for the whole of the flock.

Not Causing Others to Stumble (Rom 14:13-23)

As Paul moves on to Romans 14:13, his emphasis shifts. His main point now is that Christian liberty must be balanced and controlled by Christian love. Even though a Christian may feel free to do some things that are not sin in themselves, he must always consider the effect of his actions on others. If he loves his brothers in Christ, he will try to avoid anything that would offend them or cause them to stumble.

Beginning back in Romans 14:10, Paul points out a relationship between Christians that makes consideration for one another very important: we are brothers. Notice the emphasis Paul puts on this relationship as a basis for what we do.

QUESTION 8

How many times do you find the word *brother* in Romans 14?

    A. Four times

    B. Five times

    C. Six times

    D. Seven times

Paul's discussion here is on the problem of eating meat. Some Christians were eating the meat of animals that had been sacrificed to idols. Some accepted invitations from pagan friends to banquets in pagan temples. They knew that the idols were nothing and they were not going to the temples to honor the idols. But to others it appeared that they were taking part in sinful, forbidden idol worship.

Let's imagine what probably took place more than once when a new convert saw one of the older Christians eating in an idol temple. "Ah!" he might say, "I thought we were to give up worshipping idols when we accepted Christ. But Brother Aristarchus is a deacon in the church and there he is eating in an idol temple. If he can worship idols and still be a Christian, so can I." And so he went back into idol worship. Maybe Brother Aristarchus was even telling his friends about Jesus there at the banquet. But the new convert had misinterpreted his actions. His good action was spoken of evilly (Rom 14:16), and his example had caused his brother to stumble and fall into sin (Rom 14:21-23).

QUESTION 9

Compare Romans 14:13-23 with 1 Corinthians 10:23-33. The principle in 1 Corinthians 10:31-33 for determining what our conduct should be is, "We should do all for the glory of God and we should not be concerned about the spiritual welfare of others." *True or False?*

QUESTION 10

Which verses in Romans 14 let us know that as Christians we are free to eat anything we want to?

    A. Verses 14, 16, 19

    B. Verses 14, 17, 19

    C. Verses 14, 17, 20

    D. Verses 14, 17, 21

QUESTION 11

Romans 14:17 compares what the kingdom of God is to what it is not. The kingdom of God is not which of the following items? *(Select all that apply.)*

    A. Drink

    B. Meat

    C. Righteousness

    D. Joy

In Romans 14:17, Paul gives us a basic truth about the Christian life. The words *kingdom of God* refer to the realm in which the Christian lives. It is the realm of the Spirit. Paul says that the kingdom of God is not eating and drinking. The material world is not of primary importance in God's kingdom. The kingdom of God is righteousness, peace, and joy in the Holy Spirit. All three of these blessings come through the work of the Holy Spirit. As members of God's kingdom, we live in the realm where the Holy Spirit moves. It is His ministry that brings us these blessings. He helps us live righteous lives, even though our old human nature tries to hinder us. He gives us peace of mind in spite of problems and difficulties. He fills us with a joy that remains even in the most trying circumstances.

Helping and Pleasing Others (Rom 15:1-6)

"Even Christ did not please himself" (Rom 15:3). These are powerful words. May we remember them every time we have to make a choice between pleasing ourselves and helping pleasing others. We do not always want to do what is best for our brothers and sisters in Christ. But when we think of Jesus in Gethsemane, it is easier to say, "Lord, not my will but Yours be done."

QUESTION 12

Paul is still talking about Christian liberty and Christian love. In Romans 15:1-2, what three responsibilities do we, as strong Christians, have toward our weak brothers and sisters? *(Select all that apply.)*

    A. Bear the weaknesses of the weak.

    B. Not please ourselves

    C. Please them for their benefit.

    D. Confront them so they will grow.

QUESTION 13

If we fulfill our responsibilities in Romans 15:1-2, the effect on our weak brother will be to edify him and build him up in the faith. *True or False?*

QUESTION 14

According to Romans 15:6, what brings glory to God?

    A. Our harmony--Praising Him together in brotherly love

    B. Our obedience--Following His teachings

    C. Our love--Showing love to Him and others

    D. Our faith--Walking by faith in Him

QUESTION 15

Do you need more patience to get along well with others? What are the sources of help mentioned in Romans 15:4-5? *(Select all that apply.)*

    A. God

    B. Brothers

    C. Church

    D. Scripture

Accepting Others (Rom 15:7-12)

After talking about accepting weak members, Paul goes ahead and makes a broader application of the same principle. All Christians are to accept one another.

QUESTION 16

If we look back at Romans 14:1, the theme verse for this main division of our lesson, and compare it with Romans 15:7, what parallel or similar instructions do we find? *(Select all that apply.)*

    A. Receive the Word.

    B. Receive the filling of the Spirit.

    C. Receive the weak in faith.

    D. Receive one another.

Happy is the person who has learned to accept others as they are! And happy the church whose members really accept one another as brothers and sisters in Christ!

QUESTION 17

Compare Romans 12:2-5 with Romans 14:10. Acceptance of one another is necessary because of two relationships that Christians have to one another. What are they? *(Select all that apply.)*

    A. Leader/follower

    B. Witness

    C. Brothers

    D. Members of the body of Christ

QUESTION 18

In what way and on what basis are we to accept other Christians as brothers and sisters and members of the same body? (Rom 15:7)

    A. Because of our good attitude

    B. Because of our obedient nature

    C. As Christ has received us to the glory of God

    D. Because of our sacrificing spirit

Cross-cultural acceptance was a real problem in the early church, and it still is in many places today. Do you remember from your study in the Galatians course how Paul dealt with the problem of cross-cultural acceptance? The Jews thought that as a holy people they should not eat with the Gentiles. God had revealed to Peter that he should not consider Gentile Christians unclean. He was eating with them in Antioch before some Christians came from the Jewish church in Jerusalem. Then he withdrew from the Gentiles. Paul rebuked him for his hypocrisy and attitude.

Cross-cultural acceptance means more than accepting those of a different race or nation. The epistle of James deals with acceptance between the rich and the poor, those of high social standing, and the outcasts of society. Can they all come together in one local church and worship together in harmony? Can they treat one another as brothers and sisters in Christ? Are we satisfied to take the gospel to people on our own social level or do we consider the spiritual need of those on other levels too?

The church of Jesus Christ is made up of thousands of congregations on different social levels and speaking thousands of languages. Their customs differ. But every true Christian is our brother or sister in Christ. Let us accept them as Christ has accepted us for the glory of God.

The following is from Romans 15:8-9 in the Good News Translation:

> For I tell you that Christ's life of service was on behalf of the Jews, to show that God is faithful, to make his promises to their ancestors come true, and to enable even the Gentiles to praise God for his mercy.

QUESTION 19

How does Paul prove his statement of Romans 15:9 that one purpose of Christ's ministry was the salvation of the Gentiles, that they might glorify God for His mercy? (Rom 15:9-12)

    A. He quotes four Scriptures to prove it.

    B. He quotes five Scriptures to prove it.

    C. He quotes six Scriptures to prove it.

    D. He refers to God's purpose for the Gentiles.

Paul goes back to the Old Testament to prove that the salvation of the Gentiles was clearly predicted there as a part of God's plan. You may want to look up the passages and underline them in your Bible. They are: Psalm 18:49; Deuteronomy 32:43; Psalm 117:1; Isaiah 11:10. You will notice that some of these texts speak of nations instead of *Gentiles*. That's what *Gentiles* means: the people of other nations than the Jews.

QUESTION 20

Romans 15:12 talks about the root of Jesse. What does it mean for the Gentiles to trust in Him?

    A. They must obey the Law

    B. Gentiles trust Him for salvation

    C. They are left desolate

    D. They will live in peace

    E. He will rule over them

In these verses, we have been reviewing a doctrine that Paul has presented in both Romans and Galatians. The Jews and the Gentiles together, who trust in Christ, form His church so that we may all glorify God together. We must apply this part of the gospel to our lives in the church for God's purpose to be accomplished in us.

Topic 2: Responsibilities of the Church (Rom 15:13-33)

In some outlines of Romans, you will find that the practical division ends with Romans 15:13. The rest of the epistle is treated as an epilogue--something added as a personal postscript to the main part of the letter. It is much more personal than the preceding part.

We have already studied Romans 15:13-16:24 in this lesson as part of the historical background of the epistle. It does not contain many exhortations to Christians such as we have studied in Romans 12; 13; 14 and Romans 15:1-12. So why should we include it as part of Paul's application of the gospel? Why do we use the title *Responsibilities of the Church* for the rest of this lesson?

The answer is that we can learn more from seeing how a person does something than from just being told how to do it. God uses examples in His Word to teach us basic principles and our responsibilities. So in Romans 15:13-16:24 we will look at Paul and the early church in order to see how the gospel applies to the church.

Teaching and Spirituality (Rom 15:13-15)

> Objective 2 – At the end of the topic, you will be able to state two areas of responsibility of a local church toward its members.

Romans 15:13 is a prayer and Romans 15:14 is an expression of Paul's confidence in the church at Rome. From them we can see two vital areas of responsibility. Romans 15:13 speaks of spiritual experience. Paul has written of joy, peace, faith, and hope. Now he prays that as they accept and believe the gospel truths, the God of hope will fill them with these blessings. If they are to enjoy this wonderful hope at all times, it must be through the supernatural work of the Holy Spirit.

But spiritual experience is not enough. We must know the Word of God, teach it to others, and help them to apply it to their lives. The goodness that the Spirit of God produces in our lives will make us want to share His blessings. In summary, this passage refers to two areas of responsibility that a local church has toward its members--spiritual experience and teaching and applying God's Word. How well does your church handle these responsibilities?

QUESTION 21

Open your Life Notebook and answer the following question. Record your thoughts with enough detail to sharpen your thinking in these areas. What provision is made in your church for…

Helping people receive spiritual life and grow spiritually?

Teaching the Bible, applying it, and training others to teach it?

QUESTION 22

In the church at Rome were the responsibilities of Bible knowledge, exhortation, and helping Christians spiritually limited to the pastor?

    A. Yes, he was God's chosen instrument.

    B. No, but they should have been.

    C. No, they also included the deacons.

    D. No, all Christians have the responsibility to help and admonish one another.

World Evangelism (Rom 15:16-21)

> Objective 3 – At the end of the topic, you will be able to describe Paul's missionary policy and point out ten things in Romans 15 that contributed to his success in the ministry.

Let's go back now to Lesson 1. Review what we studied there about this passage. Then let's apply what we see in Paul's ministry as an example for the ministry of the church today.

QUESTION 23

Compare Romans 1:1 with Romans 15:16. What does Paul call himself in both verses?

    A. The servant of Jesus Christ to the Gentiles

    B. The missionary to the Gentiles

    C. The high priest to the Gentiles

    D. The pastor to the Gentiles

QUESTION 24

Compare Romans 15:15-16 with Galatians 1:15-16. Paul's call to be a servant of Christ to the nations was from the church in Jerusalem. *True or False?*

In Galatians, Paul talked about God calling people to different ministries. He also said that the church should recognize these different areas of work in carrying out the Great Commission. Read Galatians 2:7-9. It is clear from this passage that the church confirmed God's call and agreed to send Paul to the Gentiles and Peter to the Jews.

QUESTION 25

Paul views himself as a priest of God--one who prays for the people and also offers up a sacrifice to God. Compare Romans 12:1 with Romans 15:16. What is the living sacrifice that Paul presents to God in Romans 15:16?

A. His body

B. The Gentiles

C. The Jews

D. The Greeks

QUESTION 26

How did Paul serve the Gentiles? What did he give them? Compare Romans 1:16 with Romans 15:16.

A. The Scriptures

B. Personal letters

C. The gospel of God

D. New life

In Romans 15:17-19, Paul acknowledges that the Holy Spirit played a very important role in both helping him and making the Gentiles obedient to the faith wherever he preached the Gospel. This is also confirmed in Galatians 2:8.

QUESTION 27

How do you think that the power of the Holy Spirit that Paul refers to in Romans 15:17-19 should be part of the pattern of world evangelism today? How might the Spirit of God desire to work through you today? Draw some principles from this passage for your ministry and record them in your Life Notebook.

Paul states in Romans 15:19 that in every area where he established a church he "fully preached the gospel." This phrase can be interpreted in one of two ways. First, it can indicate that Paul thoroughly evangelized every area where he established a church in a metropolitan center. Or the phrase, *fully preached*, can refer to Paul's thorough preaching and teaching of the whole message. Both aspects of evangelism are important today too. Both are a part of the responsibility of the church in world evangelism.

QUESTION 28

From Paul's statement of his personal missionary plan in Romans 15:20-21, which of the following would be a useful pattern for the church today?

A. Take the gospel to those who have not heard it.

B. Live with those to whom you minister.

C. Ask for churches to support the ministry financially and prayerfully.

D. Ask for individuals to support the ministry financially and prayerfully.

In Romans 15:21, Paul gives us a scriptural basis for his missionary plan. This is quoted from Isaiah 52:15 and is one more piece of evidence that the evangelization of the Gentiles was predicted in the Old Testament.

We notice another part of Paul's missionary plan in Romans 15:22-24. When one area was evangelized and he had left workers in charge of the churches he had established there, he moved on to another unevangelized area. He planned his trip to Spain with a visit to the church in Rome on the way.

QUESTION 29

In Romans you saw some more characteristics of Paul that made him the great missionary he was. In Romans 15 are listed several things which contributed to his success, see below. Check your own life and ministry against these factors for success. Note those that you particularly want to cultivate. Talk with the Lord about it. In your Life Notebook, list the specific character qualities you are asking God to produce in your life as you come to Him through faith, believing His promises.

1. Paul appreciated other people's good points and complimented them (Rom 15:14).

2. Paul had a sense of God's call and appreciated it as a privilege (Rom 15:15-16).

3. Paul had definite guidance from the Lord for a specific ministry (Rom 15:16-20).

4. Paul considered himself the servant of Jesus to the people to whom he was sent (Rom 15:16).

5. Paul preached the whole Gospel of God (Rom 15:16-19).

6. Paul gave God the glory for what was accomplished (Rom 15:18-19).

7. Paul's ministry was in the power of the Holy Spirit (Rom 15:19).

8. Paul was diligent, thorough, and systematic in the Lord's work (Rom 15:19-20).

9. Paul followed the scriptural pattern for reaching those who had not heard the gospel (Rom 15:20-21).

10. Paul was a man of boldness and missionary of vision (Rom 15:15-24).

11. Paul enjoyed fellowship with other Christians (Rom 15:23-24).

12. Paul taught his converts their financial responsibilities to their spiritual leaders and to those who were in need and helped them carry out their duties (Rom 15:25-28).

13. Paul had faith that God would bless his ministry (Rom 15:29).

14. Paul prayed for others and begged them to pray for him (Rom 15:30-33).

Offerings (Rom 15:22-29)

Objective 4 – At the end of the topic, you will be able to describe three kinds of offerings that are a pattern for the church today, based on Romans 15:22-29.

From this section of Romans, it is possible to discover three kinds of church offerings. Paul refers definitely to two offerings but also mentions a basic principle for the third kind:

- Romans 15:24- A missionary offering
- Romans 15:26- An offering for poor Christians in need
- Romans 15:27- Offering to support ministers of the gospel

Missionary Offering

Paul planned to minister to the church at Rome when he visited them, and he naturally expected that they would want to help him take the gospel to Spain (Rom 15:24). The Great Commission is for the entire church, not just for the preachers. To give a missionary offering is a great privilege. In this way, we have a share in world evangelism. By participating with our offerings, we can help send and support others to preach the gospel where we cannot go. And so as we work to earn the money that goes into the missionary offering, we are working for the Lord just as truly as the missionary that we send. We are workers together for God.

Offering for Poor Christians in Need

Paul had three reasons for giving great importance to the offering for the poor Christians in Jerusalem (Rom 15:26).

> 1. It demonstrated a bond of fellowship and brotherly love between the Gentile Christians and the Jewish Christians.

> 2. It showed that the Gentile Christians recognized their spiritual indebtedness to the Church in Jerusalem.

> 3. It was the climax of Paul's ministry in Greece and an act of worship and dedication to God before he set out for the west.

To what extent are Christians responsible for helping other Christians who have financial needs? What problems are involved? What is the policy of your church? What is your personal policy? What would Jesus do?

All through the Bible we find the people of God helping the widows, orphans, and other poor people. Even before the law was given, Job considered it his duty to help those in need (Job 31:16-22). The law made provisions for systematic offerings and help for the poor both individually and as a nation (Ex 23:11; Lev 19:9-10; Deut 14:28-15:15).

In the books of poetry and prophecy, we see that righteousness includes helping the poor. God blesses those who meet this responsibility; He punishes those who do not (Ps 41:1-3; Ps 82:3-4; Prov 14:21; Prov 31; Prov 21:13). The prophets called people to repentance for social injustice. God told the people through Isaiah that the proof of repentance He wanted from them was not fasting, but right living, and especially right treatment for the poor (Isa 58:1-12).

Jesus both taught and practiced giving to the poor (Mt 5:42; Mt 6:1-4; Mt 19:21; Lk 6:30-38; Jn 13:29; Acts 20:35). He summed up the Law and the prophets in the law of love (Mt 22:37-40).

Paul, James, and other leaders of the early church understood that Christian love was more than affection. Loving their neighbors as themselves meant sharing with those in need (Jas 1:27; 2:15-18).

The early church accepted the responsibility of caring for those among them who did not have any other source of support. But funds were limited and families who could take care of their own relatives were not to put this burden on the church. Besides this, people who were able to work were not to burden the church with their support. Rather, they were to work and contribute to the support of those who were in need (Acts 6:1; 1 Tim 3:5-8,16; Eph 4:28). Those who were not willing to work were not to be fed by the church (2 Thess 3:10-12).

Paul taught his converts to give to the poor as part of their worship and service to the Lord. He and Barnabas carried a famine relief offering from the church at Antioch to the church at Jerusalem. Read Galatians 2:9-10 to see that remembering the poor (as the leaders at Jerusalem asked Paul to do) was part of Paul's ministry. He also taught, as Jesus had, that those who give to the poor are giving to God and will receive their reward in heaven from Him. No one can out-give God. He always gives back more than we give to Him (Mt 10:42; 1 Tim 6:17-19).

Offering to Support Ministers of the Gospel

Now let's compare Paul's words in Romans 15:27 with his application of an Old Testament principle in 1 Timothy 5:17-18. Note the responsibility of a local church to its pastor (elder) as Paul presents it.

QUESTION 30

It is the responsibility of the church to support its pastor financially. *True or False?*

QUESTION 31

How does Paul's application of this financial responsibility of the church to pastors compare with Jesus' teaching in Matthew 10:5-10 and Luke 10:1-7as He sent out first the twelve disciples and then the seventy in evangelistic ministry?

    A. Paul contradicted what Jesus taught.

    B. Paul added to what Jesus taught.

    C. Paul was repeating what Jesus taught.

    D. Paul's teaching had no relationship to Jesus' teaching.

QUESTION 32

Now let's compare Paul's exhortation to the churches in Galatians 6:6-10 with 1 Corinthians 9:1-14. Who commanded that those who preach the gospel should receive their financial support from their ministry?

    A. Paul

    B. Leaders in Jerusalem

    C. God

    D. Decided by the local church

We see from 1 Corinthians that Paul did not want the church at Corinth to support him. He did not want them to think he was preaching the gospel just to make a living. Today, gospel workers establishing a new work sometimes do not take up offerings for the same reason. Many pastors work to support themselves as Paul did and let all the offerings of the church go into paying the expenses (rent, lights, etc.). However, Paul did accept offerings from other churches (2 Cor 11:7-9; Phil 4:10-19) and called them a sacrifice pleasing to God.

QUESTION 33

To conclude this study about offerings, let me urge you to read two beautiful chapters that Paul wrote to the church at Corinth about their part in the offering he was going to take to Jerusalem (2 Cor 8–9). Then pray about this whole matter of offerings and financial responsibility. Is your church meeting its responsibility? Is teaching on this subject needed? Has the Lord spoken to you about your part in it all? If so, what do you plan to do? In your Life Notebook, write out how you plan to make application of the Scriptures to your own life and to those among whom you serve in your local assembly.

Prayer (Rom 15:30-33)

Objective 5 – At the end of the topic, you will be able to, from Paul's prayers and prayer requests in Romans 15, state the nature and power of prayer and the responsibility of the church in prayer.

Have you noticed in Paul's epistles how often, as he writes to the Christians, his spirit breaks out in prayer to God for them? Prayer interlaces his doctrine and its application. Only the Spirit of God can make it real in the lives of his readers. The Word must be mixed with faith if it is to take effect. The Holy Spirit not only gives Paul the message of God but also inspires him to pray for those who will receive it. These Spirit-inspired prayers reveal God's will and plan for us--both in the blessings He has for us in answer to prayer and in a pattern that we can follow in praying for others.

Paul's example shows us our responsibility. What should we do as we tell people about Christ or teach or preach His Word? We need to pray for them. This does not mean we must pray in an audible voice, but we can be silently asking God to work out His will in them, making the Word a reality in their lives.

Let's look now at Paul's three prayers in this chapter (Rom 15:5-6, Rom 15:13; Rom 15:33) and fill in an analytical chart such as you might use in a Bible study.

Paul's Prayers in Romans 15

Verse	Addressed to	Request	Purpose or Result
5-6	God of _____ _____	Grant you to be _____ one toward another, according to _____	That you may with _____ _____ even the Father of our Lord Jesus Christ.
13	God of _____	Fill you with _____ in_____	That you may _____ _____ through the _____ _____
33	God of _____ _____	_____ _____	

Look back over the completed chart. Notice the emphasis that Paul puts on the nature of God as it relates to the needs of the people. Is this a good pattern for you to use to strengthen your own faith as you pray? In your Life Notebook, write down specific phrases you could incorporate into your praying. You may want to keep a copy of these phrases with your Bible or journal for daily reference as you pray.

Let's review now Romans 1:7-15. Compare Romans 1:11-12 with Romans 15:29-30, 32. In these verses, we see that Paul expects to be a blessing to the church at Rome. We see, too, that Paul did not consider himself superior to other Christians.

QUESTION 34

What phrases show that Paul felt the need of spiritual help and blessing from his brothers and sisters in Christ? *(Select all that apply.)*

    A. They would join together in fervent prayer for Paul.

    B. Paul would not suffer illness in his travels and that he would have all of his financial needs met by them.

    C. Paul would be refreshed with them and that God's peace would be with them.

    D. They would be mutually comforted by each other's faith.

    E. They would overflow with hope and glorify God in unity.

    F. They would be strengthened through Paul's imparting some spiritual gift.

QUESTION 35

Romans 15:32 is a verse that shows that prayer is actually a part of the work of the church in world evangelism. *True or False?*

QUESTION 36

In Romans 15:31-32, Paul requests prayer for four things. What are they? *(Select all that apply.)*

    A. That he would arrive in Rome with joy

    B. That his ministry (offering) would be accepted

    C. That he would be refreshed by the Christians in Rome

    D. That he would have safety in travel

    E. That he would be delivered from those in Jerusalem who do not believe

    F. That he could be a fruitful witness to the guards in Rome

Were the prayers of the Roman Christians for Paul answered? Yes, all four requests, but in a different way than Paul expected. In Jerusalem the unbelievers tried to kill Paul, but God delivered him. The leaders of the church received him gladly and praised the Lord for his ministry (Acts 21:17-20). Paul was arrested, falsely accused, and imprisoned, but he used the opportunity of this arrest, trials, and imprisonment to preach the gospel to the crowds, religious leaders, and high government officials. His missionary journey to Rome was as a prisoner. But in a storm and shipwreck, his Spirit-directed leadership saved the lives of all those on board.

The shipwreck and three-month delay on the island of Malta were all part of the answer to the prayer that he might *come with joy by the will of God to Rome*. Malta was an unexpected mission field ripe for evangelism. God worked great miracles there as Paul prayed for the sick. We may be sure he preached the gospel to the people, too (Acts 28:1-10). Even before Paul reached Rome, the Christians there heard he was coming and went out to meet him and welcome him. Was he refreshed by them? Acts 28:15 says, "The brethren… came to meet us… whom when Paul saw, he thanked God, and took courage."

QUESTION 37

How well is your church meeting the responsibility to pray for definite needs of ministers and missionaries? What will you do to help meet this responsibility? In your Life Notebook, make a concrete and concise plan for making sure that this important ministry is not neglected in the life of your church.

Topic 3: Christian Fellowship (Rom 16:1-24)

At first glance, Romans 16 appears to be an insignificant list of names. First, Paul refers to Phoebe, a co-laborer for the sake of the gospel. Next, he sends greetings to people that he had met in different places. Some of them had been converted under his ministry but were now living in Rome. Finally, he sends greetings from other churches and believers who were interested in the Roman church. Although this list may seem insignificant, there is much that can be learned about the church by studying this passage.

> Objective 6 – At the end of the topic, you will be able to identify in Romans 16 three things that strengthen a church and to practice them in your life and ministry.

You may have noticed that we are reviewing many things in this lesson. This is to help you bring together what you have learned and impress it on your memory. It is also to help you prepare for the final exam.

Recognition and Commendation (Rom 16:1-16)

Please return to Lesson 1 and read again the comments on Romans 16:1-16. Take note of the words of commendation and praise that you find in Romans 16:1-16. You may want to record these in your Life Notebook. Include in your list the term "dear friend" since this shows that the person must have had qualities that made others love him or her. Then answer the question below.

QUESTION 38

Which of the following are names of the people that Paul commends or praises in any way in this chapter? *(Select all that apply.)*

 A. Phoebe, Priscilla, and Aquila

 B. Epaenetus, Mary, and Andronicus

 C. Junia, Ampliatus, and Urbanus

 D. Stachys, Apelles, and Tryphena

 E. Tryphosa and Persis

 F. Rufus and his mother

How important is it to call people by name? To recognize them personally before the church and to praise them for what they have done? To really love people and let them know it? To appreciate and remember what others have done for us? To praise other Christian workers for their labors and not just think of our own? Paul told the Roman Christians to give honor to whom honor was due (Rom 13:7), and here he sets forth the example. Words of appreciation for our efforts meet a basic need of human nature. And the more the members of a church know about what different ones are doing for the Lord, the more they appreciate one another. This strengthens brotherly love and Christian fellowship in the church.

In Romans 16:16, Paul refers to another expression of Christian love--a holy kiss. A kiss on the cheek was a greeting of friendship in oriental lands at that time, as it still is in many areas today. Christians greeted one another with a kiss. Paul is simply telling them to greet one another in the usual manner of their culture (as he might tell Christians in the West to shake hands with or hug one another). He is not ordering us to follow a certain ritual, but he is saying, "Be friendly. Show your love for your brothers and sisters in Christ."

Notice, too, in Romans 16:16 that Paul sends more than personal greetings. He strengthens the fellowship among churches by sending the greetings of the churches in one area to those in another.

Many congregations still have this custom of sending their greetings whenever one of their members visits other churches.

Warning against Divisions (Rom 16:17-20)

Satan tries to destroy a church or hinder its growth by dividing it. Sometimes this is through difference of opinion about doctrine. There were three factions in the Galatian churches: the Judaizers and those who followed them into legalism, the anti-Law party that did not want to submit to any kind of rules or restraint, and the party that held to what Paul had taught them.

Paul knew how terrible zeal for a particular doctrine could be if it was not held in check by love. It had driven him to help stone Stephen and to persecute the Christians. Time after time he had been whipped, stoned, beaten, and jailed because what he preached did not agree with what some other religious leaders taught. Doctrinal divisions in a church could tear it apart, turn people away from the truth, and destroy God's work. And although Paul had not founded the church at Rome, he could not close his epistle without a warning against anyone who might be causing divisions or who was promoting doctrines or conduct that was not in line with the gospel.

QUESTION 39

In Romans 16:17, Paul advises us, when confronted with persons who cause divisions and teach or act contrary to sound doctrine, to do what two things? *(Select all that apply.)*

    A. Watch out for them.

    B. Avoid them.

    C. Confront them.

    D. Correct them.

QUESTION 40

According to Romans 16:18, evil people often use good words and nice speeches in order to deceive people. *True or False?*

QUESTION 41

Compare Romans 1:8 with Romans 16:19. Name two well-known characteristics of the church at Rome that Paul did not want to see destroyed by troublemakers or teachers of false doctrine such as the Judaizers. *(Select all that apply.)*

    A. Generosity

    B. Faith

    C. Obedience

    D. Knowledge

QUESTION 42

Compare Romans 16:20 with Genesis 3:15. Christ has fatally "bruised the serpent's head" at Calvary, but here in this apostolic benediction we have the promise of our own personal victory over Satan. Who will bruise him under our feet?

    A. The God of peace

    B. The God of wrath

    C. The God of justice

    D. Jehovah

Fellowship between Churches (Rom 16:21-24)

In Romans 16:20, we notice again Paul's prayer for the grace of the Lord Jesus Christ to be with those who read his letter. It reminds us of the importance of grace throughout his teaching and the riches of grace that Christ has brought to our lives.

We have already noticed in Romans 16:16 that the churches in Greece sent their greetings to the church at Rome. Now we find different members of the church at Corinth joining Paul in sending greetings to the Roman Church.

Paul calls Gaius the host of the whole church. This probably means that the congregation met in his home. It could also refer to his hospitality toward all the church.

Do you enjoy reading reports about the work of the Lord in different places? Or hearing a report from someone who comes from another church? Does communication between congregations in your area encourage and strengthen the churches? What provision do you have for this? Could it be improved? *Pray about it.*

QUESTION 43

Which of the following things mentioned in Romans 16 should help strengthen Christian fellowship in a church? *(Select all that apply.)*

    A. Public denunciation of sinners

    B. Avoiding people who cause divisions

    C. Strict teaching against heresy

    D. Public recognition of the work of other Christians

    E. Being friendly

Topic 4: Glory to God (Rom 16:25-27)

The last three verses of Paul's letter to the Romans are a doxology--a beautiful expression of praise to God.

> Objective 7 – At the end of this topic, you will be able to explain why Paul concludes the book of Romans with praise to God for the gospel, for a better understanding of it, and for the opportunity to share it with others.

The contents of this climax to his epistle are very similar to its introduction in Romans 1:1-5. Compare these verses with Romans 16:25-27 now.

Paul praises the God who is able to establish and keep the people he is writing to. This may refer to the danger of divisions that he has warned them against in Romans 16:17. God is able to make them firm in their faith according to Paul's gospel.

QUESTION 44

According to Romans 16:25, Jesus Christ was the gospel and content that Paul preached. *True or False?*

The words *according to the revelation of the mystery* refer to the fact that the gospel of Christ will develop Christlikeness in those who believe it. The mystery is "Christ in you the hope of glory" (Col 1:26). Time and again Paul has shown us that this message is not just his own idea. God has revealed it in the Scriptures (Rom 16:26). Paul has obeyed God's command to make the gospel known to the Gentiles--to all nations in order that they should believe and obey God.

Revelation of the Gospel of Jesus Christ

Romans 16:25-26	
Mystery	God's Power to Save and Keep
Extent:	Made Known to All Nations
Method:	By the Scriptures
Purpose:	Obedience of Faith

In the gospel, the righteousness of God is revealed by faith. But this righteousness is to be revealed in life also. And we continue in our generation the work that Paul carried out in his--preaching Christ to the nations that they may come to the obedience of faith. Their faith and ours is manifested in faithful obedience to the only wise God, through Jesus Christ, to whom be glory forever.

QUESTION 45

Go back now and read once more the theme of Romans in Romans 1:16-17, then Paul's outburst of praise in Romans 11:33, and finally Romans 16:27. Read these words aloud to God and thank Him for His wonderful wisdom and grace that has brought the gospel to you and you to Him. How will you use praise and worship in your personal life to glorify God? In your Life Notebook, record at least three ways you plan to weave praise and worship into your lifestyle.

Lesson 8 Self Check

QUESTION 1

In Romans 14, Paul mentioned some problem areas in which the early Christians disagreed as to their Christian liberty. Which of the following was one of those areas?

    A. Which person they should marry

    B. Which church they should attend

    C. What food they should eat

    D. Where they should live

QUESTION 2

Ceremonial religion does not concern itself with what we eat or drink or the keeping of certain days as holy. *True or False?*

QUESTION 3

If we fulfill our responsibilities in Romans 15:1-2, we will edify our _____ brother.

    A. Pagan

    B. Sinful

    C. Strong

    D. Weak

QUESTION 4

In the church at Rome, were the responsibilities of Bible knowledge, exhortation, and helping Christians spiritually limited to the pastor?

    A. Yes, he was God's chosen instrument.

    B. No, but they should have been.

    C. No, they also included the deacons.

    D. No, all Christians have the responsibility to help and admonish one another.

QUESTION 5

In Romans 15:16, what does Paul call himself?

    A. A minister of Christ

    B. A slave of the gospel

    C. A redeemed sinner

    D. A preacher of the Word

QUESTION 6

How does Paul's application of the financial responsibility of the church to pastors compare with Jesus' teaching in Matthew 10:5-10 and Luke 10:1-7 as He sent out first the twelve disciples and then the seventy in evangelistic ministry?

    A. Paul contradicted what Jesus taught.

    B. Paul added to what Jesus taught.

    C. Paul was repeating what Jesus taught.

    D. Paul's teaching had no relationship to Jesus' teaching.

QUESTION 7

Romans 15:32 shows that prayer is actually a part of the work of the church in world evangelism. *True or False?*

QUESTION 8

According to Romans 16:18, evil people often use good words and nice speeches in order to deceive people. *True or False?*

QUESTION 9

Which of the following things mentioned in Romans 16 should help strengthen Christian fellowship in a church?

    A. Public denunciation of sinners

    B. Inviting people who cause divisions

    C. Strict teaching against heresy

    D. Public recognition of the work of other Christians

QUESTION 10

According to Romans 16:25, Jesus Christ was the gospel and content Paul preached. *True or False?*

Unit Two Exam: Romans

QUESTION 1

What did Paul mean in Romans 9:3 when he said, "I could wish that I myself were accursed"?

    A. He was willing to give up his eternal salvation.

    B. He was willing to endure divine discipline.

    C. He was willing to give up his life in order that they might be saved.

    D. He was willing to endure the judgment of God in time if that would save his people.

QUESTION 2

To whom is Paul primarily referring to as "children of the living God" in Romans 9:26?

    A. Spiritually restored Israel

    B. Gentiles who believe in Christ

    C. The whole nation of Israel

    D. The Jewish remnant

QUESTION 3

Which of the following prophecies does the Bible not teach?

    A. The religious leaders of Israel ("the builders") would not recognize the Messiah.

    B. Israel's leaders would "stumble over" the Messiah, reject Him, and kill Him.

    C. The efforts of the religious leaders would fail because they had chosen the wrong "cornerstone."

    D. Because the religious leaders rejected the Messiah, God would reject them and give His salvation to others.

QUESTION 4

According to Romans 10:8-9, what was the "word of faith" that the early Christians preached?

    A. If a person confesses with his mouth that Jesus is Lord, salvation will result.

    B. If a person believes in his heart that God raised Jesus from the dead, it is enough for salvation.

    C. Either confession with the mouth or believing in the heart will bring salvation.

    D. The combination of confession and belief will result in salvation.

QUESTION 5

In light of Romans 10:18-21, who are we to reach with God's Word and invite to trust Christ?

    A. Especially where people are responsive to the message

    B. Especially to the unevangelized Gentiles

    C. Especially to the Jews

    D. To everybody, everywhere, whether they want to hear the message or not

QUESTION 6

When Paul said, "By the mercies of God I plead with you, give yourselves to God," to which of the following mercies was He was referring?

    A. The grace mentioned in Romans 1–11

    B. The love mentioned in Romans 1–11

    C. The blessings mentioned in Romans 1–11

    D. All of the above

QUESTION 7

What lesson does Matthew 7:24-29 not teach us about putting into practice what we know about God and His Word?

    A. It is dangerous to hear the Word of God and then fail to apply it to our lives.

    B. Our lives will have a strong foundation if we follow Jesus' teaching and apply what we know.

    C. It is easy to be distracted and foolishly fail to apply what Jesus has taught us.

    D. We should look for opportunities to demonstrate true faith in Him.

QUESTION 8

According to Romans 12:19, why shouldn't we avenge ourselves?

    A. Because most people do not know how to properly take revenge

    B. Because it is God's responsibility to judge and punish wrongdoing

    C. Because the Scriptures teach us to be tolerant rather than judgmental

    D. Because we might get hurt

QUESTION 9

According to Romans 13:1-2, why should a Christian submit himself to the authority of the government?

    A. To help assure that governments will not make life difficult for believers

    B. To keep from embarrassing the church

    C. To honor God, who has given governments the right to rule

    D. To avoid resistance and anarchy in the community

QUESTION 10

What is the one basic rule that should guide us in all our relationships with others?

    A. Pray for our enemies.

    B. Love our neighbors as ourselves.

    C. Love the Lord our God with all our hearts, souls, strength, and minds.

    D. Do not owe anything to anyone.

QUESTION 11

In Romans 14, Paul mentioned some problem areas in which the early Christians disagreed as to their Christian liberty. Which of the following was one of those areas?

    A. Which person they should marry

    B. Which church they should attend

    C. What food they should eat

    D. Where they should live

QUESTION 12

What should the attitude of a Christian with strong convictions about food, dress, etc., be toward another Christian who does not conform to his standard?

    A. He should not judge or criticize him.

    B. He must not look down on him for being immature.

    C. Realize that he is in sin and God will eventually convict him.

    D. He should take him aside privately and confront him on the issues at stake.

QUESTION 13

In the church at Rome were the responsibilities of Bible knowledge, exhortation, and helping Christians spiritually limited to the pastor?

    A. Yes, he was God's chosen instrument.

    B. No, but they should have been.

    C. No, they also included the deacons.

    D. No, all Christians have the responsibility to help and admonish one another.

QUESTION 14

Paul viewed himself as a priest of God--one who prays for the people and also offers up a sacrifice to God. What is the living sacrifice that Paul mentions as presenting to God in Romans 15:16?

    A. His body

    B. The Gentiles

    C. The Jews

    D. The Greeks

QUESTION 15

In Romans 16:17, Paul advises us, when confronted with persons who cause divisions and teach or act contrary to sound doctrine, to do what two things?

    A. Watch out for them and avoid them.

    B. Watch out for them and confront them.

    C. Confront them and correct them.

    D. Correct them and pray for them.

QUESTION 16

According to Romans 10:17, it is by hearing the word of Christ preached that faith comes to people so that they can believe in Christ. *True or False?*

QUESTION 17

According to Romans 11:25-26, Israel will not be restored. *True or False?*

QUESTION 18

Romans 13:5 gives the following reasons why a Christian should obey the laws. They are: 1) Because of the authorities' wrath, 2) because the Christian should be more spiritual, and 3) because of the Christian's conscience. *True or False?*

QUESTION 19

According to Acts 4:1-31 and 5:12-42, the apostles disobeyed an order not to speak against the government. *True or False?*

QUESTION 20

If we fulfill our responsibilities in Romans 15:1-2, the effect on our weaker brother will be to edify him and build him up in the faith. *True or False?*

QUESTION 21

According to Romans 16:18, evil people often use good words and nice speeches in order to
_____.

    A. Preach repentance

    B. Deceive people

    C. Slander Paul

    D. Encourage believers

QUESTION 22

In Romans 11:17, the broken off branches refer to unbelieving Gentiles. *True or False?*

QUESTION 23

According to Romans 12:3, John 15:5, and Philippians 4:13, you should have modesty and what other quality?

    A. Hope

    B. Faith

    C. Love

    D. Peace

QUESTION 24

Ceremonial religion puts emphasis on what we eat or drink and on keeping certain days as holy. *True or False?*

QUESTION 25

Which of the following things mentioned in Romans 16 should help strengthen Christian fellowship in a church?

    A. Public denunciation of sinners

    B. Public recognition of the work of other Christians

    C. Inviting people who cause divisions

    D. Strict teaching against heresy

Lesson 8 Answers to Questions

QUESTION 1
- A. What food they could eat
- D. Religious observance of certain days

QUESTION 2: True

QUESTION 3
- B. Fellowship with them and do not quarrel over these issues.

QUESTION 4
- A. Should not judge or criticize

QUESTION 5: *Your answer*

QUESTION 6
- A. God has accepted each one of us.
- C. God will judge us all.
- D. Each of us must give an account to God.

QUESTION 7: *Your answer*

QUESTION 8
- B. Five times

QUESTION 9: False

QUESTION 10
- C. Verses 14, 17, 20

QUESTION 11
- A. Drink
- B. Meat

QUESTION 12
- A. Bear the weaknesses of the weak.
- B. Not please ourselves
- C. Please them for their benefit.

QUESTION 13: True

QUESTION 14
- A. Our harmony--Praising Him together in brotherly love

QUESTION 15
- A. God
- D. Scripture

QUESTION 16
- C. Receive the weak in faith.
- D. Receive one another.

QUESTION 17
- C. Brothers
- D. Members of the body of Christ

QUESTION 18
- C. As Christ has received us to the glory of God

QUESTION 19
- A. He quotes four Scriptures to prove it.

QUESTION 20
- B. Gentiles trust Him for salvation

QUESTION 21: *Your answer*

QUESTION 22
- D. No, all Christians have the responsibility to help and admonish one another.

QUESTION 23
    A. The servant of Jesus Christ to the Gentiles

QUESTION 24: False

QUESTION 25
    B. The Gentiles

QUESTION 26
    C. The gospel of God

QUESTION 27: *Your answer*

QUESTION 28
    A. Take the gospel to those who have not heard it.

QUESTION 29: *Your answer*

QUESTION 30: True

QUESTION 31
    C. Paul was repeating what Jesus taught.

QUESTION 32
    C. God

QUESTION 33: *Your answer*

QUESTION 34
    A. They would join together in fervent prayer for Paul.
    C. Paul would be refreshed with them and that God's peace would be with them.
    D. They would be mutually comforted by each other's faith.
    E. They would overflow with hope and glorify God in unity.
    F. They would be strengthened through Paul's imparting some spiritual gift.

QUESTION 35: False

QUESTION 36
    A. That he would arrive in Rome with joy
    B. That his ministry (offering) would be accepted
    C. That he would be refreshed by the Christians in Rome
    E. That he would be delivered from those in Jerusalem who do not believe

QUESTION 37: *Your answer*

QUESTION 38
    A. Phoebe, Priscilla, and Aquila
    B. Epaenetus, Mary, and Andronicus
    C. Junia, Ampliatus, and Urbanus
    D. Stachys, Apelles, and Tryphena
    E. Tryphosa and Persis
    F. Rufus and his mother

QUESTION 39
    A. Watch out for them.
    B. Avoid them.

QUESTION 40: True

QUESTION 41
    B. Faith
    C. Obedience

QUESTION 42
    A. The God of peace

QUESTION 43
    B. Avoiding people who cause divisions
    D. Public recognition of the work of other Christians
    E. Being friendly

QUESTION 44: True
QUESTION 45: *Your answer*

Lesson 8 Self Check Answers

QUESTION 1
　　C.　What food they should eat
QUESTION 2: False
QUESTION 3
　　D.　Weak
QUESTION 4
　　D.　No, all Christians have the responsibility to help and admonish one another.
QUESTION 5
　　A.　A minister of Christ
QUESTION 6
　　C.　Paul was repeating what Jesus taught.
QUESTION 7: True
QUESTION 8: True
QUESTION 9
　　D.　Public recognition of the work of other Christians
QUESTION 10: True

Unit 2 Exam Answers

QUESTION 1
    D. He was willing to endure the judgment of God in time if that would save his people.

QUESTION 2
    B. Gentiles who believe in Christ

QUESTION 3
    C. The efforts of the religious leaders would fail because they had chosen the wrong "cornerstone."

QUESTION 4
    D. The combination of confession and belief will result in salvation.

QUESTION 5
    D. To everybody, everywhere, whether they want to hear the message or not

QUESTION 6
    D. All of the above

QUESTION 7
    C. It is easy to be distracted and foolishly fail to apply what Jesus has taught us.

QUESTION 8
    B. Because it is God's responsibility to judge and punish wrongdoing

QUESTION 9
    C. To honor God, who has given governments the right to rule

QUESTION 10
    B. Love our neighbors as ourselves.

QUESTION 11
    C. What food they should eat

QUESTION 12
    A. He should not judge or criticize him.

QUESTION 13
    D. No, all Christians have the responsibility to help and admonish one another.

QUESTION 14
    B. The Gentiles

QUESTION 15
    A. Watch out for them and avoid them.

QUESTION 16: True
QUESTION 17: False
QUESTION 18: False
QUESTION 19: False
QUESTION 20: True

QUESTION 21
    B. Deceive people

QUESTION 22: False

QUESTION 23
    B. Faith

QUESTION 24: True

QUESTION 25
    B. Public recognition of the work of other Christians

Made in the USA
Coppell, TX
27 October 2024

39226214R00122